S0-BAX-376

DEATH VALLEY DAYS

LONGSTREET PRESS
Atlanta, Georgia

DEATH VALLEY DAYS

THE GLORY OF CLEMSON FOOTBALL

BOB BRADLEY

Published by
LONGSTREET PRESS, INC.
2150 Newmarket Parkway
Suite 102
Marietta, Georgia 30067

Copyright © 1991 by Bob Bradley

All rights reserved. No part of this book may be reproduced in any form or by any means without the prior written permission of the Publisher, excepting brief quotes used in connection with reviews, written specifically for inclusion in a magazine or newspaper.

Printed in the United States of America

1st printing 1991

Library of Congress Catalog Number 91-061931

ISBN 1-56352-006-0

This book was printed by R. R. Donnelley & Sons, Willard, Ohio. The text was set in ITC Clearface Regular by Typo-Repro Service, Inc., Atlanta, Georgia.
Jacket design by Tonya Beach.
Book design by Jill Dible/Audrey Graham.

Photo credits: Color and black-and-white photographs courtesy of Clemson Sports Information Office; Jim Moriarty—pages 16, 24, 117, 127, 133, 135, 141, 143, 145, 153, 156.

Special acknowledgment to Sanford Neal Rogers and John Samuel (Sam) Blackman for their generous donation of time and effort.

FROM HEISMAN...

"At Clemson we have a style of football played radically different from anything on earth. Its notoriety and the fear and admiration of it has spread throughout the length and breadth of the entire Southern world of football. All colleges should have fixed athletic traditions and should be as loyal to them as to the institution itself. The complete unity and harmony of athletic opinion and sentiment existing at Clemson is due in no small part of credit to her glorious athletic record."

—John Heisman, 1903

From Heisman to Howard to Hatfield — the rich tradition of Clemson football.

John Heisman coached the Tigers to their first undefeated season (1900); Frank Howard coached the second undefeated team (1948); and Ken Hatfield's senior class of 1990 won more games (40) than any other group in Clemson or Atlantic Coast Conference history.

Heisman started the football program at Clemson, and though he stayed only four years, his 19–3–2 record raised a few eyebrows, especially at Georgia Tech, where he went on to greater heights.

After Clemson thrashed Tech 73–0 in 1904, the Yellow Jackets hired the brash

Heisman as their first full-time football coach.

Two years earlier, Heisman, often described as ingenious, clever, devious . . . always trying to outfox his opponent, had brought his Clemson team to play Tech in a game billed as the Country Bumpkins against the City Slickers.

An account in the Clemson school paper after the game said:

"We had already won a couple of games, and word`drifted to Clemson that Georgia Tech would spare nothing to beat us. When the train with the Clemson team and baggage arrived in Atlanta the day before the game, the Tech supporters made it a point to entertain our players royally.

"The Tech supporters marveled at the ease with which they were able to get our players to sneak out that night and participate in the wild parties around town. There was quite a lot of eating and drinking, and the more the Clemson men indulged in such pastime, the more were the Tech men willing to back with money their belief that they would win the next day.

"Boy, did we clean up the Tech money. Clemson won 44 to 5.

"The Tech people wondered at the hardiness of the Clemson men after a night of

Legendary Clemson coach John Heisman.

"John had little use for players who could not quickly learn his signal system and remember the intricate and changing plays. This eliminated much otherwise eligible material (players). John used very few substitutes, three or four at best. . . . This may have been due to scarcity of first-class material, or the expense of travel and upkeep and extra equipment. Also, the rules of the game limited return of players to the game. A player had to have stamina to remain the full 70 minutes of the game."

The coming of Heisman to coach was the beginning of the "Golden Age" of football at Clemson. In the first decade (1896 through 1907) the Tigers won 44 games, lost 17 and tied seven, with staggering scores against their opponents (1,311 points to 396).

"It may well be to say just here, that football at Clemson has been a success from the very beginning," said an article in the school yearbook in 1908." But 1907 was the last of the great teams. The "Golden Age" came to an abrupt close, April 1, 1908, with the Pendleton Escapade."

For several years prior to this on each April Fool's Day, a large majority of the student body would cut classes and go over to Pendleton (four miles) and 'kill the day' playing April Fool jokes on each other . . . nothing destructive . . . just having a good time. A new commandant of cadets came to Clemson in the summer of 1907 and he announced well in advance that there'd be no toleration of anyone who cut classes April 1, 1908, to make the annual trek to Pendleton. A good number of cadets decided to defy the commandant's order and did go to Pendleton. Being a military school, the commandant had the last say. This prank resulted in the expulsion of 306 cadets, including many of the football players. It was a blow from which football was to suffer for a long time.

revelry until they discovered that Coach Heisman had sent a bunch of bohunks to Atlanta with the team's equipment and had kept the varsity at Lula, Georgia, a small town some miles from Atlanta, the night before the game."

Heisman's ingenuity in originating plays was one of his strong points. He usually had something new for every game.

C. R. "Bob" Williams, who was head coach at Clemson twice, the first time two years after Heisman left for Georgia Tech, said: "It availed little to case [scout] one of his games, for he rarely used the same trick over.

Clemson Tigers, 1902.

The "Dark Ages" would last—except for a few years of light—for two decades.

The "Renaissance" started for the Tigers with Josh Cody as coach in 1927. His four years of success (29–11–1) put Clemson on the upgrade. Players on those four teams are quick to tell anyone willing to listen that they defeated South Carolina four consecutive years.

The late Bob Jones played for Cody in 1928-29-30 and then Cody put him on his staff. When Jess Neely came in he kept Jones on his staff, and likewise did Frank Howard. Altogether Jones was on the Clemson coaching staff 44 years.

"There's no doubt who had the best team in the state when I was an undergraduate," he once recalled. "During my playing days, we only lost one game to a state school in three years. We were 15–1, the only loss coming to the Citadel my sophomore year. We beat South Carolina in Columbia three straight years and outscored them 73–21. We also had a big rivalry with Furman and beat them three times. I remember I scored a touchdown against Furman while lying flat on my back in the end zone."

Jess Neely took the coaching job at Clemson in 1931. Then came what is sometimes called "Neely's Seven Lean Years." It's true that the Tigers won just seven games his

John Heisman (top right) with his 1902 team.

first three years, but after the IPTAY Scholarship Club was formed in 1934, Neely didn't have a losing season and coached the team in its first post-season game—the 1940 Cotton Bowl.

When Neely left to go to Rice Institute following the victory in Dallas over Boston College, Frank Howard came along.

He stayed for 30 years, and never missed a game as head coach.

After Howard came "Hootie" Ingram for three years, "Red" Parker for four, Charlie Pell for two and Danny Ford for 11 before Ken Hatfield took over for the 1990 season.

Ford took the Tigers to their highest pinnacle—the national championship in 1981. Clemson started the year unranked and stayed that way until upsetting fourth-ranked Georgia in the season's third game. The Tigers gained from one to five places each week after that, and took advantage of teams above them getting beat. After defeating Wake Forest 82–24 in the eighth game, Clemson went from third to second and stayed there through the regular season. When Penn State whipped top-ranked Pittsburgh two weeks later, the Tigers jumped to No. 1 and stayed there by defeating Nebraska in the 1982 Orange Bowl.

Hatfield's first Clemson team recorded the school's 500th football victory and went on to win the Hall of Fame Bowl.

As the Tigers begin their 96th season of football, their rich tradition continues.

IPTAY

In September, 1896, a group of students met in the barracks and formed the Football Aid Society. They asked Prof. Walter Merritt Riggs, who would later become the school's president, to coach the school's first team.

Prof. Riggs, who had played football at Auburn, was well equipped to guide the team through its formative period. This is attested to by the success of the two seasons he coached (1896 and 1899) and by his leadership during the next quarter of a century as head of the Athletic Association at Clemson.

Riggs, who coached those two early teams without pay, defeated Georgia Tech in 1899 by a score of 41–5.

It was about this time that the students decided that Riggs, who had brought them the game of football, should be allowed to devote all of his time to academics.

As his replacement, Riggs brought in John Heisman from Auburn.

It is not known how long the Football Aid Society functioned. It is known that the group raised $372.50 on its first fund drive.

Heisman departed in 1904, and for the next 23 seasons, Clemson made 15 coaching changes. During this period the football record was 83–91–15. And there is

no record of any organized financial backing of sports at Clemson until the coming of IPTAY in 1934.

An incident that perhaps led to the forming of the IPTAY Club took place in a parked automobile in Florence, South Carolina, on October 31, 1932.

The car was parked outside the stadium in Florence, where Clemson had just lost a 6–0 game to The Citadel. In that group were head coach Jess Neely, end coach Joe Davis, Capt. Frank J. Jervey and Capt. Pete Hefner. Hefner, a member of the military staff at Clemson, was keenly interested in the school's sports, and during his spare time assisted with the coaching of the football team.

It was agreed that something should be done to help athletics at Clemson and the group asked Neely how much money he would need to field a good team. He said he believed if he had $10,000 a year, he could turn out a winning team for the Clemson fans.

There is no irony in the fact that the first time IPTAY crossed that $10,000 mark in a year of fund raising, Clemson went to its first post-season game, the 1940 Cotton Bowl.

As a result of that conversation, those

Dr. Rupert H. Fike, organizer and charter member of IPTAY.

present went their various ways seeking to promote an idea of a $50-a-year club which they felt would produce the money Neely had asked for. They contacted other Clemson boosters and sent out letters.

One such letter went to Dr. Rupert H. (Rube) Fike, an alumnus of the Class of 1908 and a cancer specialist in Atlanta. Fike was at once interested in such an effort, but he and some others thought that perhaps $50 might be too high and that a lesser sum should be sought.

However, the $50 effort was launched. There were some responses, but the net result was nowhere near the $10,000.

Fike, though discouraged, did not give up the idea of monetary assistance to athletics.

With the country still gripped in the Depression, Fike enlisted the assistance of a couple of Clemson men also living in Atlanta, J. E. M. Mitchell, Class of 1912, and Milton Berry, Class of 1913. After some ground work was laid, a meeting was held August 20, 1934. In addition to Fike, Mitchell and Berry, also attending were George Suggs, Gene Cox, E. L. Hutchens,

Bill Dukes, J. R. Pennell and George Klugh.

The next day Fike wrote Neely and the first sentence read: "Last night we had a little meeting out at my house and organized the IPTAY Club."

The initials of the club stood for "I Pay Ten A Year" and it was to be a secret organization. People would be initiated in as members. Each member would be given a card signed by the Clemson head coach, whose title in the club would be the Exalted Iryaas, which stood for "I receive yours and acknowledge same."

In his letter to Neely, Fike wrote of mystic symbols and secret words of recognition that sounded like the makings of a high school fraternity.

The president, vice president and secretary would be known as the Bengal Tiger, Persian Tiger and the Sumatra Tiger, respectively. A "lair" would be a unit of the order, and a "region" would designate a state, province or foreign country. Coin-like pocket pieces were issued. One had the initials of "WDWE" and "WDWD" on it which stood for "When Do We Eat" and "When Do We Drink." Another had "GOCAMS" on it, which meant "Give Our Clemson All My Support."

This secret society only lasted about five years. IPTAY then dropped its ritual and invited everyone to join in support of Clemson athletics.

In that first year of operation, 162 members gave a total of $1,623.70. Because of the Depression, it wasn't uncommon to get post-dated checks, or two checks of $5 each. Some would even divide their $10 payment four ways. Others would pay off with eggs, sweet potatoes, milk, turnip greens and the like.

But those people who were out beating the bushes for money, or anything that could be turned into money, were working to put Clemson in with the athletic elite.

Coach Jess Neely benefited from the first IPTAY donations.

The purpose of the club, according to its constitution, "shall be to provide annual financial support to the athletic department at Clemson and to assist in every other way possible to regain for Clemson the high athletic standing which rightfully belongs to her."

On a visit back to Clemson in 1980, Neely recalled that workers met a lot of curious people while making their rounds and asking for money. "And it took about three or four years before we could start helping a lot of boys," Neely said.

Although bringing Clemson from its lowest ebb to the 1940 Cotton Bowl was one of Neely's career highlights, he said that one even more important was getting the athletic department on sound financial footing. "When we came to Clemson in 1931," Neely said, "there was not hardly 20 cents in the treasury and when I left here (in 1940), there was over $20,000."

The Tigers had a winning season (5–4–0) in 1934, the year IPTAY was formed, but it wasn't until the 1938 season when the club's work really began to pay off. That year the Tigers went 7–1–1. The 1939 team was 8–1–0 in regular-season play and beat the Frank Leahy-coached Boston College team, 6–3, in the '40 Cotton Bowl.

Just a little before World War II started, IPTAY membership had risen to 1,620, but

dropped to a low of 297 during the war years. With athletes lucky to play one whole season, or maybe getting leave to play on the weekend, Clemson football took another dip. In six seasons (1942-47) the Tigers had a 23–30–2 record.

After the 1947 season, when the Tigers finished 4–5, a group of students met with head coach Frank Howard to see if he would resign. He had won 36, lost 34 and tied 3 in his first eight years.

When the students emerged from Howard's office, they had agreed to form the IPOAY Club (I Pay One A Year) to supplement the efforts of IPTAY. The club thrived, but disbanded after three years, in part, due to lack of leadership.

Of course, the next year Clemson went undefeated and won the 1949 Gator Bowl championship, and Howard had heard the last from the students about resigning.

The late Walter Tilley, Jr., was IPTAY's first permanent executive secretary, holding the job in 1947 and 1948. Membership rose to 2,684 and collections to $40,723.

Tilley was succeeded by Cary Cox in 1949. Incidentally, Cox is the only person to captain both the Clemson and South Carolina football teams. He first enrolled at Clemson, then was called into the service and was assigned to the Navy V-12 program, stationed at South Carolina. He captained the Gamecocks, and returned to Clemson after the war, where he captained the 1947 Tigers.

In the one year he held the IPTAY post, Cox saw the membership rise to 4,314 and contributions jump to $48,629.

Eugene P. "Gene" Willimon became executive secretary in April, 1950, opening what might be called the golden era of IPTAY. It was during his 27 years of service that IPTAY was organized into its present-day structure of directors, officers and workers, called representatives, throughout

Executive Secretary Eugene P. Willimon initiated the "golden era" of IPTAY.

the six districts of South Carolina and in other states.

The "T" in IPTAY was changed from $10 to $20 in 1969 and to $30 in 1976, indicating the minimum contribution, which today stands at $100. The Gold Card was created in 1967, inviting members to contribute from $100 to its present value of $5,000.

Willimon raised more than $50,000 in his first year and saw the first $1 million year in contributions before retiring. Memberships increased to more than 10,000.

George Bennett succeeded Willimon, and stayed not quite two years as executive secretary. Between Bennett and his successor, Joe Turner, the club topped the $2 million mark during the 1978-79 fiscal year. Before Turner resigned in favor of Allison Dalton, he saw the membership go over 20,000 and contributions top $5 million.

IPTAY is expected to experience its ninth consecutive year of raising over $5 million in 1990-91 and the 28th straight year where funds exceeded the previous year.

Thousands of athletes have received an education through IPTAY. All of Clemson's 18 sports, 11 men's and seven women's, receive IPTAY support. The university itself has also benefited from IPTAY contributions, and a number of athletic and university facilities have been built with IPTAY funds.

The Clemson IPTAY Club is administered by the executive secretary (now Allison Dalton). He is employed by and reports directly to the Clemson athletic director (Bobby Robinson). The athletic director is also, by IPTAY constitution, the executive director of IPTAY and has final financial authority over the club.

The organization, however, is governed by a board of directors. Six are elected by the membership from the six districts in the state, three are appointed by the school's athletic council chairman, and all past presidents are lifetime members of the board. Officers are elected by board members.

Fike served as president of IPTAY for 20 years. Successive presidents have been Dr. Robert C. Edwards, Calhoun Lemon, Willie Green DesChamps Jr., Harper S. Gault, Glenn J. Lawhon Jr., Woodrow H. Taylor, Marshall E. Walker, Chris Suber, T. Carroll Atkinson Jr., Lewis F. Holmes Jr., Forest E. Hughes Jr., George G. Poole Jr., F. Reeves

Allison Dalton, Executive Secretary of IPTAY, 1984-present.

IPTAY Round-Up, 1961.

Gressette Jr., Charles W. Bussey Jr., Dr. John H. Timmerman, Bill M. Reaves, Lawrence Starkey, James V. Patterson and Eddie Dalton.

Fike liked to tell the story of how determined he was to come to Clemson.

The Fike family lived in the Spartanburg area, and as a child he and a friend went to see Clemson and Wofford play, through a knothole in the fence at the Wofford stadium. The Terriers came out first, dressed in clean, sharp uniforms. Fike's friend said: "Now, that's my team."

A few minutes later Clemson took the field, and the Tigers were a straggly bunch, Fike recalled. Some of the players didn't even have on stockings. Fike's knothole partner said, "Now, that's your team."

The Tigers may have looked ratty, but they were much more talented than Wofford and won the game 21–0. The outcome was decided before the kickoff. It was 1900, John Heisman's undefeated season.

After the game Fike went home and told his folks: "When I go to college, I'm going to that Clemson school." His mother, in no uncertain terms, said: "You'll do nothing of the kind. We moved here just so you could go to Wofford."

But Fike did come to Clemson, graduating in '08, and has been referred to as the "Father of IPTAY."

Just what has IPTAY meant to Clemson, to the State of South Carolina, to the nation, and to the many individuals it has afforded an education in the past 57 years?

Maybe Prof. Riggs had the right idea when he spoke these words on football, and athletics in general, in 1899:

"So long as the game of football helps to make better men of our students, stronger in body, more active in mind; men full of energy, enthusiasm and an indomitable personal courage; men . . . who can deal honorably with a vanquished adversary, and can take victory moderately and defeat without bitterness.

"And so long as football properly controlled and regulated helps the student in his college duties, instead of hindering him. . . .

"So long as it helps to bring about a closer bond of sympathy between students and members of the faculty by creating interest apart from the routine duties; so long as in all these ways the best interests of this and other colleges are advanced, and the course of education aided in its highest mission . . . long may it live and prosper."

Although those words were spoken some 35 years before the formation of IPTAY, the ideas expressed by Prof. Riggs are exemplified today in the total education program at Clemson.

Bowman Field, circa 1910.

Riggs Field, with goal post, upper left.

FIFTY YEARS IN "DEATH VALLEY"

The Clemson football team has had three "homes" on campus. For the first quarter of a century, all athletic events were played on Bowman Field in front of Tillman Hall. Football then moved to Riggs Field (the present soccer stadium).

It was only natural that Clemson's first permanent stadium built for football would be named for Prof. Riggs, the school's first coach back in 1896. The wooden stands were in the shape of a "U" — running behind where the quadrangle now stands, parallel to Highway 93.

Bowman Field was named for Prof R. V. T. Bowman, who assisted in coaching during the early years of football at Clemson. Football, basketball and baseball were among the sports played there.

When Jess Neely went to Rice in 1940, he gave Frank Howard some advice, which went in one ear and out the other. In essence, Neely told Howard to do a little sprucing up on Riggs Field, maybe add a few seats, but not to go over 10,000 because Clemson would never need more than that.

During Neely's stay at Clemson there were about 9,000 seats available, but the Tigers never played more than four games at home in his nine years as coach, and only played four once. In six of his seasons the Tigers played only two home games.

But Neely hardly had time to get unpacked in Houston when Howard had plans on the drawing board for a new stadium at Clemson. There would be 20,000 seats, and it would be in a natural valley a little west of Riggs Field.

Clemson played two years at Riggs Field after Howard became head coach. The Tigers got into their new stadium in time to open the 1942 season against Presbyterian . . . but just barely. Gates were still being hung an hour before game time, and an estimated crowd of 5,000 showed up. In the first four seasons at Memorial Stadium — which was named in honor of all Clemson men who died in all the nation's wars — Howard was probably thinking that Neely knew exactly what he was talking about when he said 10,000 seats would serve Clemson's needs. In the first four years of the new stadium, the Tigers played 11 games and only three of them drew more than 10,000. But these were World War II years — most able-bodied men were in service, gas was rationed, and family life was disrupted for the duration. Football just didn't fit in.

But as America adjusted after the war, so did college athletics, and Clemson was no exception.

A capacity crowd (20,000) in Memorial Stadium for the Villanova game in 1952.

Beginning with the Wake Forest game in 1945, Clemson's attendance began to increase, and with one exception has drawn 10,000 or more spectators in every home game since then. The lone game that did not attract that much attention was The Citadel in 1954. An all-night and all-day rain kept nearly everyone at home. The announced attendance was 1,500, but that might have been stretching it some. Howard said there were more players dressed on the two teams than there were fans in the stands, and that he personally waved at each spectator.

All four home games in Clemson's undefeated season in 1948 drew 15,000 or better, but it wasn't until the Wake Forest game in 1949 that the stadium enjoyed its first full house of 20,000.

The stadium is widely known as "Death Valley" nowadays, but this term was first used prior to the '48 season when the late Lonnie McMillian, head coach at Presbyterian, said he had "to take his team up to Clemson and play in death valley."

The Blue Hose were the opening-game opponent for the Tigers for years, getting a $25,000 guarantee but generally taking a pretty good licking. Nobody much picked up on McMillian's comment, and it wasn't

until Howard started using the "Death Valley" term a few years later that the name really caught on.

In the first 10 years the stadium was used, Clemson's record was 25–8–1. The Tigers have won better than seven out of every 10 games played at home in the last 49 years. The 1991 season will be the 50th anniversary of the stadium.

When the stadium was being built, there was little mechanized equipment and much of the dirt was moved by mules and a scoop. The original cost was around $6.25 a seat. On the last addition to the stadium, in 1983, the cost was $866 a seat.

When the original part of the stadium was built, much of the work was done by scholarship athletes, including a number of football players. The first staking out of the stadium was done by two members of the football team, A. N. Cameron and Hugh Webb. Webb returned to Clemson some years later and was an architecture professor. Cameron moved to Louisiana to be a civil engineer.

The building of the stadium did not proceed without a few problems. One of the football players said he was not allergic to poison ivy and waded into a patch of it with a sling blade, throwing vines in every direction. The next day he was swollen almost twice his normal size and had to be put in the hospital.

Howard left his mark on the new stadium. When each of the four corners was poured, the coach took the chew of tobacco he had in his mouth and threw it into the wet concrete.

So there's a little Howard legacy in each corner of the stadium where, on November 16, 1974, the playing surface was named Frank Howard Field for the long service and dedication he gave the university.

When the original grass was being laid, Howard now recalls what a slow process it was for a few weeks.

"About 40 people and I laid the sod on the field," Howard remembers. "After around three weeks, I remember it was July 15th, we had only gotten halfway through. I told them that it had taken us three weeks to get that far, but that I would give them three more weeks' pay for however long it took (to finish). I also told them I'd go over to the dairy barn and get 50 gallons of ice cream when we got through.

"You know, it didn't take 'em but three days to finish the rest of the field . . . and we sat down in the middle of the field and ate up that whole 50 gallons of ice cream."

There wasn't another major expansion of the stadium until before the 1958 season, when 18,000 sideline seats were added. But the talk of additional seats started during the 1955 season when Maryland played there. Every available bleacher seat in a three-county area was rented to take care of the overflow.

At that time the Big Eight Conference and the Atlantic Coast Conference had an agreement with the Orange Bowl. Oklahoma had already won its league title and the winner between the Terps and Tigers was going to play the Sooners in Miami.

With 30,000 people filling every possible nook and cranny, the Tigers jumped to a 12–0 lead, but melted in the second half and lost 25–12.

Those new seats were ready by the time Virginia came into the valley to open the '58 season.

Jim Tatum came to Clemson for the first time as the North Carolina coach the following Saturday, and it was a game of milestones.

The Tigers came from behind three times to win 26–21 — Howard's 100th collegiate coaching victory. It was also Clemson's first 40,000 home football crowd.

It was one of those hot September days. The concession people were caught by surprise by the size of the crowd. They ran out of cups in the third quarter and of ice early in the fourth quarter. Although no count was kept, a record was certainly set that day with the number of heatstroke patients. Emergency medical crews reported that people were laid out like cordwood underneath the stands after being overcome by the heat.

Increasing demands for seating space brought the stands in the west end zone. The new 5,658 seats were in place prior to the opening of the 1960 season, bringing the stadium capacity to more than 43,000.

The area behind the east end zone has always been used for overflow crowds and has been tagged as Section GG (green grass). It used to be a good baby-sitting place where parents could send the children. Now these seats sell for the same price as a 50-yard-line reserved seat. Howard once said he didn't see why everybody wanted to sit on the 50. "There's never been a touchdown scored there yet," he observed.

Section GG used to accommodate around 10,000 fans, but that has been about

Overhead shot of Death Valley.

FIFTY YEARS IN "DEATH VALLEY"

cut in half with additional permanent stands.

There have been two other major additions to the stadium in the last dozen years. The south stands (press-box side) were double decked in 1979. (Actually, the last game of 1978, South Carolina, was the first time the south top deck of 8,964 seats was occupied. That audience, 63,050, set a new home attendance mark.)

The north stands were double decked prior to the 1983 season with 14,125 seats. With about 1,500 seats known as the east bleachers, and the new handicapped areas put in place in 1978, and the VIP boxes, the total seating capacity is 79,575.

However, crowds in excess of 80,000 are not uncommon when standing-room patrons, the press, stadium security, stadium employees and the like are included in the final count.

In the last eight seasons, the Tigers have played before 19 home crowds that were over 80,000. Clemson and South Carolina have drawn four of the top 10 crowds, Georgia has a pair, while Florida State, Duke, N. C. State and Georgia Tech have the others.

Memorial Stadium also has more private boxes than any other college stadium in the nation. There are 98 of these VIP havens, ranging from boxes that accommodate six people to the largest that can hold 44. Boxes are leased to individuals and companies for a period of five years.

Clemson fans have the reputation of following their team on the road. It is common for 8,000-12,000 to attend a regular-season away game. When it comes to post-season bowl games, the Tigers usually will sell about as many tickets as are available, sometimes numbering 25-30,000. At the 1978 Gator Bowl game with Ohio State, Tiger fans were in every section of the stadium and were able to spell out C-L-E-M-S-O-N around the oval.

Howard's Rock.

The Gator Bowl will probably always have a soft spot in its heart for Clemson. After losing money on its first three games, Clemson played Missouri in the fourth Gator Bowl, January 1, 1949. At that time the stadium held around 39,000. Clemson sold about 21,000 of those tickets and put the game in the black for the first time. Clemson won the game, 24–23, and it was voted the most exciting Gator Bowl game at the 25th anniversary celebration.

Clemson's home attendance is the envy of many schools. In fact, the all-student production, Tigerama, which is the world's largest pep rally on the night before homecoming, annually draws around 40,000.

For the past five years, Clemson has sold over 55,000 season tickets, and this does not count around 11,000 seats which are saved for students. Additional season tickets could be sold were it not for ticket commitments to certain visiting teams.

In the past 10 years, more than four and a half million fans have attended Clemson's

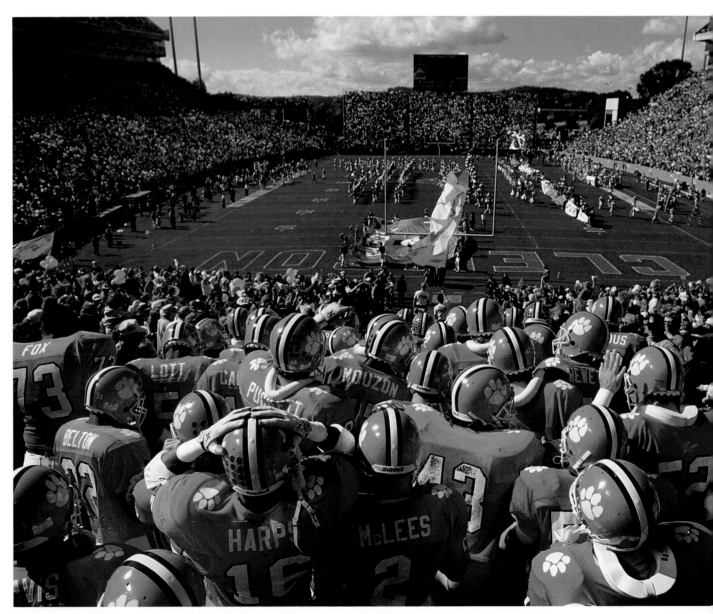

Players atop "the hill" preparing to touch Howard's Rock on their run down to the field.

FIFTY YEARS IN "DEATH VALLEY"

62 home football games, for an average of 73,985 per game. The biggest season was 1988, when the average was 81,750 — fifth best in the nation. On two occasions the Tigers have drawn over a half million fans in a season. Clemson played eight home games in 1987 and 602,526 streamed through the gates.

With Clemson being one of the national leaders each year in attendance, it's no surprise that the Tigers have led the ACC in home crowds for 13 consecutive seasons, several times by more than 20,000 a game.

Besides the fans who come to games in motor homes — some of which stay from Thursday till Monday — that park around the old Seneca River bed, there are thousands of others who come early Saturday morning and set up tables for tailgating, complete with candelabra. Most do not come inside the stadium proper until about 15 minutes before kickoff. But they are in place in time to see the players run down the hill.

Real Clemson fans will not miss the color and pageantry of those 30 seconds as the Clemson players and coaches run down a rug more than a hundred feet long onto the stadium floor just before kickoff.

This ceremony actually started in 1942, when the stadium was completed. The players dressed at Fike Field House, and the shortest distance to the stadium was down Williamson Road.

Howard continued the tradition after locker rooms were built inside the stadium. After the final briefing by coaches in the west end zone locker rooms, team members board buses for the short ride around to the east end zone bank. When everyone is off the bus, the cannon sounds. The players take off down the hill, touching Howard's Rock as they pass. The band strikes up Tiger Rag and the celebrated entrance is made through a human chute of band members.

The Tigers have done this for every game since 1942, except for 1970, 1971 and four games of the 1972 season. In all, the Tigers have run down the hill 217 times, counting the six runs of 1990.

The Tigers have a 158–53–6 record when they run down the hill and 6–9 record when they don't. Coach Ken Hatfield didn't think twice when he decided to continue this tradition in his first year at Clemson in 1990.

Rubbing Howard's Rock is another tradition that is now 25 years old. The late S. C. Jones, Class of '19, took a trip to California, and came by Howard's office and presented the coach with a rock "from Death Valley, California, to Death Valley, South Carolina."

The rock, about twice the size of an adult's head, sat on the floor in Howard's office for a couple of years. Finally, he told Gene Willimon, executive secretary of IPTAY, to "get rid of this rock."

Instead, Willimon had it mounted on a pedestal underneath the main scoreboard in the east end zone where the players come down the hill. It was in place in time for the opening game of 1966 against Virginia. The Tigers, down 18 points with 17 minutes to play, came back to defeat the Cavaliers 40–35.

Before the 1967 season opened against Wake Forest, Howard told his players: "All of you who're going to give me a 100 percent when you go into the valley today, you can rub my rock. It'll give you good luck. Any of you who isn't going to give 100 percent, keep your filthy hands off my rock. Don't you touch it."

Clemson won the game 23–6, and Howard made reference to his speech about the rock on his television show the next day.

A lady from North Carolina wrote and said: "Dear Coach: If you'd believe more in God and less in that rock, you'd be a lot better football coach."

Walter Riggs (center top, with hat) coaching his last team in 1899.

THE COACHES

The first four years of Clemson football has been likened to "the Stone Age." The players were rugged individuals, who had spent most of their years before coming to Clemson behind a mule and a plow. "Horny-handed sons of toil" was the way South Carolina Sen. Ben Tillman described the Clemson student body during these early days.

Due to the lack of helmets or any other head protection, all the players wore long hair. They were called "lions" because of their manes, and "tigers" because of their orange and purple striped jerseys. The latter nickname stuck, although many say that Clemson's nickname came from Auburn, where all of the early coaches came from.

Clemson professor Walter M. Riggs, who was a student at Auburn, coached that first team for no pay in 1896; W. M. Williams, also an Auburn man, was hired to coach the 1897 team; J. A. Penton, an assistant coach at Auburn, was hired by the Tigers for the 1898 season. Due to lack of funds, Riggs came back for his second season in 1899; and he hired John Heisman from Auburn in 1900.

Heisman was successful from the beginning, taking the Tigers to their first undefeated season in his first year. Heisman believed that even the scanty uniforms of the day were a deterrent and eliminated the shin guards and stockings, thinking that would afford more free movement and give his players a little more speed.

The "sons of toil," indeed.

The forward pass was not in use at that time. Bob Williams, who was Clemson's head coach three times (1906, 1909 and 1913-15), was the first coach to use the forward pass at Clemson. This came against Georgia Tech, on Thanksgiving Day in 1906, and was from George Warren to Powell Lykes. It was thrown with the team lined up in punt formation.

Heisman used handoffs and lateral passes long before they came into general use. He loved to confuse the opposition.

A number of schools refused to play Clemson when Heisman was coach. They said the Tigers' play was unnecessarily rough. Heisman's theory was "hit 'em and hit 'em hard."

Heisman's teams at Clemson won 85 percent of their games in his four years. Nearly every one of his players had a nickname — "Peg" Douthit, "Buster" Hunter, "Pee Wee" Forsythe, "Beef" DeCosta, "Vet" Sitton, "Jock" Hanvey and "Puss" Derrick, just to name a few. In later years, some would earn a nickname because of a brother, cousin or the like who had played before him, and instead of being "Big John" he might be "Little John."

During the four years after Heisman, coaches Eddie Cochems, Bob Williams, Shack Shealy and Frank Shaughnessy won 65 percent of their games with stars from the Heisman era.

The first decade of the "Dark Ages" following the Pendleton Escapade in 1908 produced few outstanding teams or players. Only a handful would have measured up to Heisman's standards. Some of the best in those years were "Tanny" Webb, "Shorty" Schilletter (for whom one of Clemson's dining halls is named), "Mule" Littlejohn, "Sarg" Poole (Dr. Robert F., who would later become Clemson president), "Rummy" McGill, "Dopey" Major, "Bub" Hart, "Red" McMillan, Bill Harris and "Warhorse" Bates. This group toiled for the Tigers anywhere from 1909 to 1916. It only won 45 per cent of its games.

Jiggs Donahue, in his four years as head coach (1917-1920) raised the winning percentage to 60 per cent.

The two years of E. J. "Doc" Stewart and the four of Bud Saunders, covering 1921-26, produced only 16 victories and three ties to go along with 32 losses.

Josh Cody came on the scene in 1927. Cody started out with a scoreless tie with Presbyterian, but then won five of the next six before suffering back-to-back shutouts to Georgia and Furman. But the 5–3–1 season, compared to the 2–7 the year before, started Cody on four successful seasons which would produce 29 wins, one tie and only 11 losses.

Cody left the cupboard bare for Jess Neely, who came to Clemson in 1931 and managed only one win and two ties. Tennessee beat him 44–0 and Alabama, where he had come from, slammed the Tigers 74–

7 in Montgomery.

Neely's 1932 and 1933 teams did manage three victories each, but seven wins in three seasons are not the makings of a coaching legend.

When IPTAY was formed in 1934, things began to turn around, and Neely did not have a losing season in his last six at Clemson.

Neely's '38 and '39 teams produced 15 wins and a tie. This caught the eye of officials of Rice Institute in Houston, who were searching for a head coach. Some contact had been made with Neely by Rice before he took his '39 team to play Boston College in the Cotton Bowl, and other meetings were held after his arrival in Dallas.

One night in a hotel room prior to the bowl game, Neely confided to a few people, including Bill Sullivan of Boston College, that he had decided to accept the offer from Rice to be its new head coach.

Sullivan was Frank Leahy's publicity director and would follow the legendary coach to Notre Dame. Sullivan would later become owner of the NFL's New England Patriots.

Sullivan related years later that when Neely announced to the small group that he was going to Rice, Frank Howard, who was Neely's line coach, said: "Well, I'm not going with you." And Neely retorted: "I hadn't planned to ask you."

Howard knew something that Neely didn't. J. C. Littlejohn, who was Clemson's business manager, had told Howard before the team went to Dallas that if Neely did go to Rice, he wanted Howard to be the next Clemson head coach. Following the triumphant return from Dallas and Neely's departure to Rice, the Clemson Athletic Council met to name a replacement.

After spending a half hour or so with council members, Howard stepped to the back of the room "just to listen to what they were going to say about me." After some discussion, which Howard says "seemed like an eternity," Prof. Samuel "Slim" Rhodes said: "I'd like to nominate Frank Howard to be the new Clemson head football coach."

Howard recalls there was no reaction from the other board members and so he blurted out: "I second the nomination." He got the necessary votes and then hung around for the next 30 years as the Tigers' head man.

A contract for four years was drawn up, but Howard said after about three months he lost it and he did not have another contract his entire stay at Clemson. Quite a contrast to what head coaches demand nowadays. "We didn't need no contract," Howard says. "Back then a handshake was worth more than something written in many cases. We always had a good relationship with the Clemson administration and didn't worry about a job."

Wally Butts became head coach at Georgia in 1939, a year before Howard took over at Clemson and Neely was named at Rice. The three coaches ranked highest for a number of years in longevity at one school. After Butts stepped aside following the 1960 season, Howard and Neely were neck-and-neck in tenure. It stayed that way until 1966 when, after 27 years in as Rice head coach, Neely, who was several years older than Howard, decided he had had enough and retired. That left Howard with the longest tenure of any football coach in the nation.

He held that distinction for another three years. He retired from head coaching after the 1969 season, and Cecil W. "Hootie" Ingram, an assistant on the staff of Frank Broyles at Arkansas, was named the new coach.

The day Howard's retirement was announced, a reporter asked him how long he thought it would be before a new coach

Josh Cody coached the Tigers from 1927 to 1930.

was named. "Well, son," Howard said, "when the president gets shot or killed or dies in office, they got another one in about 15 minutes. I 'spect it'll take 'em two or three weeks to replace me." Actually, Ingram was named coach a week later.

Howard retained his title of athletic director, which he held almost as long as he had been football coach. When university President Frank Poole gave him the extra title of A.D., he gave Howard a little extra stipend to go with the added responsibility. But he asked Howard not to tell anyone what his new salary was. Howard said: "Don't worry about that, Dr. Poole, I'm just as ashamed of it as you are."

Howard was relieved of his duties as athletic director February 4, 1971, and he was succeeded by Bill McLellan (now at Southern Mississippi), his long-time assistant. Since he was three years shy of reaching his 65th birthday and full state retirement benefits, the Clemson administration gave him the fancy title of "Assistant to the Vice President of Student Affairs." His boss happened to be Dean Walter T. Cox, who would later become the university's president, but who, before going into administrative work, had played under Howard in 1940.

Hootie Ingram succeeded Frank Howard as Tiger coach in 1970.

Nobody remembers Howard giving Cox too much advice on how to run the student affairs office, or even visiting the office for that matter. But anybody who wanted to drop by Howard's office in the athletic building could get plenty of advice on any subject. All you had to do was slow down long enough to get a conversation started.

Ingram did not have a winning season in the three he stayed at Clemson, and resigned to be an assistant commissioner of the Southeastern Conference. Red Parker came on board from The Citadel in 1973. His first team finished with a 5–6 record, and his second went 7–4—Clemson's best since 1967.

Parker's third team dipped to 2–9, and even though one of his wins in the 3–6–2 season of 1976 was over arch rival South Carolina, he resigned.

Charley Pell, an assistant coach on Parker's staff, was named head coach at a news conference one night following a home basketball game.

Pell got in almost two seasons. His first team had an 8–3–1 season in 1977 and went to Clemson's first bowl game in 18 years. More than 50,000 Tiger fans fought over about half that many tickets for the Gator Bowl game against Pittsburgh. The Panthers took the Tigers apart, 34–3, but fans found out that going to post-season games was still nice.

Clemson has been to a bowl game 10 of the last 14 seasons and in three of those years the Tigers were ineligible for post-season play because of NCAA and Atlantic Coast Conference probation.

In 1978, after beating South Carolina in the regular-season finale, Pell announced he was resigning at Clemson to take the head coaching job at the University of Florida. Clemson had already accepted an invitation to play coach Woody Hayes and his Ohio State Buckeyes in the Gator Bowl.

Pell's resignation came on a Monday, and two days later Danny Ford, Pell's assistant head coach, was named Clemson's head coach by the university Board of Trustees.

The night Pell told Clemson President Dr. Bob Edwards that he was resigning, he left to fill an engagement as speaker at the Jacksonville Beach Quarterback Club. He did not return to the Clemson campus until the following Saturday night. He held a press conference Sunday night and announced he was relinquishing the team to Ford for the Gator Bowl game.

Frank Howard on bench with players, 1944.

Ford now had 19 days to get his team ready to face Ohio State, and without the services of two assistant coaches who had gone with Pell to Florida. Woody Hayes had been coaching football longer than Ford had been living.

There have been many coaches who have ended their careers with bowl games, but Ford was the first to start there. The second coach to do this was John Gutekunst. And wouldn't you know it, the game was against Ford and his Clemson Tigers.

Coach Red Parker exhorts the troops on the sidelines.

In 1985, Gutekunst, a former Duke assistant who had scouted Clemson on many occasions, was named head coach at Minnesota, replacing Lou Holtz, who had gone to Notre Dame. His first game was against Clemson in the Independence Bowl in Shreveport, Louisiana, on a cold December night.

Both Ford and Gutekunst were successful in their head coaching debuts. Ford went on to coach the Tigers through 1989, including the national championship season of 1981.

Ken Hatfield faced the difficult task of replacing the enormously popular Ford in 1990, but had won full support of Clemson loyalists by the end of the season.

Coach Charley Pell with assistant (and future head coach) Danny Ford.

Current coach Ken Hatfield.

FRANK HOWARD

For years Frank Howard has said that he had to quit coaching because of health reasons — "the alumni got sick of me," he'll say to whoever will listen.

Howard told a packed news conference Wednesday, December 10, 1969, that the decision to retire from coaching "was not what I wanted personally, but what I think is best for Clemson."

He said he "made the decision last April or May to resign as head coach and had informed several persons at Clemson of my decision.

"I had to do it sooner or later," he declared, "and the reports get out every year and it ruins my recruiting. The only way we're going to build up is to get a coach in here who isn't retiring every year."

Howard stressed that his health "is as good as it ever was" and that it was not a factor in his decision to step-down as coach.

The bald 60-year-old said he got into coaching "for the derndest fool reason — I heard you got to take a shower bath every day. That sounds crazy, but it's true. That was a luxury in those days. A coach always got to take a shower bath, but not many other people did. And that's why I became a coach."

Despite better financial offers on numerous occasions, Howard stayed at Clemson. "When I die I want to be buried up there on that (Cemetery) hill near the stadium. I want to be there so I can hear all them people cheering my Tigers on Saturday and where I can smell that chewing tobacco in every corner of the stadium. Then I won't have to go to heaven. I'll already be there."

During his 39 years as a coach at Clemson — nine as an assistant to Jess Neely and 30 as the head man — Howard had built up a following of sportswriters who knew a call to him would mean a readable story or column the next day. And stories he told were more plentiful than the writers. "Most of 'em ain't so," he says, "because I started them myself."

Jack Gallagher, longtime Houston sportswriter, said that "Frank's ample stomach identified a profile as prominent on Clemson's campus as the nearby Blue Ridge Mountains."

Gallagher recalled when Howard came to Houston for a testimonial dinner for Neely. "I really ain't much of an after-dinner speaker," Howard said. "I'm just after a dinner and I don't mind talking for it."

Then he directed his remarks to the alumni.

Coach Howard going over final game plans on Friday afternoon.

"Everywhere you go these days they talk about oe-ganizin' the alumni," he offered. "They want to help with recruiting. I don't know whether that's good or not. The alumni give you enough hell when they dis-oe-ganized."

On faculty members:

"We got a lot of PhD's at Clemson. They're OK after four or five years, but when they first come they all want to make a name for themselves by flunking football players. We straighten them out pretty soon."

On politicians:

"Senator Strom Thurmond (a 1923 graduate of Clemson) wanted to go with me on some speaking trips when he was president of our alumni association. Trouble was, he'd talk a half hour about Clemson and an hour and a half about Strom."

On his first ambition in life:

"I've often wondered where I'd be today if my first ambition in life had been realized. Then my chief aim was to go to Auburn and be a chicken farmer."

Howard never went for gimmicks to try to psyche his players into winning. "Blocking and tackling wins games," he said.

As an example, he cited his first season at Clemson when the Tigers won five in a row and then lost two straight.

He promptly received a letter from his mother in which she said: "Frank James ('she always called me Frank James when she was annoyed at me') you tell those boys to win and I'll bake them some cookies."

Howard said he had to write his mama and tell her that you don't win games promising the players to give them some cookies.

Howard said that his successor would not be anyone on his staff. "They [the alumni] are ambitious," Howard said. "They want Knute Rockne for football coach, Casey Stengel to coach baseball and Adolph Rupp for basketball."

Soon after Howard announced his retirement, the Atlanta Touchdown Club made known it would dedicate the luncheon of its 31st Jamboree to Howard "for his contributions to football and the Touchdown Club over the years."

His reaction was: "It will be a fitting tribute to a great coach, and I sho appreciate it. I don't want to change my image too fast now that I'm just a dignified athletic director, so this'll give me a chance to ease out of it and bring old Hootie Ingram down to Atlanta to hear what a great coach he's succeedin'."

Ingram was named Clemson head coach

seven days after Howard retired. Ingram was on the Arkansas staff of Frank Broyles.

"I guess y'all saw on that there satellite TV how I finished real good (as a coach) when me and Chuck Fairbanks (Oklahoma) coached the South in the Hula Bowl and beat the heck out of them Yankees, 35–13.

"I told 'em at the banquet in Hawaii why they got me down there. Dee Andros (Oregon State) was there 'cause it was the year of the Greek—him, Onassis and Agnew. Fairbanks had to be invited so he'd bring his Heisman Trophy boy Steve Owens along. Jack Mollenkopf (Purdue) had to bring Mike Phipps. The University of Hawaii coach had four players in the game. They decided they'd better have a coach . . . so they invited me."

Frank Howard stories abound like blackberries in July. Some are worth picking, others aren't.

He has been known as a "kisser" at times.

Clemson had beaten North Carolina in 1961 and 1962, which were the sophomore and junior years of the Tar Heels' bruising back Ken Willard. But in 1963, when UNC came to The Valley, Willard literally wore the Tigers out. The final score was 29–0.

At that time there was a door connecting the home and visiting dressing rooms and Howard was one of the few who had a key to the lock.

After he had a few encouraging words to his beaten players, Howard unlocked that door and yelled: "Wheah's that Willard?"

When Willard came to the door, Howard planted a big kiss on his cheek and said, "Son, I'm glad I won't have to see you in that light blue uniform again."

And the same year, after the Tigers had won on a late field goal against South Carolina, Howard burst into his own dressing room and inquired: "Wheah's that Rodney Rogers, that boy whut kicked the field goal

Frank Howard in his playing days at Alabama.

and won the game for me?

"Come heah, boy, I's going to kiss you."

Rogers tried to run, but Howard caught him and planted a kiss on him.

Howard saw numerous coaches come and go at both the Southern Conference and Atlantic Coast Conference schools while he was in his 30-year hitch at Clemson. There were 52 of them, to be exact.

One was Douglas Clyde "Peahead" Walker at Wake Forest. He and Howard were two veteran ribbers who always had a "feud" going between them.

Someone once asked Howard why his wife always went with him on trips. Walker, standing nearby, piped in, "She'd rather go with him than have to kiss him goodbye."

Howard always had favorite nicknames for his opposing coaches. Once when N. C. State was playing at Clemson, Wolfpack coach Earle Edwards (whom Howard had called "Midnight" for a number of years) elected to receive the kickoff instead of kicking off despite a blustery wind that was gusting to more than 30 miles an hour. Clemson, trailing 6–0 on two Gerald Warren first half field goals, naturally took the wind, scored 14 points and won 14–6.

After that, Howard began calling

Coach Howard with a worried look in his early days as Clemson's coach.

Edwards "West Wind" instead of "Midnight." Howard said that original name came about because anytime he walked into the William Penn Hotel in Pittsburgh at midnight during recruiting season, Edwards was sitting there watching all of the high school players being hustled by all of the major colleges.

Other people may have called South Carolina coach Paul Dietzel "Pepsodent Paul," but Howard called him "Colgate Paul," "because that's the only team he could beat when he was at Army." He used to call Bill Murray at Duke "Preacher" because even in regular conversation he sounded like he was giving a sermon.

In 1990 and 1991 several major conferences re-aligned themselves by taking in one or more teams, hoping it would be of mutual benefit to both the school(s) and/or the conference.

Howard said he didn't know why so much was being made about the ACC expanding to nine teams by admitting Florida State.

"I advocated adding two teams to the conference around 1960," he said, when the ACC raised the college board score to 800. One of the officials asked me why did I want a conference with 10 teams, and I told him then we could just play each other and

nobody would know how sorry we were."

When the conference was thinking about putting restrictions on football scholarships, Howard sent them a message:

"If you're gonna kill the game, also do this:

"Pool all gate receipts.

"Pay all coaches the same, win, lose or draw, and rotate coaches among schools every four years, like the Methodists do ministers."

Howard was always ready to talk about his players, whether they were still in uniform or were already out in life on their own. He got ragged quite a bit for not having as many pro players as some of his counterparts.

"The most satisfaction is seeing some ole guard or tackle or halfback become a lawyer, or a doctor, or a successful businessman and good citizen," he once said. "It's worth more than a hundred touchdowns. That's the truth, if I ever told it."

One morning at the Clemson Holiday Inn, where the "First-Liar-Ain't-Got-A-Chance Coffee Club" meets every day, members of the group had ganged up on Howard again concerning the pro games of the day before. Several ex-ACC players had decent days, but former Clemson players were not mentioned prominently.

"Yeah, but my players are going to be making more than a lot of those pro players in the long run," Howard boasted. "I got boys out there who are bank presidents, engineers, college professors, diplomats, college presidents, and I even have four or five who are preachers."

About that time, as luck would have it, one of his ex-player preachers walked into the dining room.

"Rev. Bowen, come over here a minute, please, sir," Howard said reverently. "Rev. Bowen, did you ever play football for me?" Howard asked.

FRANK HOWARD

"Hell, yes," Rev. Bowen answered without batting an eye.

At a football practice in the spring one year, Howard was asked if a certain player had improved.

"I 'spect so," Howard answered. "He ain't as noticeable doing nothin' now as he was last fall."

Most any player who ever came under his command would go to bat for him in the wink of an eye.

Hugh Mauldin (halfback 1963-64-65) said: "He's one of the greatest men I've ever known. He acted like a rough, gruff old man, but he has a heart of gold. If it hadn't been for him, I never would've gotten to school. He's 99 percent down-to-earth . . . true blue."

Dr. Thomas H. Barton, president of Greenville Technical College, gave Howard more problems than many of the players because of his academic work. But "Black Cat," as he was known in college, continued on to get his Masters degree and then his doctorate from Duke.

Instead of referring to Barton's school as Greenville Tech, like most people do, Howard calls it "Black Cat University."

Barton, who played for Howard in 1951-52-53, said: "When I first saw Frank Howard, I had all my belongings—as he used to accuse me of—in a sack. I was young and just out of the service and certainly not serious about anything. But he taught me some things that have lasted all my life. He had more to do with shaping my life than anybody but my mother. I give credit to Frank Howard for straightening me out and teaching me the things of life I needed to know."

And Jackie Calvert, tailback in 1948-49-50, which included the Gator and Orange Bowls, put his thoughts this way: "He's probably one of the most honest people you'll ever meet. Outside of his public image, he's a very gentle person. Oh, he was pretty tough—except when we were winning. The happiest I ever saw him was in 1950 when we played Missouri. We were a two-touchdown underdog and we beat 'em pretty bad, 34-0 I think. Coach Howard came in the dressing room—and you know how he likes to chew that tobacco. He was going around giving everybody a hug and a kiss, which wasn't too pleasant, but we didn't mind. He's one of the best friends I guess I ever had . . . somebody you can count on."

Other former players have told the story of Howard going miles out of his way to visit a former player who was down on his luck or was having some personal problems.

"He has just dropped in on some people and said he was riding by their house and he thought he would come in to see them," a former player related.

"He knew that one former player had all kinds of problems and was thinking about committing suicide. He just thought he'd

Coach Howard and daughter Alice celebrate a big win.

drop in on the fellow to show that somebody cared."

Howard never talked much about things like that. He'd rather be known as the country-sounding clown who turned out football teams that were seldom if ever outhit by the opposition.

"I've said a lot of things I shouldn't have said," he once offered. "I often wonder if all that talk does any good. It makes me look awful stupid sometimes. But it's too late for me to change now."

In his later years, Howard said the only thing he didn't like about football was the recruiting. And he had his share of recruiting stories.

The most well-known he recalls happened when Jess Neely sent him to Charleston to see a 240-pound lineman—unheard of in those days. When Howard located the player's home, a boy weighing all of 165 pounds answered the door.

When the boy identified himself as the player Howard was looking for, the coach said, "Well, son, I'm selling the Saturday Evening Post, and was wondering if you would like to subscribe to it."

Howard recalled another time he received a letter from a coach in Virginia, telling him about a 155-pound tackle he had. Howard always said he could get up a lot better conversation with a 200-pound fullback than he could with a 175-pound lineman.

But the coach told Howard that this player was sure to grow and fill out. He explained that the boy's great-great-grandfather came over on the Mayflower, one of his uncles was a former governor of Virginia, another uncle had been a Supreme Court justice and that he didn't see how he could go wrong in giving this player a Clemson scholarship.

"I wrote this coach back real quick," Howard recalled. "I told him that I was looking for a boy to play football . . . I didn't need one for breeding purposes."

Howard said he always tried to get on the right side of the player's mama. "I found that the mama is the one behind most of the decisions made at home. I remember I did such a good job one time on selling Clemson to this boy's mama that she came to Clemson and he went to South Carolina."

One segment of the community who always seized the opportunity to talk to him was the news media. As Larry Tarleton wrote in the *Charlotte Observer* the next day after covering Howard's retirement press conference:

"Yes, the ACC and football will miss Frank Howard. But the people who will miss him most are the sportswriters. Any time you were really hurting for a column, all you had to do was make a phone call to Clemson."

Dick Herbert, *Raleigh News & Observer*, wrote:

"The easy way to talk about the end of the coaching career of Clemson's Frank Howard would be to describe him as a colorful character and comedian. The proper way, though, to one who has known and watched him for all those years, would be to discuss character.

"When you talk about that, you think about a man's work being his bond, his teams playing according to the rules, and a devotion to the profession that claimed his energies 365 days a year.

"Frank Howard was not found wanting in those things."

Writing in the *Greenville News*, Dan Foster said this: "Over half the people in this country have been born since Frank Howard took that head coaching job back in 1940. It is understandable that many devoted Clemson followers cannot separate Howard and Clemson.

"He enjoyed coaching as few coaches

ever do, because he lived it. His grief made his losses sweeter for his foes, and his victories were untenable because his joy was unrestrained.

"On the personal side, Howard was noted chiefly for his country bumpkin manner. He received much criticism for it.

"But his grammar is not the chief feature of Frank Howard. Nor is his genius, nor his humor, nor even his large ego.

"They are all part of him, but his main guns are integrity and loyalty."

The lead editorial in the *Columbia Record,* under the editorship of John A. Montgomery, pointed out:

"Frank Howard has been nothing less than Clemson College football, itself. Getting used to someone else directing the Tiger squad is going to be as difficult as breaking in a new pair of shoes.

"Ol' Howard has meant much to Clemson, to the state of South Carolina and to American football. May he sleep better at nights and enjoy long life, hearing Clemson students cheer Tiger victories, as athletic director. A legend he is; a gracious man, he is; a coach to be ranked among the greatest, he is."

Leslie Timms was sports editor of the *Spartanburg Herald* and he "scooped" the

Coach Howard holds game ball marking his 150th victory as a head coach (against Maryland, 1966).

story a month before it happened that Howard would step aside as head coach at the end of the season.

Timms ended his column on Howard when the resignation actually took place with these words:

"You could reminisce about Frank Howard for a day and still have stories left over. Just let it suffice to say that he is a good, kind man who cared about his people. He didn't make a lot of noise about that, he just performed the deeds.

"Howard is going to sit in the stands now and watch the man he chooses to succeed him direct the field action. He will probably find it hard to do. But Frank Howard will do it just like he has performed other difficult tasks to perfection in the past.

"It's the end of a long series of battles for Frank Howard the coach. Now he can enjoy life as Frank Howard the man and he deserves all of the enjoyment he can get. Like we said, Frank Howard is a good man. You can't speak much more highly of a person than that."

Furman Bisher has been in the big time a longtime as sports editor of the *Atlanta Journal.* A few of his thoughts on Howard:

"There are some, beset by youth, who

Coach Howard receiving ACC Coach of the Year Award in 1956.

cannot imagine that Frank once had hair and no stomach. The outlanders who've seen only those atrocious sideline pictures, in which Frank gives the impression of a Mississippi deputy arresting a driver with an Illinois tag, might be moved to a 'by jove' by a reading of his credentials.

'Educated at Barton Academy.' How's that for class! 'Graduated, University of Alabama, with a BS degree in business administration.'

"And get this: 'Member, Omega Delta Kappa fraternity.'

"Why, the old fraud!

"So there he goes, out in the pasture to graze. It ain't like he's dead, or anything. It's just that old coaches who become athletic directors do have a tendency to become dull. I do hope that Frank will keep his act alive and the dialogue fresh and let the other fellow see to the coaching."

Herman Helms, former sportswriter on the *Charlotte Observer* and later sports editor of *The State* in Columbia, was one of Howard's staunchest supporters in the press. Helms wrote:

"The haunting question now is this: Has football become so cruelly competitive that a contributor such as Frank Howard cannot pick his own time to go?

"No time would be the right time for an original, a one and only kind of man like Frank Howard, to go. But it was inevitable that it would happen in some season soon.

"He was 60 years old and he had coached for 39 years. No time would be the right time, but it would have been nice if he could have picked the time, if he could have given the last signal that closed a great career.

"But it didn't happen that way. He left without rancor, without bitterness. A man who has given 39 years of his life to a cause isn't about to hurt the cause. Frank Howard would not dare hurt Clemson.

"He tried to make it look right, for Clemson's sake, but he didn't succeed. The timing was the giveaway. No coach plans to quit three days before the signing date for high school recruits. No coach plans to quit at a time like that and particularly if his successor is not at his side. The timing told the story, an unpleasant story.

"An old warrior left because things had become so unpleasant for him. An old warrior left trying to look brave in the face but with tears in his heart. A contributor who gave so much to a game and a school and a state left because people have short memories.

"That's the way it was. It was sad. There is no other way to say it."

But probably the best of all the stories and columns written when Howard retired from coaching was by Donnie Woodward in the *Spartanburg Herald* the Sunday after the retirement. Woodward tried to reach someone in Barlow Bend who knew or remembered Howard. This is his experience:

Last Wednesday afternoon after Frank Howard announced his retirement as Clemson's head football coach, it seemed interesting to find out what the people of Barlow Bend, Alabama, had to say about the announcement.

It was in Barlow Bend on March 25, 1909 that Frank James Howard was born. He has recalled Barlow Bend by saying, "The only white families within 10 miles of where we lived in Barlow Bend were my mother and father and my father's father. I never saw a little white boy until we moved into Mobile when I was five."

While Howard lived in Barlow Bend, the town was a prosperous rural community. Today, it doesn't even have a police department. Most of the old families have moved away, leaving a general store, a post office, and about 250 residents.

The first attempt at reaching someone in Barlow Bend failed when the long-distance operator was unable to locate the town in her directory.

"Are you sure there is such a place?" she asked.

I decided to call the Chamber of Commerce in Jackson and ask the people there for assistance. Mrs. Bessie McCrary, executive secretary, answered the call.

"I'm afraid that I can't help you very much. You see, Barlow Bend isn't a very large town and there aren't many people living there today.

"No, they don't have a mayor. They don't have a police department, either. But there is a post office and a general store."

Mrs. McCrary recalled that her late husband was a doctor who frequently made calls in Barlow Bend. "He knew about everybody there, but most of them have gone now.

"Frank Howard? No, that name doesn't sound familiar.

"What did he do?

"I'm sorry I can't help you, but I've never heard of a Frank Howard. You say he's a football coach at Clemson University. Oh, I see. I'm terribly sorry I can't help you.

"You might try the general store in Barlow Bend and see if the owner can help you. Wait a minute and I'll get the number," Mrs. McCrary said.

B.C. Carr operates the general store, which he says, "has a pot-bellied stove in the middle of the floor for heat." The news about Howard's retirement hadn't reached the "Baron's" hometown.

"I haven't heard about it yet and I'm sure none of the folks here have either," Carr said over the telephone. "Probably wouldn't make too much difference, though, 'cause not too many people who live here now know him.

Strongman Howard proves in 1965 that he is stronger than any of his players.

"You might try Smith's Bakery in Mobile, though. I understand that Howard worked there when he was a small boy. I read that somewhere in a magazine article.

"Yeah, I've heard of Howard. But I've never met him. Seems like a real character," Carr said.

This time the operator found Mobile without any trouble.

"Sure, I've known Frank Howard since he was 12 years old," said Roy Smith.

Smith is the owner and president of Smith's Bakery in Mobile, fifty miles northeast of Barlow Bend. His father, the late Gordon Smith, founded the business. Some 48 years ago, Howard went to work at the bakery to help pay his way through school.

Roy Smith was 24 at the time. He and Howard soon became friends and are still close friends today.

"When Frank came to work at the bakery, we started him out with a job on the wagon as a wagon boy. He went around the town delivering things from the bakery. Then we put him in the shop, where he helped bake and wrap pies.

"The work enabled him to go to school," Smith remembered.

Howard recalls that he "got up at 3:30 a.m. every day" to work at the bakery. "I left at 7:30 to go to school."

Howard is thankful to Smith and the late J. C. Vaughn for the help they gave him as a young boy. Vaughn is a former school teacher who died earlier this year.

"If it hadn't been for Roy Smith at the bakery, Mr. Gordon's son, and for a professor, J. C. Vaughn, I don't know what would have happened to me. I did not have a father; I thought I was a pretty tough boy. I'd get in one fight at little recess and two fights at big recess," remembers Howard.

"That's true," said Smith. "Frank was a real fighter. Nobody ever bothered him.

"I sometimes wish he'd cast his lot with us at the bakery. I know he would havemade it to the top of the bakery business without a doubt. Sure, he could have been a bakery president or maybe owned one of his own."

Smith then turned to the serious side.

"Frank Howard is an outstanding man and I know he's been a marvelous influence on a lot of people. He has really turned out to be a wonderful man."

Coach Howard stalks official Jack Vest.

"We keep in touch. He was here last summer for a visit. And whenever I can get to Clemson for a game, he'll put me on the bench during the game. Whenever he runs out of tobacco to chew, he asks me for a cigarette and chews it.

"When he was here, he didn't mention retiring. But I figured Frank was fixing to do something. In a way, I'm glad to see him retire, because he'll live longer.

"I don't know anything else to say about Frank Howard except he is a good man and a real character. He's my friend," Smith said.

But Smith did have something else to say. He reminded me about Howard and the home run. Howard tells it this way:

"I'll never forget something that happened to me in Mobile playing baseball. The Smith Bakery team had a team in the City Twilight League. They had college boys and some what you might call semipros. I was a little ol' boy, 15. They needed a catcher in the championship game. They sent word to me at school to come on out to the field.

"We got down to the ninth inning. We was losing, 1–0. There was two outs and a man on first base. I was the batter. I was a good, tough catcher with a mean peg to second base. I hit three ways: right handed, left handed and seldom. They got two strikes and no balls on me. The next pitch I hit; I musta closed my eyes; I hit it hard as I could hit it. It went slap over the tennis courts at the end of the field for a home run.

"I played in the Rose Bowl. I coached in the Cotton Bowl, Orange Bowl, Gator Bowl, Sugar Bowl, Bluebonnet Bowl, but I never had a thrill like hitting that home run."

Smith went on. "That's the Frank Howard I remember—all that color and talk, yet a real warm man. I'm glad I've known him."

Color . . . excitement . . . talk . . . jokes . . . tales about "The Bear" . . . head football coach at Clemson . . . booed one week, carried off the field the next . . . Frank James Howard.

Sure is a pity that Mrs. McCrary hadn't heard of him. She's missed a lot.

Howard did not seem to miss coaching, but he showed some signs of restlessness before Clemson's opening game of the 1970 season . . . the first time in 30 years that he had not been on the sidelines as head coach.

Just as Clemson and The Citadel were about the kick off, the press box door swung open. Howard let his intentions be known right away. "Have you got a seat up here for me?" he asked.

After being escorted to a chair, he had one more question: "Have you got a cup for me?" He had brought his usual chew with him.

Clemson president Bob Edwards had given Howard and his wife Anna two seats in the president's box, which was directly in front of the press box.

"I can't sit out there with all of them PhD's and other academicians," Howard said. "They don't talk my language."

With a rare exception, Howard has been in the Clemson press box for every home game since. About his only misses have been to attend the Georgia-Florida game in Jacksonville, or the Alabama-Auburn game.

Nowadays, Howard doesn't exactly live a Life of Riley, but he comes and goes as he pleases. Unless he's out of town on a speaking engagement, he's in his office at the Jervey Athletic Center seven days a week.

A reporter recently asked him how his health was. "Pretty good for a person my age, I guess," Howard said. "Most people old as I am got grass growing on top of them."

Long live the Bashful Baron of Barlow Bend!

The Paw.

FRANK HOWARD

THE PAW

Catchy nicknames and symbols are a big part of athletics. Some don't get out of the dormitory, others are rather localized. But then there are others that become part of the vocabulary — O.J., Magic, The Catch, The Game, Juice, The Refrigerator, Black Cat, Pistol Pete, Bear, Wilt the Stilt.

A little over 20 years ago (1970) "The Paw" came into being at Clemson.

Dr. Robert C. Edwards, then Clemson president, decided he would like "to upgrade the image of the university" and hired the Henderson Advertising Co. in Greenville to start to work on this idea. Company president Jimmy Henderson had attended Clemson and had an idea of what Edwards was thinking about.

"We've asked these people (Henderson) to come in and help us examine and evaluate our program. In fact, they are helping us with a positive approach on all communication matters university-wide," Edwards said.

Among the possible changes being discussed were new uniforms and a new logo that would not replace the tiger but complement it.

After about six weeks of "thinking out loud on several angles" Henderson presented what was first called a "tiger track" as the new logo.

Henderson's people wrote to every school in the nation that had "Tigers" as its nickname, asking for a picture of its mascot. After most of them had responded the conclusion was reached that a tiger is a tiger regardless if it was a Persian, Bengal or Sumatra.

Several other ideas were kicked around, one being the impression of a tiger's foot, or paw. In order to get the real thing, Henderson wrote the museum of Natural History in Chicago, asking for a plaster of Paris cast of the imprint of the tiger's paw.

The imprint was changed to a print, tilted about 10 degrees to the right and presented to the Clemson committee working with Henderson.

The plan was to use the paw on football helmets, schedule cards, bumper stickers, as a pocket patch on blazers, painted on the football field and basketball court, and, in many cases, to replace the "O" in the word Clemson.

Someone even suggested that all of the typewriters on campus be changed where the tiger paw would replace the "o" on the keyboard. That seemed a bit far-fetched and didn't get off the ground.

Now the gospel had to be spread. Football coach Hootie Ingram, basketball coach Tates Locke, all-conference tailback Ray Yauger and Wright Bryan, the university's vice president for development, made a one-day whirlwind trip to six cities . . . Florence, Columbia, Charleston and Greenville in South Carolina, Charlotte and Atlanta.

At each stop a press conference was held. Bryan told the gatherings: "At any university from time to time, there needs to be a modernization. There needs to be some symbol which keeps the whole thing together" and the university hierarchy believed that the paw was the answer.

"Symbols like the tiger paw won't help us to win football games," Ingram said at one of the stops, "but we hope they will help retain the enthusiasm Clemson people are known for."

With tongue in cheek, Locke said: "For three months I've been making speeches extolling the virtues of the tiger. Now, all of a sudden, I have to talk about his feet."

Some people around Clemson, and that included Frank Howard, didn't like the paw in the beginning. But it has created such a bonanza for souvenirs that few people now show up at an athletic event without either wearing orange or some item with the paw on it.

Before Georgia Tech became a member of the ACC, the Yellow Jackets did not relish playing Clemson on a home-and-home basis.

Finally Howard and Bobby Dodd, Tech's athletic director and head coach, decided that the Yellow Jackets would play at Clemson for the first time in 1974, then in Atlanta the next three years and back in Clemson in '78.

When Pepper Rodgers brought his '74 team to Death Valley, the Tigers won 21–17. Rodgers found out that the proposed '78 meeting at Clemson was only a handshake deal between Howard and Dodd, and that

nothing had been signed. So Tech backed out of the deal.

The last game on any signed contract was 1977, and despite the efforts of Clemson athletic director Bill McLellan, no agreement could be reached between the two teams. So the series was broken off.

But George Bennett was executive secretary of IPTAY at the time and he wanted to show the business and commercial people, the Atlanta Chamber of Commerce, and anybody else who was interested in the Atlanta economy, just what 10-12,000 Clemson fans spend on a two-night stay in Atlanta.

Bennett suggested that all Clemson fans who were going to attend the '77 game to take all of their money in $2 bills with an orange tiger paw stamped on it.

People were seen paying for their hotels with fifty $2 bills, or a meal with ten of the stamped bills. One waitress was heard to say: "If I see one more $2 bill with a tiger paw on it, I think I'll throw up."

Bennett's point was pretty well proven. Some fans still take their $2 bills with them on all road games, but this tradition is more prevalent at bowl games.

The paw was becoming more of what the Henderson people had visualized. Their press release introducing the paw print philosophy was entitled: Tiger On The Loose — A quick history of Paw Power.

For years Clemson's roaring tiger was a dead ringer for more than 35 other college cats across the country.

The Paw changed that.

Paw prints, stretching all the way from the stadium to the library, serve as constant reminders that Clemson's Tiger is alive and kicking. Not only are those unique prints on concrete and turf; they've blossomed on notebooks, book covers, bumper stickers, blazers, sweatshirts . . . and the list goes on.

Since 1970, The Paw has engulfed the

Tiger faithful. The SAE fraternity annually paints huge tiger paws on all of the streets on campus leading to the stadium. At some point, all of the major highways leading into Clemson have had paws painted on them.

The fraternity members had to get permission to paint the paws on state and federal highways, as well as some of the streets on campus that are maintained by the state.

Fraternity members came to the athletic department to see coach Bob Jones. Jones had actually been on the coaching staff of

Clemson for a year longer than Howard because Jones was an assistant for one year for Josh Cody, who preceded Jess Neely and Howard.

Jones graduated from Clemson in 1930 and one of his classmates was Silas N. (Si) Pearman, who was the South Carolina Highway Commissioner at the time. The fraternity members asked Jones to write to Pearman for his blessings in painting paws in the highways and streets in the Clemson area, which was done and permission was granted.

Whether or not the P.S. Jones put on his letter to Pearman had any bearing in the decision is not known. But to paraphrase, Jones said that he had a hunch that if permission were not granted the paws would show up on the streets anyway . . . painted after midnight when not much traffic was around.

When Clemson was invited to play in the 1977 Gator Bowl, some enterprising students had a stencil cut of a tiger paw some 22–24 inches high. From Clemson to Jacksonville, every five miles or so, the student spray painted a paw on the road.

When Clemson played in the Orange Bowl for the national championship in 1981, these tiger paws were extended on from Jacksonville to Miami.

But highways were not the only place the tiger paw found its place.

Hardly anything has escaped having The Paw placed on it. Anything wearable has been imprinted.

When veteran trainer Herman McGee passed away, his casket had a tiger paw on the lining of the lid of the casket.

Birth announcements proclaim a new tiger on the block with a paw.

And you can buy a baby bottle with paws just so the newborn can get a close-up look of The Paw.

Eyeglasses have been seen with a tiny

Young fan demonstrating Clemson loyalty.

paw down in one corner of a lens.

One has even been seen on a tooth.

Telephones, watches, all kinds of athletic equipment such as golf balls and club covers, bath towels, tumblers, drinking glasses, coffee mugs, car flags . . .

Orange wigs? Sure.

And there's all kinds of school materials, from notebooks to pencils to book satchels to rubber stamps.

There's gift wrapping.

And don't forget the orange bib overalls.

Incidentally, some of those watches play "Tiger Rag" with the push of a button.

There is a group on campus known as the Central Spirit Committee. The main concern of these students, numbering 35–

The Paw points the way to Death Valley.

3,000 balloons released from Death Valley at Maryland game, 1983.

40, on game day is to make sure that every person attending the game who wishes a tiger paw painted on his nose, cheek, or even bald head, has the opportunity sometime between getting out of his car in the parking lot and reaching his seat.

At one game several years ago the committee set a Guinness Book of Records mark for the number of paws painted on people's faces at one game—more than 43,000.

Clemson fans hold another Guinness Book record—most balloons released at a football game.

When Maryland played in Death Valley in 1983, the committee worked on a balloon project. At first, there were going to be about 300,000 balloons released as the Tigers came down the hill.

But someone heard a rumor that another school was planning to release 325,000. More balloons were purchased, and when the time came more than 363,000 were sent skyward. The helium-filled mostly orange balloons drifted toward the northeast. Some were found as far away as Laurinburg, North Carolina—more than 200 miles from Clemson.

The committee asked for 1,000 students to come to the stadium at 7 o'clock on the day of the game to assist with the blowing up and tying of the balloons. More than 2,000 showed up and the job was accomplished in less than three hours.

At first the Tiger paw was not registered because as much exposure as possible was sought and officials thought that the frequent appearances would be worth many dollars of advertisement. People would identify The Paw with Clemson.

But because many people took advantage of using The Paw in many ways, the decision was made to have the symbol registered with the United States Patent and Trademark Department, making it a national registration and not just in the state of South Carolina.

This would keep anyone or any institution from using the exact paw print. A variation (say with claws protruding) would be acceptable, but not the identical print.

Now, if a company wants to market a product using The Paw, the company must get permission from Clemson. It must also submit a sample and sign a non-exclusive license agreement, pay a licensing fee and agree to pay a royalty fee on all sales at the manufacturer's level at the rate of six and a half percent.

The national championship of 1981 brought about these changes. "The Paw had become synonymous with Clemson," said Robert Ricketts, assistant athletic director and business manager. "We felt any publicity for Clemson would be beneficial. But the 1981 national championship changed all of that. It was obvious that Clemson needed to register The Paw because everyone wanted to use it. We had to have some control over what our university was becoming associated with in terms of products and other things."

Clemson's program is administered by Collegiate Concepts, Inc., a consortium of 90 schools from across the country that provides services in contractual registration, and accounting at a much more efficient and cost effective level.

Bill Battle, former head football coach at the University of Tennessee, is president of the group and is the Clemson representative.

During the week Clemson fans wear many hats—doctor, engineer, farmer, truck driver, lawyer, preacher, policeman, orchardist, coach, merchant . . .

But come Saturday in the fall, when Clemson is playing football, they all show up wearing the same thing . . . THE TIGER PAW!!

Clemson fan George Burns cradles The Paw.

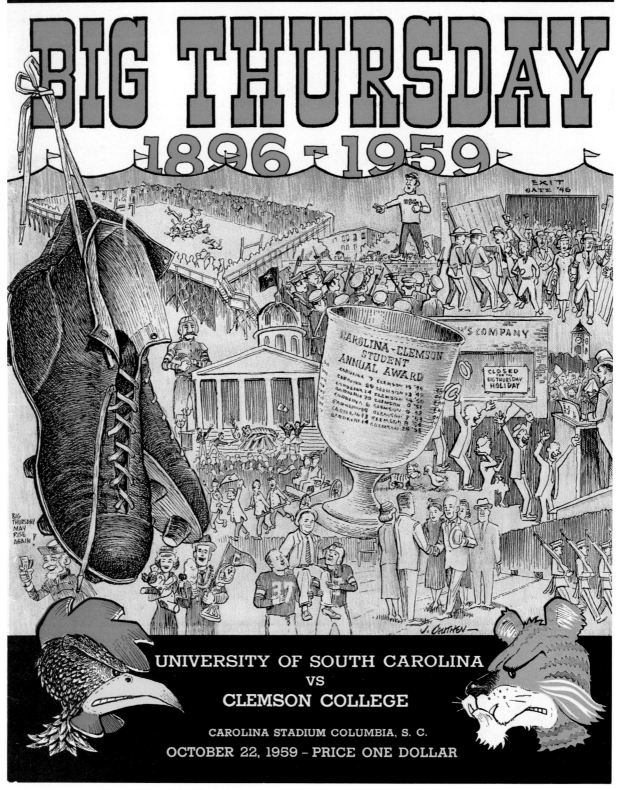

Big Thursday, a Clemson tradition for more than sixty years.

BIG THURSDAY

It has split the state since 1896. If you're a college football fan, you're on one side or the other. No straddling the fence for this one.

It is not unusual to see a carload of fans heading for the game with a Tiger flag flying from one side of the car and a Gamecock banner fluttering on the other side.

Clemson vs. South Carolina.

Many friendly wagers are made, and most of the time, not for money. Maybe the loser has to wash a car once a week for a month; or buy a champagne-steak dinner; or eat a hot dog while he watches the winner devour a juicy T-bone.

The game wasn't played in 1901 or in a seven-year stretch between 1903 and 1909 because of strained relations between the two schools. It was last played on a Thursday in 1959. The rivalry is no less serious now that the game is played on a Saturday, but the history of Big Thursday is something special in South Carolina — something special in college football.

Students from the two schools got out of class on Big Thursday for what was known as State Fair Holidays. There was no business transacted in state government. All offices were closed.

Clemson fans held a big pep rally on campus the Tuesday night before the game. After World War II, Frank B. "Gator" Farr would come up from his home in Palatka, Florida, and hold burial services for the Gamecock.

His entourage would enter the outdoor theater complete with coffin and military escort. As the band played the Funeral March, Farr would enter, wearing a derby hat, complete with orange and purple ribbon, and a split-tailed coat.

The coffin used in the ceremony was given to Clemson fans in Dallas by Boston College supporters following the 1940 Cotton Bowl. The BC fans had planned to use it to bury the Tiger mascot, but a 6–3 Clemson win ended that idea. The coffin was brought back on the team train and stored in Tillman Hall. It was pulled out of storage once a year for the solemn rites.

Farr made the same speech in every year of his burial performance. It came from the fall edition of a Sears Roebuck catalog, ladies ready-to-wear section, corset page.

Farr would recite: "And Sears Roebuck saith, 'No chicken shall strike a tiger and be permitted to live.'"

Then, for 20 minutes or so, Farr would say nothing except what good Tigers would want to hear about Gamecocks. All of his 'sermon' would be in prose and he would review the season of each team up to that time.

Farr always made this announcement: "There will be a big baptismal service in Carolina Stadium this Thursday afternoon. All Methodists will be baptized on the north end of the field, all Baptists will be baptized on the south end of the field, and the South Carolina Gamecock will be baptized at both ends of the field."

And Farr would close out his service with: "And so my little Gamecock friend, it's ashes to ashes and dust to dust, you're gonna catch it Thursday, you little cuss."

No bona fide minister ever put as much emotion in his sermon and Farr did in his. At the end of every verse, rolls of toilet paper would fill the air and the Tigers would scream in delight. But they would quickly quiet, knowing Farr was ready to add additional insult to the remains lying in the casket.

While Clemson fans were having their fun on Tuesday night, the South Carolina faithful made their yearly trek to the steps of the state capitol the Wednesday night before the game for the annual Tiger burn. There, a king-sized stuffed tiger filled with firecrackers would be set afire. After about 15 minutes of explosions there wasn't much left of the animal, much to the joy of all Gamecock fans.

That same night the freshmen teams of the two schools would square off in what became known as "Little Wednesday." First-year players were not eligible for varsity competition during most of those years.

But Thursday was the big day around the state.

The game originally was played at noon, so most fans could be back home by dark. But kickoff was changed to 2 p.m. for most

of the last thirty Big Thursdays.

One of the highlights of the afternoon would come at halftime, when the presidents of the two schools would meet at midfield and exchange guests. The governor would sit on one side during the first half, while the state's two U.S. senators would sit on the other side. At halftime, the school presidents would swap politicians.

Everyone dressed up for the game. Regardless of the temperature, furs and hats were the order of the day. The wives of the dignitaries meeting at midfield at halftime would all have on spiked heels as they trudged along in the grass of Carolina Stadium.

There were never enough seats to meet the Big Thursday demand. For a number of years South Carolina allowed Clemson to transport folding chairs to Columbia and set them up between the Tiger bench and the permanent stands.

About the only thing a person could see from those seats were the punts in the air. But seeing the game was not that important to some of those people. Just being inside the stadium was enough. There was no television and no transistor radios, and people were willing to spend just about anything to get inside.

In 1946, there was a counterfeit ticket scandal, the only one known in the long-standing series. Several thousand bogus tickets were printed up and sold. Arrests were made but not before the tickets were in circulation.

Pressure at the stadium entrances was so great that one of the big wooden gates was broken down and the stampede was on. Naturally, with so many people holding tickets for the same seats, there was only one place to go—to the sidelines.

People were six deep from the sideline back to the Clemson bench. Coach Frank Howard said he accidentally stepped on several fans during the game, and remembered a soft-drink vendor between him and the sidelines selling his wares to the fans.

South Carolina won that game 26–14, but most fans there that day will not remember the score as much as the gate crashing and the sea of fans who filled every available space except the playing field. The game was delayed several times to get fans to pull their feet back off the out of bounds line.

Big Thursday started as an extra attraction for the State Fair. It brought thousands of dollars to the State Agricultural and Mechanical Society, because fans who wanted to attend the game still had to pay an admission to the fair, even if they never set foot on the midway.

A new stadium was constructed and used for the first time in 1934 on land next to the fairgrounds, where the present Williams-Brice Stadium stands today. It didn't take long to outgrow the new field. Sellouts were commonplace, and led South Carolina coach Rex Enright to remark: "If these two teams played in Nome, Alaska, on July 4th, it would be a sellout."

Shortly after that statement was printed in the paper, Enright received a letter from the mayor of Nome, inviting Clemson and South Carolina to play there July 4th.

Enright coached the Gamecocks against Howard for 15 years. Howard won their first meeting in 1940, but the following year the heavily favored Tigers were beaten 18–14. Clemson missed a first down by a foot on a late drive, and the Gamecocks held on for the win.

It was South Carolina's first victory over Clemson in eight years, and was called the biggest upset in Big Thursday games to date. Gamecock fans were so enthralled that they put on a fundraising drive and got enough money to buy the Enrights a silver service and a new car.

Frank "Gator" Farr conducts ceremonial Gamecock burial on Big Thursday.

Pearl Harbor was attacked that December, and World War II was underway. Because of the war, Clemson's talent was drained, while South Carolina had access to athletes in its Naval V-12 program. The Tigers managed just one win, one tie and three losses in 1943-47.

But Howard got his car following the 1948 season, thanks in large part to a sophomore fullback named Fred Cone.

Cone came from Pineapple, Alabama, slightly larger than Howard's birthplace of Barlow Bend, Alabama. Cone was recruited for Clemson by Howard's sister, Hazel, who lived next door to Cone's aunt in Biloxi. Although Cone had never played high school football, Hazel was sure he'd make her brother a great football player.

She proved prophetic, and Howard questioned his sister later on how she knew Cone was going to be such a great football player.

"I saw him dive off a diving board one time," she replied.

Cone became Clemson's first 2,000-yard career rusher, and still is ninth best on the career list. He led the Tigers to only their second undefeated season in history in 1948, and Clemson won two out of three from South Carolina in Cone's playing time.

Clemson went into Columbia undefeated in 1950. The Tigers were still undefeated when they left town, but there was a tie instead of another win on their record. That day the most dazzling display of rushing ever performed against the Tigers took place. Steve Wadiak rushed for 256 yards. The entire Clemson team only had 191 yards on the ground and Cone had 117 of that.

South Carolina then enjoyed its longest winning streak of the entire series — four games. But Clemson won four of the last five Big Thursday games before the series went home-and-home in 1960.

In the 95-year, 88-game series between Clemson and South Carolina, tensions have always been high. At times there have been mass free-for-alls by the two student bodies out on the field.

The most serious trouble did not happen on the field, but on the South Carolina campus following the 1902 game. The series was stopped for the next six years.

Since 1900, Clemson had been running roughshod over everybody under John Heisman. But in 1902, South Carolina beat

Gamecock burial ceremonies continue.

the Tigers 12–6, on some well-designed defenses concocted by Gamecocks' head coach C. R. (Bob) Williams and his assistant, Christie Benet. Williams would later become head coach at Clemson.

In those days the entire Clemson student body would go to Columbia for State Fair Week and camp on the fairgrounds in tents, with stacked rifles and fixed bayonets. The students would stay in Columbia the rest of the week and enjoy the fair.

The night after the game the town was wild. South Carolina won the first game between the two schools in 1896, but had lost four straight after that. With the surprising victory, it was time for the Gamecocks to flap their wings and crow.

The South Carolina students were celebrating, and fist fights were springing up here and there in the downtown area. To add insult to injury, the South Carolina students were parading around with a transparency showing an exuberant crowing rooster riding a bleeding, whipped tiger.

Against the advice of city officials and law enforcement personnel, the South Carolina students carried the transparency in a parade down Main Street in which both

Tiger captains George Rodgers (48) and Billy Hair (77) calling the coin toss before Big Thursday game, 1952.

student bodies took part.

When the parade was completed, the cadets were dismissed from formation near the state capitol building and only a few blocks from the South Carolina campus. Fuses became shorter and shorter and soon the Clemson Cadet Corps marched to the Sumter Street entrance of the campus with fixed bayonets and swords dangling at the side.

South Carolina students brought out shotguns and pistols and huddled behind the old wall at the entrance.

J. Rion McKissick, a freshman student, who would later become the university president, was asked by a senior, "Mr. McKissick, are you armed?"

"Yes, I have a pistol, sir," came the reply.

"How many rounds of ammunition?"

"Eight, sir."

"Make every shot count, Mr. McKissick."

There was no bloodshed, and much of the credit for that was given to Christie Benet, the Gamecocks' assistant coach and a Columbia businessman. Although the confrontation was on the South Carolina campus, Clemson had the numbers.

Benet, who would later become a highly successful lawyer and a Clemson trustee,

tried to reason with the shouting crowd, but made little headway. Finally, being a collegiate boxer, he offered to settle the issue by taking on any Clemson student so chosen by those present.

The Clemson students wanted the transparency destroyed. Then Benet proposed that each side choose a committee to iron out the differences. A joint committee of six students was chosen and a settlement was negotiated. One of the agreements was that the transparency would be burned, and this was done amid loud cheering from both sides.

When reports of what had happened filtered back to the administrations of both schools, the committee which governed South Carolina athletics felt it was necessary to discontinue the game. After six years, the series resumed in 1909. There have been no more interruptions.

Through the years the game continued to be played in Columbia on the third Thursday in October during State Fair Week, but more and more pressure was being applied by Clemson wanting the game to be on a home-and-home basis.

Clemson's main gripes were that the game was played on the enemy field each year, there was not an equal division of tickets, Tiger fans always had to sit in the sun field, and the school did not get to share in program sales and concessions.

In 1958 and 1960, Clemson made major additions to its stadium and the seating capacity was comparable to Carolina Stadium. Frank Howard said there was no reason for the football season to end in South Carolina in mid-October as had been the case for 65 years. Besides, he said, the up-state would also like to see some of those tourist dollars roll in.

Necessary scheduling mechanics were set into motion for the first game to be played in Clemson in 1960, and to alternate sites each year after that. So, November 12, 1960, the first Clemson-South Carolina game was played outside of Columbia.

With one exception, every game since 1960 has been played on a Saturday. That exception was in 1963 when President John F. Kennedy was assassinated in Dallas. Nearly all the nation's college football games scheduled for the Saturday after Kennedy was killed were either postponed or canceled. The decision was made by the officials of both schools to play the following Thursday, November 28, in Columbia. This is the only Clemson-South Carolina game ever played on Thanksgiving.

Big Thursday always brought out the banter in Howard. Some of his best came in 1958. Warren Giese had become the Gamecock head coach in 1956. On the Monday prior to the '58 Big Thursday, Giese was supposed to have said: "Only God and Howard know what happens to IPTAY funds."

Howard, who had shut out Giese's first two attempts against Clemson, said: "Giese knows as much about IPTAY as he does about crossing our goal line. The first time that young fellow scores on us, I'm going to tip my hat to him across the field."

South Carolina scored with 57 seconds left in the half and Howard, true to his word, doffed his hat in the direction of Giese across the field.

The Gamecocks scored once again in the third quarter and two times in the fourth as they won the game 26–6. After each score, Howard doffed his hat to Giese.

This was considered an upset of some magnitude. Clemson entered the game undefeated and ranked No. 10 in the country.

After Howard talked to his players, he opened the dressing room door and invited the press "to come in and claim the body."

During his press conference, Howard was asked about tipping his hat to Giese. "My head got mighty sunburned before the game was over with," he said.

Since 1962 the Clemson-South Carolina game has been played on the last game of every season except one — when the Tigers played Wake Forest the week after the South Carolina game in Tokyo in 1982.

But whenever and wherever the game has been held, all kinds of practical jokes have always been part of the festivities. In the past, it wasn't unusual for a Clemson fan to bring a live rooster to the game and see it tossed up in the air all through the student section.

One year a brave student ended up on the 50-yard line wringing the neck of a White Leghorn rooster during halftime. Naturally, that brought members of both student bodies onto the field. When peace had been restored, white feathers were strewn from goal line to goal line.

In 1961 one of the most clever practical jokes occurred. A South Carolina fraternity borrowed some uniforms from Orangeburg-Wilkinson High School that were almost identical to the Clemson uniforms. They came out of the south end of the stadium in Columbia for pregame warmups, followed by a paunchy gentleman with many of Frank Howard's traits.

As they began their calisthenics, it was clear that this was not the real Clemson team. The side-straddle hop had never been performed so badly. Punters were falling over backward. There was still smoke coming from the cannon and the band was still playing "Tiger Rag" when the Clemson students stormed the field to go get these people ridiculing their team. However, through the effort of the heavy security forces always on hand at one of these games, very little skin was lost.

As part of its performance, the fraternity had borrowed a cow from a farmer across the river in Lexington County and had planned to lead her out and introduce her as Clemson's homecoming queen. But the cow suffered a heart attack underneath the stands and died.

Nothing quite as elaborate has been tried since, but there usually is something going on between the two student bodies. Maybe the most daring trick ever pulled by the Clemson crowd was by a group of students that got into Carolina Stadium on the weekend prior to a Big Thursday game and planted rye grass seed down the center of the field spelling out "C-L-E-M-S-O-N." On the day of the game the seed had sprouted enough where the word Clemson was quite legible from the South Carolina stands.

Since the home-and-home rotation started, each school has increased the size of its stadium, and most of the time the largest crowd to see the teams play each year is when they meet each other.

The Clemson game ranks No. 1 and No. 2 in South Carolina's largest home crowds and No. 2 and No. 3 on Gamecock road trips, with only a trip to Michigan being larger. At Clemson, the South Carolina attendance is listed as first and third. Florida State is second.

There hasn't been a seat sold to the general public in years.

Down through the years, there have been exciting games, so-so games, dull games and four ties.

For pure excitement, the 1977 game in Columbia (even years are played at Clemson, odd years in Columbia) would have to be No. 1.

South Carolina entered the game with a 5–5 record, but four of their losses had been by a touchdown or less.

The Tigers opened that season with a loss to Maryland, but then won seven in a row before a tie to North Carolina at Chapel Hill and a four-point loss to Notre Dame.

Two freshman runners, George Rogers and Johnny Wright, highlighted the South Carolina offense. Clemson countered with a passing combination of Steve Fuller to Jerry Butler and depended on Jim Stuckey and Randy Scott to keep the defense honest. Rogers, Fuller, Butler and Stuckey all would be first-round NFL draft picks.

To add a little more hype to the day, ABC Sports decided to show the game as one of its regional telecasts — the first time a network had chosen to televise the game. Kickoff would not be until 4 o'clock, making it the first of the series to end after dark.

Coach Howard kisses Big Thursday goodbye.

Danny Ford shows the rivalry lives on after Big Thursday has died.

It was a pretty safe bet that if Clemson won the game, the Gator Bowl would invite the Tigers. Jim Ade, the bowl's president, was at the game. Clemson had been to seven bowls, but not to one since the 1959 Bluebonnet.

It was obvious from the beginning that the Tigers did not want the season to end after this game. They drove 90 yards to score on their second possession. A field goal and another touchdown made it 17–0 at the half.

A 52-yard run by tailback Ken Callicutt gave the Tigers a 24–0 lead in the third period. South Carolina finally scored in the final seconds of the period to make it 24–7 — still a very comfortable lead for the Tigers.

Heading into the twilight of the fourth quarter, the excitement began.

When Clemson lost a fumble, South Carolina wasted little time in moving the ball into scoring range. Ron Bass completed a 40-yard pass to Phillip Logan than carried to the Clemson 11 and Steve Dorsey scored one play later.

After a 10-yard Clemson punt went out of bounds at the Tigers' 39, Spencer Clark, Rogers and Dorsey quickly drove the ball to the one. Dorsey got the touchdown from

there, making the score 24–20 with just over seven minutes left in the game.

Another shanked punt — this one for only 18 yards — traveled out of bounds at the South Carolina 48. A first down moved the ball to the Clemson 40, and here the Bass to Logan combination worked again for a touchdown. Britt Parrish's point-after gave the Gamecocks a 27–24 lead and just 1:30 remained to be played.

Willie Jordan gave the Tiger faithful a lift when he returned the kickoff 26 yards to the Clemson 33.

Fuller huddled his team and told them: "Get ready fellas, we're going down the field and score." But after the first two plays, things looked bleak. Faced with a third and seven, Fuller connected on a clutch pass to Rick Weddington for 26 yards. Fuller stopped the clock with a throw-away, then found Dwight Clark open for an 18-yard completion at the USC 20.

The next completion — which became known as "The Catch" in Clemson lore — was good for the winning touchdown.

Fuller, a righthander, moved to his left and threatened to run. Instead, he threw to Butler on the goal line. Butler leaped as high as he could and made a two-handed catch on the ball, falling backward into the end zone for the score.

While Clemson prepared to meet Pittsburgh in the Gator Bowl, the Tigers' sports information office was deluged with requests for photos of "The Catch" for the den or office. The State newspaper allowed Clemson to purchase the print and hundreds of copies were run off to meet the demand.

Other Clemson-South Carolina games have had exciting finishes, but never has one team been that far behind and rallied to go ahead. And never has a Tiger-Gamecock game been decided this late (49 seconds to play) in the game.

```
S. 23   18-0   W   H    Presbyterian
S. 30    6-7   L   A    Tulane
O.  7   25-6   W   N1   N.C. State
O. 19   27-0   W   A    S. Carolina
O. 26   15-7   W   A    Navy
N.  3   13-6   W   A    G. Wash.
N. 11   20-7   W   H    Wake Forest
N. 18   21-6   W   A    Southwestern
N. 25   14-3   W   A    Furman
J.  1    6-3   W   N2   Bost. Coll.
N1 at Charlotte, NC
N2 at Cotton Bowl, Dallas, TX
```

1939: SOUTH CAROLINA'S FIRST BOWL TEAM

Cemson's invitation to play in the fourth annual Cotton Bowl created excitement in the state from the mountains to the seashore, but especially in the upstate.

South Carolina finally had a bowl team.

The mayor of Anderson, G. Cullen Sullivan, proposed a motorcade from his town to Dallas, headed by the U.S. congressional delegation from South Carolina. The Clemson student body of 2,200 scrambled for tickets.

Boston College coach Frank Leahy admitted right after his team got its Cotton Bowl invitation that he knew "very little about Clemson."

You couldn't fault him for that. The Tigers had little reputation outside the state.

The Cotton Bowl was billed as the "farmer boys" against "them city slickers."

After defeating Furman in the final game of the 1939 regular season, the Tigers waited nearly two weeks before receiving the invitation to play Boston College. The Eagles, like Clemson, had lost one game during the season. But Clemson's acceptance was not automatic.

There was a Southern Conference rule against playing in post-season games. Clemson had to ask for a waiver on the rule.

A majority of the schools had to approve the appearance. The rule had been waived a year earlier so that Duke could play in the Rose Bowl.

Head coach Jess Neely also had to get permission for several of the players to miss basketball practice until after the bowl game, including All-American Banks McFadden.

It only took the Southern Conference officials long enough to convene before granting Clemson approval to play in its first bowl. Dr. Charles N. Wyatt, Furman's faculty representative made the motion and the second came from South Carolina. A unanimous standing vote made the approval official. When news reached the Clemson campus that the Tigers could play in Dallas with conference blessings, one of the assistant coaches said: "I wish we could play right now. I've never seen such enthusiasm."

Full credit for Clemson's success was given to Neely. He had won just seven games in his first three years, but along came IPTAY in 1934, and Neely did not have a losing season in his next six. Now, what would be his final year at Clemson had been culminated with the bowl invitation.

Neely, who had the reputation of squeezing a penny until Abe Lincoln yelled "uncle," left the athletic department in the black, something he didn't find in 1931.

Jess Neely's ninth and last season as head coach did not begin well.

The Tigers were coming off a 7–1–1 season in '38, and a solid group of experienced players were returning. But in the opening game of 1939 against little Presbyterian, Clemson went to the locker room at halftime with the score still 0–0.

The season finally got going in the second half, and one of Clemson's touchdowns came on a 90-yard run by McFadden, which is still the school record for a rushing touchdown.

Neely's team was called "Road Clemson," because after the Presbyterian game at home, the Tigers would play only one more time before the home crowd, and that wasn't until the seventh game against Wake Forest.

Clemson went to New Orleans next to play Tulane, and even though the Tigers lost 7–6, many said this is where McFadden put in a real bid for his All-American honors, which he'd later earned.

He passed to Joe Blalock for the Tigers' only score, and he was the only player on either team to go the full 60 minutes without rest.

He also kept the Tigers in the game with his punts. More than 50 years have passed, and McFadden still has two punting records he established in that game. One is for the most punts over 50 yards (six) and the other is for most total punting yards (504 in 12 kicks).

The Tigers started a streak the next week against N. C. State in Charlotte that would see them win their final seven regular-season games and earn their first postseason bowl bid.

The Wolfpack fell 25–6, then South Carolina never got inside the Clemson 15-yard

Banks McFadden, Clemson's first All-American, led the Tigers to their first-ever bowl game in 1940.

line as the Gamecocks lost 27–0 in the annual Big Thursday game in Columbia.

After taking nine days off, the Tigers traveled to Annapolis for their game against Navy—but McFadden, laid up with an infected foot, didn't make the trip.

Aubrey Rion moved up to take his place, and Chippy Maness inherited the punting chore. With McFadden out, the Tigers only passed twice—once by Rion and once by Maness. One was complete for 17 yards and a touchdown (Rion to Maness) and the other was intercepted.

With the star tailback left home, Neely let his fullback (Charlie Timmons) and wingback (Shad Bryant) handle the running game.

Both played well, the defense held Navy scoreless until the fourth quarter, and the Tigers won easily.

Clemson went back to the D.C. area the next Saturday to play George Washington in a Southern Conference game. McFadden was back in uniform again and contributed to the victory by passing 15 yards to Joe Blalock for a touchdown with 15 seconds left in the first half.

Clemson's second and final home game was against Wake Forest. There were 12,000 fans crammed into every nook and cranny of Riggs Field.

The game didn't really heat up until the second quarter.

McFadden connected with Blalock over the middle, and after stumbling three or four strides, and never having complete control of the ball, he collected himself and fought off John Polanski to score on a play covering 76 yards. This is still the 10th longest pass in Tiger history.

On the ensuing kickoff, Polanski took the ball in at the eight, and 80 yards later was run out of bounds at the Clemson 12. This is still the longest non-scoring kickoff return in history against the Tigers.

The victory gave Clemson a 4–0 Southern Conference record and moved the Tigers up to No. 16 in the national rankings.

They climbed to 15th the following week after defeating Southwestern 21–6 in Memphis.

That left Furman as the final opponent. A win over the Purple Hurricane would just about cinch a bowl bid.

The Tigers stuck to the ground, gaining 216 yards rushing and only 28 passing. But their defense was even more impressive in holding Furman to just 23 yards of total offense, 16 on rushing.

Then came the wait for the bowl bid.

Carter "Scoop" Latimer, sports columnist for the *Greenville* (South Carolina) *News*, without question wrote more positive columns and stories on Clemson than anyone ever has.

His flowery columns were read by thousands. One of his columns is reprinted below, written after Clemson's invitation to the Cotton Bowl was accepted, but before the game was played against Boston College.

Clemson's skillful football team, coached to perfection and possessed of everything that goes to make it a great

All-American McFadden in his other uniform.

organization, will be ready to set off all the high explosives against Boston College in the Dallas Cotton Bowl New Year's Day.

The fire of Marse Jess Neely's squad has been rekindled for the pyrotechnics come January 1. Positively scorching was the heat generated in practice yesterday by Banks McFadden, Shad Bryant, Charlie Timmons, Joe Payne, Joe Blalock, Carl Black, Bill Hall, George Fritts, Walter Cox, Tom Moorer, Bob Sharpe and all the other boys who have combined to give Clemson and South Carolina the finest team in history.

They're practicing in an entirely different atmosphere from that of last September, although more pronounced than ever is that old spirit of "a team that won't be beaten, can't be beaten," as the late Bill Roper used to say of his Princeton Tigers.

Head Coach Jess Neely is presented with a silver service upon his departure for Rice in 1940.

In pre-season training, around Labor Day, Marse Neely shouldered the tremendous responsibility of trying to weld another powerful machine to carry on where the 1938 team left off. Gone were ten lettermen, including a half dozen boys who had been selected on All-Southern teams the year before. It may have seemed a hopeless task to everybody but Neely and the boys who were determined to step up and fill the vacancies.

Then and there was the first flash of instantaneous combustion. They blazed away, and the fire spread in a burning desire to win.

Now the team is set. The boys have finesse. They perform with rhythmic skill, and, they are practicing now to keep in physical trim and to match wits and strength with the highly touted Eagles of Boston College.

All this bullish sentiment seeping out of New England about the power and versatility of the Eagles isn't the least bit frightening to Clemson's Country Gentlemen, aristocrats of the gridiron who are afeered of nothing and you dasn't make 'em mad.

I think it is the team of the year and Jess Neely is the coach of the year. For, it just doesn't always happen for a coach and team to be bereft of as many stars as Clemson lost last year, and then return to power.

Clemson went to the Cotton Bowl as the underdog. The Tigers got 1,000 tickets for the game, at $3.30 each.

The main team (33 members) left Clemson Christmas Day by train for Dallas. Arrival there was shortly after 9 p.m. December 26th. The remainder of the team (18 more), along with the Senior Platoon drill team and the band, would come in later.

A crowd of 20,000 showed up for the game, the largest crowd that Clemson had ever played before. The cold weather was nothing to write home about.

The Eagles scored first, with a field goal in the opening minutes of the second quarter. Then Clemson drove 57 yards for a score, with Charlie "Tuffy" Timmons going over from the two-yard line.

Timmons was the leading ground gainer for the Tigers that day because Boston College had geared its defense to stop McFadden. The Abbeville native gained 115 yards on 27 carries.

With a 6–3 lead, the Clemson defense took over.

Fans who saw the game still talk about McFadden ranging from sideline to sideline knocking down Charlie O'Rourke passes. The Eagles went to the air 23 times and completed only four, with one interception.

Boston College gained just 102 net yards on the ground.

Frank Leahy, the BC coach who would later go to Notre Dame for even more fame, said following the game: "Clemson has a great team. My boys gave everything they had and we have no excuses. It was a grand game and Clemson is one of the best teams I have ever seen. I have the satisfaction of knowing that while we were beaten, the game wasn't lost on a fluke."

Oddly enough, both teams and many of their fans were on the same special train that came back from Dallas, through Memphis, Birmingham and Atlanta, into Clemson. A large contingent of fans met the train at the Calhoun station about 5 p.m., with all the Tiger players sporting Texas 10-gallon hats.

There was little rest for some of the football team members. The basketball team was waiting on McFadden, Wister Jackson and Joe Blalock while Aubrey Rion was ready to trade his pads for a pair of boxing gloves.

And within 10 days after coming back from Dallas, Neely accepted the head coaching job at Rice Institute in Houston. The Clemson Athletic Council and Board of Trustees made several overtures attempting to get Neely to reconsider, but even a bonus and a raise in pay for himself and each of his assistants could not sway Neely's leaving.

An outstanding organizer and frugal with the funds available, Neely found the athletic department $47,000 in the red when he came to Clemson in 1931. He left with $52,000 in the treasury.

McFadden, arguably Clemson's greatest athlete, pictured with other 1939 All-Americans.

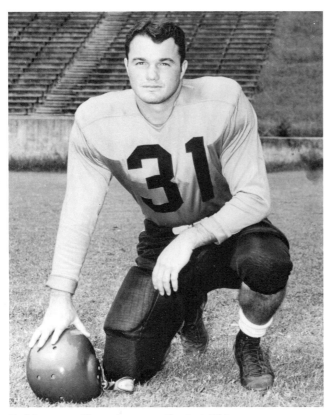

Fred Cone was still a sophomore on the great '48 team.

Bobby "Schoolboy" Gage introduced by Coach Howard at pep rally in 1948.

1948: UNDEFEATED AND UNTIED

If you had to pick a pivotal football season in Clemson history, it probably would be 1948.

The Tigers had been playing with 4-F's and 17-year-olds for five or six years, there had been only one winning season since 1942, and Frank Howard's eight-year record was 36–34–3.

A group of students had visited Howard at the end of the '47 season and talked to him about resigning, but Howard weathered the mild uprising, and 1948 proved to be a golden year for Clemson.

Not only did that team give the university its second undefeated and untied season in its 53-year history, but the Tigers were invited to play in the 1949 Gator Bowl, the first of six post-season games the Tigers would go to under Howard in the next 12 years.

And the Gator Bowl was won by the field goal—the only field goal the Tigers made all year!

Bobby Gage would close out his stellar career as the most valuable player in the Gator Bowl. Fred Cone, Jackie Calvert and Ray Mathews were all sophomores in 1948. This trio would shine in the undefeated season, then lead Clemson to its biggest plum yet—the 1951 Orange Bowl.

"I don't think that I ever had more satisfaction out of one season than I did in 1948," Howard said. "Some people were after my scalp the year before, but those three sophomore backs really put some numbers on the board. We only had three seniors on the starting team but one of them was Gage, the tailback. And he was a heady player and would take chances. Cone probably didn't say two dozen words on the field during his three years. But when we got to the 10-yard line, it was ole Freddie's the rest of the way. Mathews was a crafty passer and runner while Calvert was a more than adequate replacement for Gage. And that line in '48 was about the best blocking one I ever had. With these players, we had a lot of fun, especially in 1948 and again in 1950."

The Tigers started the 1948 season with their usual opening-game victory against Presbyterian, 53–0. The Tigers actually had only three other games that year which could be put in the "laugher" category. Furman went down 41–0 in the sixth game, Duquesne was beaten 42–0 in the eighth game, and The Citadel went down 20–0 in the final regular-season game when the Tigers went to Charleston to dedicate Johnson Hagood Stadium.

Of the other six games won by Clemson, only one was played at home and that was the second one with N. C. State. Clemson's defense would be tested many times during the season, but maybe never as much as this one.

Gage returned a punt 90 yards for a touchdown in the first quarter, a run that is still a school record. It would be the only score of the game.

Late in the fourth quarter, State drove from its own 20 and got a first down at the Clemson six. Ed Mooney got to the two, and Dick Johnson got to inches from the goal on second down. Johnson hit center again, but when the players were unscrambled, the ball was still on the six-inch line. Mooney tried the right side, but was thrown for a yard loss on fourth down. Clemson took over and ran out the clock.

A week later the Tigers were underdogs again, this time against Mississippi State in Starkville, led by former Army star Shorty McWilliams.

Clemson scored twice in the first quarter, and MSU never got close.

The Tigers had a big edge in the statistics, too. When coach Howard was asked what he thought was the turning point of the game he said: "When we went on the field."

Clemson had the next Saturday off in preparation for the annual Big Thursday battle with South Carolina at the State Fair in Columbia.

The usual sellout—this time 25,000—was on hand for the 46th game between the two schools, and the Gamecocks had the added incentive of ending Clemson's undefeated season.

South Carolina quarterback Bo Hagan passed 27 yards to end Roger (Red) Wilson after 10:30 of the first quarter had elapsed. And that's how the first, second and third quarters ended—with South Carolina leading 7–0.

Ray Mathews, also a sophomore, in the open field against Furman.

As the third quarter ended, South Carolina's Bishop Strickland fumbled a punt and Oscar Thompson covered the ball for the Tigers ten yards from the South Carolina goal line. This wasn't the closest Clemson had been to the Gamecocks' goal that day. The Tigers had driven to the five in the first half only to have Gage fumble.

But this time Clemson was not denied. On a third down from the one, Cone went into the line, and on a designed play turned and lateraled the ball to Carol Cox, who scored. But Jack Miller's extra point try went under the crossbar.

On South Carolina's last possession, the Gamecocks missed a first down by two yards on their 24 and went into punt formation.

Through the years, a story has been told that a Clemson fan stood up in the stands before the punt and waved a $100 bill, offering a bet that Clemson would score on the next play.

If there were any takers, they left the game $100 poorer. Tackle Phil Prince broke through and blocked the punt and end Oscar "Rabbit" Thompson scooped the ball up at the 11 and went in for the score. This time Miller made the extra point and Clemson won the game 13–7.

The Tigers next traveled to old Braves Field in the Kenmore Square section of Boston to play Boston College. The Tiger followers were few but loud and visible, with several waving Confederate flags throughout the night.

Boston College passed 43 times against

ndly rivals "Peahead" Walker, head coach at Wake Forest, and Clemson's Frank
~ard.

Clemson, 42 of them by Butch Songin, then an NCAA record for an individual in one game. That record stood until 1951, when Freddie Benners of Southern Methodist passed 44 times against Notre Dame.

Clemson climbed to No. 12 in The Associated Press poll after the Eagles became their fifth victim of the year, and the Tigers began to get some attention from bowl scouts.

In the next three games Clemson would score 104 points (Furman 41–0, Wake Forest 21–14, and Duquesne 42–0). The Tigers were ranked 10th when they met No. 19 Wake Forest, coached by Douglas Clyde "Peahead" Walker.

The Deacons had already accepted a bid to play in the Dixie Bowl in Birmingham, Alabama. Howard said his preference was any of three bowls — the Sugar, the Cotton

or the Gator.

It was one of the top games in the nation that day, and had the added spice of Howard and Walker jawing at each other once more.

Walker had an All-American lineman in Bill George, who later would be an All-Pro for many years with the Chicago Bears.

When George came to play for the Deacons, the school was still located in the small community of Wake Forest, about 25 miles north of Raleigh, and games were played in Groves Stadium, a facility holding around 20,000 people.

Howard claimed that when George came down to Wake Forest for his official visit while still in high school, Walker took him over and showed him the Duke campus, with its Gothic building, formal gardens and Duke Stadium, site of the 1942 Rose Bowl.

Howard said he wasn't sure what Walker told George to get him to come to Wake Forest, but he had an idea.

Anyway, Howard said, when George arrived on the Wake Forest campus that fall, he was a little surprised at the look of things.

Howard said that when George asked Walker about it, Peahead made a quick recovery. He told George: "Son, you have to go here for two years before you go over to the main campus."

Fans at the 1948 game would see one of the thrillers of the season.

The teams traded touchdowns throughout the afternoon before Clemson went ahead for good early in the fourth quarter. The victory left the Tigers as one of the nation's five unbeaten and untied teams.

The ninth-ranked Tigers had little or no trouble defeating Duquesne. Touchdowns were scored rushing, receiving, on punt returns and a blocked punt. The defense had one of its best games, holding the Dukes to 63 yards rushing and 37 passing.

A highlight of the afternoon was the presentation of a new car by Secretary of State James F. Byrnes to Howard. This would be the first of three cars Howard would receive from alumni and friends during his coaching stay at Clemson.

Clemson had two more games, both on the road. The first was against Auburn, a team that had won only one game during the year. The game was to be played in Ladd Stadium in Mobile, Alabama. Two days of torrential rains made the field a near quagmire before the teams kicked off.

Auburn surprised the Tigers by scoring first, then holding Clemson scoreless until the fourth quarter.

Late in the final period, when the Tigers finally scored, Jack Miller's extra point was the difference in the 7–6 game.

Howard announced after the game that Clemson had accepted an invitation to play Missouri in Jacksonville's Gator Bowl January 1, 1949. This would be Howard's first bowl team as a head coach, but the third he had been involved in. Howard was an assistant coach when Clemson played Boston College in the 1940 Cotton Bowl and played in the 1931 Rose Bowl when his Alabama team defeated Washington State 24–0.

Clemson's final regular-season game was in Charleston with The Citadel when the Bulldogs would dedicate their new Johnson Hagood Stadium.

A victory would mean the Southern Conference championship. Another plum Clemson wanted was the conference scoring title for Ray Mathews. In his final game of the season, North Carolina's Charlie "Choo" Justus scored twice against Virginia and had a 66–60 lead over Mathews.

The Tigers scored three touchdowns and Mathews had all three.

Clemson dropped to 10th in the polls after beating The Citadel, but the Tigers got what they wanted — the conference championship and the individual scoring title for Mathews. A few days later Howard was named the Southern Conference coach of the year. Missouri and the Gator Bowl were less than four weeks away.

At the end of the regular season, Clemson, Michigan and California were the only undefeated teams in the nation. But the Tigers went into the Gator Bowl as an underdog.

Clemson fans were ready for this game. The last bowl the team had been to was nine years earlier. There had been a world war in between.

The Gator Bowl was still struggling. The Jacksonville people had lost money on the first three games, and Clemson fans had no reputation at that time of supporting a bowl team. In four home games, the average attendance was less than 17,000.

But Clemson helped turn the Gator Bowl around. Of the 38,000 seats available, Clemson fans occupied 21,000. And many more have come to Jacksonville since then. The Tigers have played in the Gator Bowl six times and have set a new attendance mark on almost every appearance.

The crowd on hand that January in 1949 was the largest ever to see a football game in Jacksonville.

Cone scored twice early for Clemson, but Missouri came back to tie the game 14–14 at the half.

Clemson took the second-half kickoff and quickly moved down the field for another score, which came on a Cone to Gage to John Poulos lateral pass of 10 yards.

Missouri scored on a safety, then Jack Miller's field goal gave the Tigers a 24–16 lead.

Miller's kick was the only one the Tigers made all season. Only one other one was even tried, and that was in the second game against N. C. State.

Jack Miller kicks field goal to beat Missouri in the '49 Gator Bowl—the only Clemson field goal of the season.

Howard didn't have too much faith in his placement kickers. Clemson wasn't successful on another field goal from 1948 until the fourth game of the 1956 season (72 games) against Wake Forest when Horace Turbeville booted one in a 17–0 win.

People often ask Howard who he thinks were the best players he coached, or the best game he'd ever seen, or the best anything. He says Fred Cone is the best player he ever coached, and of all the plays he has seen Clemson run, the one he remembers most came in this game.

It was late in the fourth quarter, Clemson had the ball on the Missouri 41 with a fourth down and three yards to go. "I certainly didn't want to let Missouri get the ball again," Howard says, "because neither one of us had stopped the other one all day. Back then, it was against the rules to send in plays so Gage called the offense, and he decided to go for it. I turned to Russ 'Pop' Cohen, one of my coaches, and said, 'Ole man, if they make it, I'll be a great coach. If they don't, they might ride me out of Clemson on a rail with tar and feathers.'"

Gage took the snap and handed the ball to Cone, who was stopped cold. But Cone was never one to give up, and he slid off and found a little more running room to the

outside. He gained six yards to the Missouri 35. That one play enabled Clemson to keep possession and run out the clock.

Small wonder that Howard loved that player and that play. A year earlier people has been asking him to quit. Now his team was the unbeaten Gator Bowl champion.

And it's small wonder that in 1970, after the silver anniversary game of the Gator Bowl, that the 1949 game between Clemson and Missouri was voted the most exciting game in the 25-year history of the bowl.

"Anybody who saw this game would have to say it was the most exciting," said George Olsen, executive director of the Gator Bowl. "Maybe we're a little biased because this game put us in the black for the first time. But I believe the people who voted in the poll knew what they were doing."

"From a spectator's standpoint, I still think this is the most exciting game I ever saw a Clemson team play," said Frank Howard, who was the Tiger coach at the time. "We couldn't stop them and they couldn't stop us. That's the reason we went for it on fourth down late in the game. I was afraid to let them have the ball back. Guess we were fortunate, but we had some good players and they came through for us."

"Dumb Dumb" Wyndham.

Clemson ran the "Single Wing to Perfection" in the early '50s.

S. 23	55-0	W	H	‡Presbyterian
S. 30	34-0	W	A	Missouri
O. 7	27-0	W	H	‡N.C. State
O. 19	14-14	T	A	S. Carolina
O. 28	13-12	W	A	Wake Forest
N. 4	53-20	W	H	Duquesne
N. 11	35-14	W	A	Bost. Coll.
N. 18	57-2	W	H	Furman
N. 25	41-0	W	A	Auburn
J. 1	15-14	W	A1	Miami
A1 at Orange Bowl, Miami, FL				

1950: THE ORANGE BOWL CONTROVERSY

Frank Howard went into the 1950 season in a foul mood, and with good reason.

His 1949 team had been a bust, finishing with a 4–4–2 record despite a solid group of players returning from the unbeaten 1948 team.

The coach had reason for hope — some of those players from '48 were coming back again — kids like Fred Cone and Jackie Calvert and Ray Mathews, Bob Hudson and Jack Brunson and Windy Wyndham.

Clemson fans also were awaiting the varsity debut of tailback Billy "Sweet William" Hair.

Still, Howard was grumpy, and though this team would take him to another unbeaten season and the biggest game of his coaching career — the Orange Bowl — the mood would follow him all year long.

In a pre-season summation Howard said: "I see where everybody around's got the best team they ever had. Ain't nobody gonna git beat. Now, I'll tell you what . . . either football's changed since last season, or somebody's lying like hell."

Continuing to analyze the situation, Howard said: "Now at the start of the fall workouts I thought we might have a pretty good ball club. The backs were running good and my line ain't mean enough yet,

but it's been hitting hard. Then, I pick up two or three papers and see how well off everybody else is, I'm almost afraid to start the season."

Howard was full of backhanded compliments about his line play, too. "We're gonna have a better line than last year," the head coach said. "I don't see how we could be no worse. Sometimes they hit so light I think I got a bunch of gorillas around — in love with each other."

Well, maybe the opener against Presbyterian cheered up Howard a bit. The Tigers led 35–0 at the half, won 55–0 and made history.

Three Clemson backs each had more than 100 yards rushing. Cone ran for 143 yards and scored twice; Mathews ran for 131 yards and scored three times; and Calvert had 109 yards and one touchdown.

The next game, against Missouri in Columbia, Mo., would be the first big test for the "loving gorillas."

Vic Chapman, an Anderson, South Carolina, tire dealer whose blood runneth orange, had a live Missouri mule waiting when the Tigers got to the airport to leave for the game. Chapman said he did this, "to practice taming Missouri animals."

For publicity purposes, Cone mounted

the animal and Mathews held the halter as pictures were snapped.

Howard told the team in the dressing room just before the game that if they won there would be several thousand people at the airport to greet the team. "And I expect if you lose," Howard predicted, "there won't be anything there but that jack ass."

Apparently, the players took their coach to heart. On Clemson's first play from scrimmage, Calvert broke free down the sidelines and scored on an 81-yard play. Missouri had been ranked 18th in the nation in the pre-season poll and was a 13-point favorite over Clemson.

The Tigers quickly proved the polls wrong. Calvert's score came with the game just 28 seconds old. They scored again in the second quarter, twice in the third and once again in the fourth. And, in a repeat performance, the three backs made history again!

This time Calvert led the charge with 175 yards, Mathews added 120 and Cone had 111.

It was the first time in 35 games that Missouri had not scored. And Windy Wyndham, whose given middle name was Friendly, had eight unassisted tackles and broke up two passes.

The weather was quite hot that afternoon in Columbia and Howard was substituting as often as possible to keep fresh players in the game. Clemson was playing some two-platoon football that year, but Wyndham would go both ways — a blocking back on offense and a linebacker on defense.

Wyndham had been given the nickname of "Dumb-Dumb" by Howard because he had the tendency to go the wrong way on a play. Howard told him one day: "Son, you're so dumb you ought not to be one, you oughta be twins." So he became "Dumb-Dumb," and he carried that nickname to

his grave, as do most nicknames Howard has given people.

Howard recalls that Wyndham came up to him when a number of inexperienced players began to show up on the field and said: "Coach, how about not putting more than six of them sorry ones in on defense with me at one time. I can protect six of them, but I don't think I can protect more than six."

Howard agreed to do that, and even go a step farther. "I told Dumb-Dumb that I'd stand on the 50 and that I'd have all of the players I wanted to get in the game on defense to stay on my left with the offense standing to my right. Then I told him he could be in charge of the defensive substituting as long as he saw that everybody got in the game."

Most Clemson football historians agree that Wyndham was one of the hardest hitters who ever put on a Tigers uniform. In the 1949 Gator Bowl against Missouri, the Mizzou quarterback, Bus Entsminger, was running the Split-T down the line when Wyndham broke through and, just as Entsminger pitched the ball back to his trailing halfback, Wyndham hit him and knocked him into the runner. Both Missouri players were on the ground, stunned from the hit.

In the 1950 game, Wyndham put hits on three different Missouri players who had to be assisted from the game. That's when the Missouri captain approached the referee and asked him to "get that wild man out of the game before he goes completely berserk and kills every one of us."

Clemson blanked N. C. State the next weekend 27–0, the third straight shutout for Tigers, who up to that time had scored 116 points themselves.

In the Big Thursday game two weeks later, Steve Wadiak put on the greatest rushing performance ever against a Clemson team—256 yards. That is still the best individual performance against the Tigers.

The game ended in a 14–14 tie, which would turn out to be the only blemish on Clemson's record that season.

Next came Wake Forest in Winston-Salem, and Bowman Gray Stadium, which held about 15,000, was popping at the seams with 22,000 people. Clemson was ranked 16th in the nation at 3–0–1, and the Deacons were 17th nationally at 4–0–1.

Indications were that this would be a defensive battle. Clemson had given up 14 points in four games and Wake Forest had allowed 21 in five games.

The action went just about the way the script was written, but with two unexpected players, who were anticipating watching most of the game from the sidelines.

Both Ray Mathews and Fred Cone received rib injuries in the first four minutes of the game. Jim Shirley moved in for Cone and Frank Kennedy replaced Mathews at wingback. These were two sophomores replacing two seniors. Kennedy had not played five minutes in the first four games, but he scored Clemson's first touchdown in the second quarter.

A 57-yard touchdown run by Calvert gave the Tigers a 13–0 lead at the half.

In the second half, Wake Forest recovered Clemson fumbles on the Tiger 24, 37, 22 and 35, but couldn't score.

In the fourth quarter, Jim Staton broke through and blocked a Billy Hair punt and the Deacons recovered at the Clemson eight. It took Bill Miller four tries, but he scored on fourth down. Ed Kissell was wide right on the PAT, and Clemson held to a shaky 13–6 lead.

With two minutes left in the game, Wake Forest got the ball back on its own 13-yard line, and the lead seemed safe.

But the Deacons quickly moved up the field and scored with 20 seconds left in the game. Bob Patton broke through and blocked Kissell's PAT to preserve the 13–12 win.

The next four games were cakewalks—Clemson outscored Duquesne, Boston College, Furman and Auburn by a score of 186–36.

Sophomore tailback Hair had 100 or more yards against Duquesne (104), Boston College (124) and Furman (141).

Possibly the most significant game of these four was Auburn. The War Eagles had not won a game all year long, but there was a rumor that if Clemson won by more than 40 points, a bid to the Orange Bowl would be locked up.

The final score was 41–0, and Cone had a career day, scoring four times. It was Auburn's first ever Homecoming loss.

Now the Tigers sat back and waited for the bowl invitation. And waited. And waited. And Howard slipped back into his bad mood.

The home-based University of Miami team was a unanimous Orange Bowl pick, but the selection committee was split on who should oppose the Hurricanes.

Howard was becoming a little impatient, and was quoted by sportswriter Furman Bisher as saying that the "Orange Bowl Committee can drown in its own orange juice."

Howard said that wasn't exactly his quote. He called Bisher and asked him if he was trying to get him fired by misquoting him. Bisher was said to have told Howard: "If I had quoted you with what you actually said, we'd both be fired."

Anyway, Clemson's selection to play Miami proved to be unpopular in some places. Students at the University of Alabama openly protested the decision, and a number of derogatory articles appeared in newspapers around the South.

Gene Plowden, a Clemson alumnus, was a sportswriter for The Associated Press in Miami and he wrote a letter to Howard which appeared on the national AP wire and was published by many papers. It said:

"Dear Frank:

You and your players can do a great job of 'educating' South Florida football followers when the Tigers meet the University of Miami Hurricanes in the Orange Bowl here New Year's Day. The storm that broke when the selection was announced almost a week ago hasn't subsided yet."

"Who is Clemson?" was a familiar cry. "Who have they played? What town is it in? Never heard of it. Is it a new wonder drug or something?"

Many seem to have taken the choice as a personal affront. Some said even Miami's beloved Hurricanes were insulted. One writer commented that he thought Clemson was some sort of animal being added to the Ringling Brothers and Barnum and Bailey Circus.

"The choice of Clemson to meet the Hurricanes was a surprise," said one of the more charitable writers. "Some will applaud. Others will object. Some of the fans are yelping over the choice of Clemson. I concur from a publicity standpoint we did not come up with a scoop, but I do think that Clemson has a good football team and that our chances for an exciting contest are very good. If you are disappointed, accept it in good spirits. After all, it's not the first time the Orange Bowl Committee has disappointed you."

Another writer wrote: "There's no use having apoplexy over Clemson's selection. We're stuck with it, so let the disappointment go at that.

"We know Clemson was ranked 10th in the Associated Press football poll, while Miami was 15th; and you had a good point when you said, 'Tell them to read the AP poll if they want to know about Clemson.' You saw Miami whip Missouri, 27–0, on the Hurricanes' home ground, the same team Clemson walloped, 34–0, early in the season in Missouri.

"I thought you summed it up nicely the other day when you said: "They don't have to worry about us. The people will see a good football game. There are a lot of schools with older traditions than Clemson, but there aren't many with a better team. You can't play tradition.

"You are right, Frank, and the records show Clemson fared pretty well against Boston College in the Cotton Bowl in 1940 and against Missouri in the Gator Bowl two years ago. As a Clemson alumnus, I may be a bit biased; but I do believe this Orange Bowl will rank with the best, and I've seen some thrillers. So, bring your boys down and show these Miamians a thing or two, Frank. They can stand a little enlightening.
          Sincerely,
          Gene Plowden (Clemson '24)

P.S. By the way, you don't happen to have a couple of Orange Bowl tickets lying around, do you, Frank? There isn't a one left in town."

There were 65,181 people at the game, the biggest audience ever to see the Tigers play. This was the only bowl being played that featured two undefeated teams. Miami, like Clemson, entered the game with an 8–0–1 record.

This 1950 team was one of the most prolific offensive teams in Clemson history, and the defense wasn't all that shabby either. It had four shutouts to its credit, and only one team scored as many as 20 points.

Forty years later, the 1950 team has no less than seven offensive records still in the books, such as most rushing per attempt (5.25), most touchdowns per game (4.8), most rushing touchdowns a game (3.5),

Sterling Smith holds onto miami's Frank Smith for a safety and a 15–14 win in the 1951 Orange Bowl.

Post-game celebration in the locker room (Smith, center).

most yards per play (6.16) and most points per game (32.9). Also, it is tied with two other teams for the most 400-yard games of total offense (7) and the most 500-yard total offensive games (3).

As already mentioned, only four times in Clemson history have three backs gained over 100 yards rushing in one game, and the 1950 team did it twice on back-to-back weekends.

The Orange Bowl turned out to be a wild one.

Clemson scored on a one-yard run by Cone to lead 7–0 at halftime and added a 21-yard scoring pass from Hair to Glenn Smith in the third quarter, but Charles Radcliff missed the extra point after the second score.

The Hurricanes came roaring back when Harry Mallios went in from five yards out

and Frank Smith scored on a 17-yard pass from Jack Hackett. Gordon Watson made both of his extra points, and the third quarter ended with Miami ahead by one, 14–13.

Clemson won the game 15–14 when Miami's Frank Smith tried to sweep right out of his own end zone and Sterling Smith brought him down for a safety.

The Hurricanes got one more chance when they recovered a Cone fumble on the Tigers' 34-yard line, but lost the ball back on an interception two plays later.

Howard still has a soft spot in his heart for both the 1948 and 1950 teams. They were his first two bowl teams, and they were both undefeated. The Tigers were now 3–0 in bowl competition, but their total margin of victory in the three was only five points. This led Howard to remark: "We humiliated all three of 'em."

The team ready to board plane on the way to the 1952 Gator Bowl.

Gator Bowl action: Billy Hair returns opening kickoff 72 yards—but does not score.

S. 22	53-6	W	H	‡Presbyterian
S. 29	20-14	W	A	‡Rice
O. 6	6-0	W	A	‡N.C. State
O. 13	7-21	L	A	‡Pacific
O. 25	0-20	L	A	S. Carolina
N. 3	21-6	W	H	Wake Forest
N. 10	21-2	W	H	Bost. Coll.
N. 17	34-14	W	A	Furman
N. 24	34-0	W	H	Auburn
J. 1	0-14	L	N1	Miami (FL)

N1 at Gator Bowl, Jacksonville, FL

1951: THE DEFIANT GATOR BOWL

Clemson's 1951 season included its share of "firsts."

The first four games were played at night—for the first time.

The Tigers played against a black player—for the first time.

A full-blooded Catawba Indian played with the Tigers—for the first time.

And the Tigers defied the Southern Conference by playing in the Gator Bowl, setting the stage for the birth of the Atlantic Coast Conference.

By winning its last four games, Clemson was 7–2 and an odds-on favorite for the Gator Bowl invitation to face Miami. When the invitation came from Jacksonville, the Tigers had to decide whether to accept and go against the wishes of the Southern Conference presidents, who in September had voted not to allow their schools to play in post-season games.

In recent years, the faculty chairman of athletics has been the school representative at conference business meetings when votes were taken. Nowadays, the faculty chairman, athletic director, head football coach and head basketball coach attend the annual meetings of the conference. The presidents are also invited, but the faculty chairmen cast the votes after conferring with other parties from their institutions.

In 1951 the Southern Conference presidents did the voting, and they were quoted as saying that they did not want their conference to become known as a football conference, which was the reason for their vote against post-season football.

Included in the group was Clemson's president, Dr. Robert Franklin Poole.

After a number of meetings between governing bodies of the college and athletic department, the decision was made to defy the conference rule and accept the bid. Clemson's official statement of acceptance, under the signature of athletic council chairman Dr. Lee W. Milford, read:

"The Gator Bowl Committee of Jacksonville, Fla., has extended to the Clemson College Athletic Council, through our head coach and athletic director, Frank Howard, an official invitation for our football team to participate in a bowl game with the University of Miami on January 1, 1952.

"At a called meeting of the Athletic Council, including our president, Dr. R. F. Poole, we discussed and considered the invitation and the results from all possible angles if we accepted. As a result of this meeting I have asked the Southern Conference officially, and in the usual way, for

Billy Hair in action in 1951.

its approval.

"The Southern Conference did not approve our request. This is the first time in the history of the Southern Conference that a member institution has been denied this privilege. We have again studied and discussed the various issues that have brought about the unusual denial of a Southern Conference member participating in a bowl game on New Year's Day.

"I have discussed this with our president, Dr. R. F. Poole, who in turn has consulted every member of the college Board of Trustees and upon our recommendation, they have given their hearty approval of our accepting the bowl bid mentioned above.

"Our acceptance of this bowl bid, which has not met the usual approval of the Southern Conference, is not intended in any way to be a defiance of the action of the Southern Conference."

Clemson acted on the belief that the September conference vote against bowl games was a "recommendation" and not a directive. Maryland, which was going to the Sugar Bowl to play Tennessee, held the same view, but unlike Clemson, accepted its bid without polling the other conference schools.

Clemson and Maryland could be expelled from the conference, according to Commissioner Wallace Wade. He said that Clemson violated the conference bylaws by refusing

to go by the league vote on the bowl issue. He said he "couldn't even guess" what the league would do about it, but that under the bylaws this could mean expulsion.

Clemson went to the Gator Bowl and prepared to take the conference consequences.

The season had started quietly enough, with the usual drubbing of Presbyterian.

The first test came the following week in Houston against Jess Neely's Rice Owls.

It had been 12 years since Neely left Clemson for Rice. Frank Howard replaced Neely at Clemson, and they didn't like to play against each other.

Billy Hair, now a junior tailback, sparked Clemson to a pair of first-quarter touchdowns, and freshman Buck George scored in the third quarter to give the Tigers a 20–14 victory.

The Tigers shut out North Carolina State the following week, with fullback Jim Shirley running 36 times, a school record that still stands.

Now undefeated after three games, Clemson fans were already talking about a second consecutive bowl appearance. It was then that the presidents of 14 of the Southern Conference's 17 schools held a meeting at the University of North Carolina at Chapel Hill. They pledged to enact legislation at their December meeting that would not allow any conference football team to play in post-season bowl games.

The Tigers went about as far away from home as they could for the fourth game of the season. College of the Pacific handed Clemson its first loss since 1949 with a 21–7 victory. Eddie Macon and Tom McCormick, at that time the third top ground gainer in the nation, bore the brunt of Pacific's ball carrying.

Pacific scored all of its touchdowns in the third quarter and Clemson did not score until 31 seconds remained in the game.

One of Pacific's touchdowns came on an

18-yard run by Macon, the first black player the Tigers had ever played against.

On Big Thursday, the South Carolina defense stole the show from the offense. Safety Billy Stephens started the scoring at 12:35 of the first quarter when he returned a punt 74 yards. Before the afternoon was over, Stephens would recover a Tiger fumble, break up a pass in the Gamecocks' end zone and grab another interception out of Billy Hair's arms.

Stephens was not the only Gamecock defensive player to shine. Harry Jabbusch had a 15-yard pass interception for a touchdown, and Leon Cunningham recovered two fumbles.

Altogether, Clemson lost four fumbles and saw three passes intercepted in the 20–0 loss.

With three of the last four games at home, that would be the last defeat the Tigers would suffer in the regular season.

Wake Forest was first. As "Scoop" Latimer wrote in the Greenville News: "Clemson's infuriated Tigers rebounded from their sluggishness in two previous games and reached their strength, sciences and senses to crush the favored Wake Forest Demon Deacons."

A crowd of 24,000—the largest ever to see a game at Clemson—saw Hair record more than 100 yards rushing and 100 yards passing for the fourth time in his career. He rushed for 102 yards—including a 42-yard scoring run, and completed seven passes for 147 yards, one a 15-yard touchdown.

Boston College was next. Hair and Company jumped on the Eagles with two first-quarter scores and never let up.

Then came Furman in Greenville, which was almost a home game for the Tigers. From a 7–7 tie in the second quarter, Clemson pushed over the go-ahead score before halftime for a 14–7 lead.

One of Clemson's two scores in the third period was a 90-yard scoring dash by Buck George, which tied Banks McFadden for the longest run from scrimmage in Tiger history. George, a full-blooded Catawba Indian as well as a freshman, also had the honors of scoring Clemson's last touchdown in the fourth quarter.

George Olsen, business manager of the Gator Bowl, attended the game. When asked about the bowl controversy, Olsen only would say that "the invitation might be forthcoming if Clemson plays well and wins against Auburn."

Howard was quizzed about the possibility of not playing in a bowl and said: "I can't say a thing at this time." Supposedly the conference had been polled that day, but he was mum. "(Maryland coach) Jim Tatum opened his mouth too fast, and it's got us all in trouble. So I can't give out a statement of any kind."

The Clemson coach was careful in his wording because the school cannot accept the bid without the permission of the conference. But 10 days earlier Maryland had accepted the Sugar Bowl bid without first seeking permission.

Clemson was hoping that the action taken by the presidents in September to outlaw all bowl games for all league teams would either be rescinded or changed in some way.

Eight representatives from the Gator Bowl were on hand when Clemson took to the field against Auburn. What they saw was a lot of sputtering and backfiring by the Tigers for three quarters—and a 6–0 Clemson lead.

The Tigers finally woke up in the final period, scoring four touchdowns.

For the third time during the season and the fifth time in his career, Hair recorded over 100 yards rushing and 100 yards passing with 113 on the ground and 184 through the air. Steve Fuller later performed the same feat twice, once in 1976 and again in 1978, but no other Clemson player has done this more than once.

At the Gator Bowl, the Tigers took a 14–0 licking from the Hurricanes.

Miami quickly recovered from Hair's opening kickoff return of 72 yards and kept the Tigers out of the end zone, and this proved to be the turning point of the game. Probably still winded from the long return, Hair ran four consecutive times, and Clemson lost the ball on downs.

Miami senior defensive back Jim Dooley had four interceptions, and shut down Glenn Smith and Otis Kempson with his tight coverage throughout the game.

The Tigers were inside the Miami 20-yard line five times, but either had to give the ball up on downs or saw Dooley intercepting in the end zone. Clemson had 233 total yards to 174 for Miami and had a 14–5 edge in first downs. But between the four interceptions, one blocked punt and one fumble lost, the Tiger offense was always shortchanged.

The Miami players said they really wanted to win this game for Frank Smith, who was tackled in the end zone for a safety that gave Clemson a 15–14 victory over Miami in the 1951 Orange Bowl a year earlier. Smith had to sit this Gator Bowl game out with an injury.

As expected, Clemson and Maryland were punished by the conference for playing in post-season games. The two were denied permission to play any other conference teams in 1952 except each other. There was one exception—legally required games against conference opponents could be played.

So is the South Carolina General Assembly passed a law or resolution requiring the playing of the traditional State Fair game in 1952, so that Clemson and South Carolina could continue their series unbroken.

Clemson being declared an outcast by the conference was voted the top sports story in the state in 1951. And the biggest story at Clemson was getting a new schedule together for the '52 season.

The Tigers opened their home schedule with the traditional Presbyterian. The next Saturday the Villanova Wildcats came to town for Clemson's homecoming. This was a little early in the season for the "ole grads" to come back, but it was necessary—Clemson's last seven games would be on the road.

Then came the first meeting between the Tigers and Maryland. The Terrapins clobbered the Tigers 28–0, and went on to finish No. 3 in the nation.

Villanova, Maryland, Florida and South Carolina all defeated Clemson after the Tigers had beaten Presbyterian. Clemson then beat Boston College, tied Fordham and lost to Kentucky and Auburn to end the season with a sad 2–6–1 record.

Talk had already started about forming a new conference, one reason being the Southern's ban on post-season bowl games. At the Southern's annual meeting May 8, 1953, seven schools withdrew to form the Atlantic Coast Conference. Clemson, Duke, Maryland, North Carolina, North Carolina State, South Carolina and Wake Forest were the ACC charter members.

These seven schools met again in Raleigh on June 14, 1953, and named Dr. James T. Penney of South Carolina as the first conference president. On that same day a set of bylaws was adopted. December 4 of that same year, Virginia was officially admitted as a member of the league.

South Carolina tendered its resignation from the ACC on June 30, 1971, and the league stayed at seven members until Georgia Tech was admitted April 3, 1978, and Florida State was taken in as the ninth member July 1, 1991.

S. 22	27-7	W	H	‡Presbyterian
S. 29	20-20	T	A	Florida
O. 6	13-7	W	A	‡N.C. State
O. 13	17-0	W	A	Wake Forest
O. 25	7-0	W	A	S. Carolina
N. 3	21-6	W	H	Va. Tech
N. 10	6-6	T	A	Maryland
N. 16	0-21	L	A	‡Miami
N. 24	7-0	W	H	Virginia
D. 1	28-7	W	H	Furman
J. 1	21-27	L	N1	Colorado
N1 at Orange Bowl, Miami, FL				

1956: ACC CHAMPS AND THE ORANGE BOWL

The Atlantic Coast Conference and the Big Eight Conference signed a five-year contract with the Orange Bowl to play each other in the January 1 festival in Miami. The first game pitted Maryland against Oklahoma on New Year's Day, 1954.

The team representing the ACC would probably be its conference champion, but the eight league schools were required to take a vote after all conference games were completed.

Clemson played five conference games in 1956, and five games outside the conference against Presbyterian, Florida, Virginia Tech, Miami and Furman.

The Tigers finished the year with a 4–0–1 conference record to win the title, but because of their 3–2–1 record outside the conference, there was talk that Clemson might not be the best ACC representative in Miami.

Clemson did get the bid to play Colorado, but Howard summed up the team's feeling following the game by saying: "I'm glad we gave them a good game down here, after all we had to take."

It was a telling quote, but it was what Howard had said at halftime of the Orange Bowl that stands out as the highlight of the '56 season.

Clemson was no match for Colorado in the first half. John "The Beast" Bayuk pounded the Tigers' line time and time again. The Buffaloes' quarterback was Boyd Dowler, who would later become an outstanding NFL receiver. Colorado also had an outstanding sophomore lineman, John Wooten, who would also play in the NFL and is now an administrator with the Dallas Cowboys.

Down 20–0 at halftime, the Tigers had been outgained 196 yards to 71, and Jess "Mule" Yarborough, a Clemson graduate and a member of the Orange Bowl Committee, was looking for the nearest hole.

In the Clemson dressing room, Howard tore into his team. Howard has never denied that he minced few words in letting the players know that he was ashamed of them, and hurt as deep as he was ever hurt.

As close as can be pieced together, this is pretty close to what Howard said at the close of his tirade:

"I'm just not going to be a part of a football team that lays down and quits like that. If you guys don't want me to be your coach, I can take a hint. I'll quit. I'm not in the habit of being ashamed of my football team. If that's the way it's gotta be, I'll get out."

Fullback Bob Spooner, with Banks McFadden in background.

Howard has never admitted or denied that he threatened to resign that night. But whatever he said, he set his football team on fire.

Charlie Bussey, Clemson's quarterback, said that tales of Howard's halftime talk have not been exaggerated. "No matter what you've read or heard about it, it was all of that," Bussey has said.

Clemson got the second-half kickoff and began an 18-play, 69-yard scoring drive that took nearly nine minutes off the clock. With the exception of one play when Bussey ran for a yard, either Bob Spooner (11 times) or Joel Wells (6 times) carried the ball. Not a single pass was thrown.

On Colorado's first possession of the second half, it was four plays and out.

Then it was Spooner and Wells again, with Wells scoring on a 58-yard run. When Bussey kicked the extra point, the Tigers were within six.

Early in the fourth quarter, Clemson's Tommy Sease recovered a Colorado fumble at the Buffaloes' 11-yard line, and three

plays later Spooner scored from the one. Bussey's extra point gave Clemson a 21–20 lead.

Twenty-one points had been scored in just over 18 minutes. Colorado had the ball for nine plays during that time, Clemson for 31.

Then Bussey tried an on-sides kick, which Colorado recovered. To this day, Bussey can give no logical reason for his short kick. "My teammates say I called an on-sides kick and didn't even bother to tell them about it," Bussey says. "I always tell them that I only told the players who were fast enough for it to do any good. "I really don't know why I called that kick," Bussey said. "I'd been hit in the head earlier in the game, and that's the only explanation I've ever been able to come up with."

Howard always said that Bussey couldn't run, he couldn't punt or kick extra points and that he was a pitiful passer. "He couldn't do any of these on-the-field things," Howard said. "But just look up at the scoreboard when the game was over and see who the winner was."

After that short kick, which was recovered by John Wooten (and more than 35 years later he still reminds Howard when they meet up that "I'm the one who recovered that kick in the Orange Bowl"), Bussey came off the field and Howard said: "Razz, (Howard's nickname for Bussey), why did you kick it short?"

"I kicked it that way up at Raleigh (against N. C. State) and we won," was Bussey's explanation.

"Yeah," Howard replied, "Up there you were one point behind and you wanted to get the ball back. Down here you were ahead and you shoulda tried to put that thing in Biscayne Boulevard and make 'em go the length of the field."

Starting at their own 47, the Buffaloes moved down the field. After one running play netted eight yards, Eddie Dove ran at Clemson's left side four consecutive times for a total of 26 yards. With the ball at the Clemson 19, Bayuk ran three straight times to score, giving Colorado a 27–21 lead with 7:13 left to play. And that's how it ended.

The early season had gone well for the Tigers, with five wins and two ties. The most disappointing game was a 20–20 tie with Florida in Gainesville.

Though the Tigers were decided underdogs, they jumped into a 14–0 lead in the first quarter. The Gators scored twice in the second period, but missed an extra point for a 14–13 Tiger lead at halftime.

Florida went ahead by six in the third period, then Willie Smith started the Tigers on their final touchdown drive in the fourth quarter by recovering a Gator fumble at the Clemson 32.

Quarterback Bussey directed the 11-play drive, and the final yard was made by fullback Spooner.

After a five-yard penalty for delay of the game, Horace Turbeville kicked the extra point and the scoreboard flashed a 21–20 Clemson lead. However, one of the officials called holding in the Tiger line and the kick was nullified.

On the second attempt, Florida's Bill Bolton bolted through and blocked the kick.

All of the scoring the following week was crammed into the fourth quarter. N. C. State scored first, and Clemson came right back but missed the extra point.

Bussey's on-sides kick was recovered by Clemson's Charlie Horne, who scored the winning touchdown a few plays later.

Clemson defeated Wake Forest 17–0, at Winston-Salem. Nothing odd about that score, but what made it unusual was Horace Turbeville's field goal. It was the first successful field goal the Tigers had kicked since Jack Miller's game-winning boot in the 1949 Gator Bowl.

After beating South Carolina 7–0 on Big Thursday, Clemson had a tough Homecoming game against Virginia Tech.

With Clemson leading 7–0 in the third quarter, VPI quarterback Jimmy Lugar passed the Hokies to the Tiger 11-yard line on three straight completions. But on his fourth attempt, Rudy Hayes intercepted the pass and ran 77 yards before being overtaken. Hayes' return is still the longest non-scoring interception return in Clemson history.

Joel Wells, who had 108 yards rushing, went over from the three for the winning score.

This was the fifth straight year that Clemson had played Maryland and the Tigers had yet to win, but were getting closer each year. First it was 28–0, then 21–0, then 16–0 and then 25–12 in 1955.

Clemson was 5–0–1 going into the 1956 game while the Terps were a disappointing 1–6–0. The Tigers scored in the third period and Charlie Bussey, who had not missed a PAT since the N. C. State game, attempted to make his 10th conversion in 12 attempts on the season, but the kick went slightly to the left.

Following a Maryland punt Wells fumbled a handoff, and Maryland guard Jack Davis recovered on the Clemson 3-yard line. On fourth down, Tom Selep plunged over from

Bill Hudson (75) and Bill Thomas (57) blocking for Charlie Bussey against North Carolina State.

Clemson president Dr. R. F. Poole and Coach Howard on Miami Beach prior to '57 Orange Bowl versus Colorado.

the two. Bill Komolo missed the extra point, and the game ended in a 6–6 tie.

Miami, in one of its usual Friday night home games, finally knocked the Tigers from the unbeaten ranks with a 21–0 drubbing before a crowd of more than 47,000, which included Vice President Richard Nixon.

Clemson beat Virginia 7–0 to win the ACC championship. Bussey sneaked over from the half-yard line in the first quarter for the only score.

The Cavaliers, incidentally, had a big,

bruising fullback named Jim Bakhtiar, who was an Iranian prince, and he led all rushers with 83 yards.

In the final game of the regular season, against Furman, Joel Wells had one of his best days of the year, gaining 106 yards rushing. The Tigers won easily, 28–7.

One person looking on was ACC Commissioner James H. Weaver. He had taken a poll of the league's schools six days earlier, and an affirmative vote had been given to Clemson to represent the ACC in the Orange Bowl.

S. 20	20-15	W		H	Virginia
S. 27	26-21	W		H*	N. Carolina
O. 4	8-0	W		A	Maryland
O. 11	12-7	W		A	‡Vanderbilt
O. 23	6-26		L	A	S. Carolina
N. 1	14-12	W		H	Wake Forest
N. 8	0-13		L	A	Ga. Tech
N. 15	13-6	W		A	N.C. State
N. 22	34-12	W		H	Bost. Coll.
N. 29	36-19	W		H	Furman
J. 1	0-7		L	N1	LSU

*Frank Howard's 100th win at Clemson
N1 at Sugar Bowl at New Orleans, LA

1958: CLOSE CALLS TO THE SUGAR BOWL

After winning the conference championship in 1956 and playing in the Orange Bowl, Clemson's record dipped to 7–3 in 1957. The Tigers were 4–3 in the ACC and finished third.

But in the summer of 1958, Clemson was ready to go big time. The administration decided to enlarge Memorial Stadium for the first time since it was opened in 1942.

Plans called for 18,000 new seats, nearly doubling the size of the stadium.

"This will give us one of the best facilities in the nation," Howard said.

More than 20,000 people showed up for the season opener in '58, and they were treated to the type of game that this team would become famous for—close till the end.

To add color to the opening-game pageantry, the Tigers entered the field by running on the world's largest banner. Actually, it was a carpet made by the Wunda Weve Company of Greenville and presented to Howard by W. W. Pate, Sr., president of Wunda Weve.

The banner was made with an orange border and a purple background with "CLEMSON" spelled out in orange down the middle. The carpet was woven 13 feet wide and 104 feet long.

Although that original carpet is no longer used, the Tigers still come down that east bank on an orange and purple carpet.

And there was something else very different about this opener. It was against Virginia.

For the first time since 1929, the Tigers did not open the season with Presbyterian. In 1957 Clemson defeated the Blue Hose 66–0. The next week the Tigers went to Chapel Hill and North Carolina wore Clemson out, 26–0.

As the game was winding down, Howard made the decision not to play Presbyterian anymore. He turned to Bob Jones, his long-time assistant and confidant, and said: "I ain't playing PC no more. Those guys don't even know they got hit last week. That game sure didn't help on this one here."

Schedules then weren't made out years in advance like they are today, so Howard quickly was able to replace Presbyterian with Virginia.

The Tigers, rated 18th in pre-season polls, got their expected victory over the Cavaliers, but by the unexpected margin of only five points, 20–15. Virginia led 7–0, 7–6 and 15–14, but the Tigers finally over-powered the Cavs with a 10-play, 91-yard

Charlie Horne, Harvey White, Rudy Hayes, George Usry—1958 stalwarts.

touchdown drive in the final quarter to go ahead for good.

Sophomore Lowndes Shingler directed the Tigers to what turned out to be the winning score, a four-yard run by Bill Mathis.

"We didn't know exactly what to look for," Howard said after the game. "What we scouted for, we stopped pretty good. But they hadn't put in those outside flankers (which Virginia used on almost every play) when we scouted them. It was like going out there and playing in the dark.

"The things I didn't like about my ball club," Howard continued, "was they were jumpy and jittery, and that's not the mark of a good team."

South Carolina upset Duke that Saturday, and Howard was asked if that might help his team's chances of winning the ACC title. "It never helps us for South Carolina to win," he snapped.

Next up was North Carolina and Jim Tatum, who was in his second year as Tar Heel head coach. He and Howard had kept up their usual banter all summer, a custom since 1952, the first year Clemson played Maryland when Tatum was there.

All they were trying to do was fill up the stadium the Saturday they played each other, and they usually succeeded. And as one observer said, "They'd go off the field, arm in arm, counting their money on the way to the bank."

Tatum started early in the summer of 1958 in letting people know the kind of team Clemson was supposed to have. At a civic club speech he said "Howard has six backs that can make any club in the conference."

Howard violently denied this by saying he had ten backs instead of the six Tatum had mentioned.

"Tatum is the best publicity man I ever had at Clemson," Howard admitted. "I think he's talking too much. But, then, when I check the ticket sales for this in my capacity as athletic director, I ain't so sure that he's not smarter than I give him credit for."

He certainly succeeded this time. Extra bleacher seats were situated at every possible place, and the crowd of more than 40,000 broke the single-game attendance mark by 10,000.

This game might to this day still be one of the Top 10 ever played in The Valley—and there have been 232 of them through the 1990 season. If the fans thought they were wrung out after the 20–15 win over Virginia the week before, this one would leave them limp.

Howard said after the game: "If everyone didn't get their money's worth . . . then we'd better call off the rest of the season. It's my opinion it was one of the best games ever played here."

Howard also called the victory "one of the happiest in my 28 years of coaching. Not only was the 26–21 win over North Carolina the 100th of my career, it was also against Jim Tatum, whom I had never before defeated." (Howard lost four Maryland games to Tatum and one North Carolina game).

A Sonny Folckomer to John Schroeder pass for 16 yards staked the Tar Heels to a 6–0 first-quarter lead, but on the last play of that period, Jim Payne blocked an attempted quick kick and tackle Jim Padgett picked the ball up and ambled 28 yards to score. Harvey White passed to George Usry on the conversion.

The Tar Heels scored again in the second quarter to go up, 14–8. But Clemson came back and George "Pogo" Usry went over from the one to end a 68-yard drive. When the two-point run failed, the teams went to halftime tied.

Doug Cline scored in the third quarter for Clemson as the Tigers regained the lead, but missed on another two-point attempt. Don Coker's one yard run and Phil Blazer's conversion PAT put the Tar Heels back in the lead in the third quarter.

Late in the fourth quarter, Usry scored from the three for a five-point lead that would stand up. The Tigers missed another two-point pass conversion.

Some of the 40,000 on hand did not get to see the exciting finish. In the 93° heat, several hundred were overcome with heat exhaustion as every concession stand ran out of ice.

With the largest crowd in CLemson his-tory watching the game, and the town's population swelled more than 10-fold, traffic after the game was horrendous.

Some said a person could tell when the traffic light changed in Anderson, 16 miles away, when the cars moved in Clemson.

The governor and the chief highway commissioner got balled up in the traffic, the story goes, and it didn't seem like more than a few weeks before bulldozers, scrapers and highway crews were in town laying down four-lane roads in and out of town.

When someone mentioned this to Howard, he winked and said: "I had some of my highway patrol buddies make sure the governor and commissioner got in the slowest moving line of traffic out of town so they could see we needed a better highway system to accommodate all of those big crowds we were going to have each home game."

Today, the highways around Memorial Stadium are such that an 80,000-plus crowd can be clear of the parking lots in 45 minutes to an hour.

Clemson had to play Maryland the next weekend in College Park, a place the Tigers had never won. Howard saw his 10th-ranked team score just once, but made it stand up for the win. The touchdown came

Doug Cline (37) heads through some Deacons of Wake Forest; quarterback Harvey White looks on.

on a 50-yard pass from Harvey White to Wyatt Cox.

The Tigers went out of the conference for the first time for their fourth game, playing Vanderbilt in Nashville. It was another down-to-the-wire affair.

Tom Moore led the Commodores to a 7–0 third-quarter lead when he scored from nine yards out.

On the third play of the fourth quarter, Vandy was forced to punt, and the Tigers started a drive that was to last nearly eight minutes and go 76 yards to score. All thirteen plays in the drive were on the ground, and there were no third down conversions and only one on fourth down.

Hayes, White and Usry handled all of the rushing, and White got the touchdown on a quarterback sneak. White's two-point pass conversion attempt was intercepted, leaving the Tigers trailing, 7–6.

After the Commodores went three downs and out, Clemson regained possession with just under six minutes left and 69 yards from the goal. This time the Tigers used 15 plays (13 runs) before White scored the winning touchdown with nine seconds left in the game.

For the record, White ran 14 times and gained 104 yards, and he completed eight of 12 passes for another 60 yards. Howard praised his team, especially White, whom he kissed on the cheek in the locker room after the game. "He was the coolest man in the stadium," Howard said. "The winning drive was entirely his own choosing. We did not send in a single play."

Two weeks later Clemson played its next to last Big Thursday game against South Carolina. This was the game in which Howard promised to tip his hat "to that young fella" (Gamecocks' coach Warren Giese) if his team scored on the Tigers. Howard did a lot of hat tipping in South Carolina's 26–6 victory.

The loss knocked Clemson from 10th to 19th in the national polls.

Back home against Wake Forest, the Tigers would go down to the wire again.

The Deacons had a sophomore quarterback—Norman Snead—who was getting rave notices, and before he completed his eligibility he had left his niche in both the Wake and ACC record books. Snead had an end, Pete Manning, who would make all-conference with Snead that season.

Clemson scored on the first play of the second quarter on White's one-yard run. He then passed to Wyatt for the two-point conversion.

The Deacons came back later in the quarter with a one-yard score by Bobby Robinson, but Snead's two-point conversion pass to Bob Allen was no good, and Clemson kept an 8–6 lead.

It stayed that way until the fourth quarter, when Clemson reserve quarterback Johnnie Mac Goff scored. The extra-point kick was blocked.

But, my, how Snead could move his ball club.

Facing a third and 10 late in the quarter, Snead threw complete to Robinson for 26. Then he hit Manning, first for 10 yards, then for 31, and Wake Forest was at the Clemson 8-yard line. Two runs and a pass got three yards and Snead circled Clemson's left end for five yards on fourth down for the score.

Charlie Carpenter tried to hit Manning with the two-point conversion, but the pass was knocked down.

Trailing 14–12, the Deacons' Eddie Ladd tried a short kickoff, but Jim Payne fell on the ball for the Tigers.

Rudy Hayes could get only nine yards in four carries, and Wake Forest was in business again at its 41. Snead's pass to Jim Dalrymple was incomplete, but Clemson was charged with interference, which amounted to a 35-yard penalty. This stopped the clock, and with one second showing, Shingler knocked down Snead's pass inside the five to preserve another win that was not decided until the very end.

The following week against Georgia Tech in Atlanta, White was hobbled by an ankle sprain from the Wake Forest game, and Shingler did not play at all. The Yellow Jackets scored twice in the second quarter, and the Clemson offense never got going.

Back to the conference wars, and another fourth-quarter victory, this time over N. C. State in Raleigh. The win over the Wolfpack gave the Tigers the ACC championship, although two regular-season games remained to be played.

The N. C. State game wasn't actually as close as some of the earlier games—it was just that no one scored until the fourth quarter.

The Tigers went up 13–0 on touchdown runs by Usry and Bobby Morgan, and the Wolfpack got a late touchdown to make the final score 13–6.

The next game wasn't close. The 16th-ranked Tigers came home and clobbered Boston College.

Clemson's defense let the Eagles have

Doug Cline breaking tackles versus the Gamecocks.

only 80 yards rushing while ten runners amassed 210 rushing yards for the Tigers. Clemson only completed seven passes, but two of them went for touchdowns. Wyatt Cox had a 10-yard scoring reception and Bill Mathis caught one for a 47-yard score.

With a 7–2 record, the bowl talk started.

"I'm sure this game didn't hurt us," Howard said. "Three (bowl committees) have been in touch with us, but what they are thinking, I don't know. We'll just have to wait and see what move they make."

There had been reports that if Clemson defeated Furman, the Tigers would have the opportunity to play the No. 1–ranked team in the nation—the LSU Tigers and the famed Chinese Bandits defense—in the Sugar Bowl.

The way the Tigers started out, there was no question that the Sugar Bowl, or any other post-season bowl, would be happy to have Clemson. Fourteen points rolled up in the first quarter and 16 went up in the second.

Whatever Coach Bob King told his team at halftime must have shocked them more than Clemson did with its display of the first half.

Furman outscored the Tigers 19–6.

"After that display in the second half," Howard told Sugar Bowl president "Monk" Simons, "I don't know if you would even want us."

But about a half hour after that statement, Clemson had its invitation to play in the Sugar Bowl. And then the critics went into high gear.

Newspapers in Louisiana and Mississippi, and some of the better-known national columnists, scalded the Tigers. It made the pregame publicity of the 1951 Orange Bowl look like a Sunday School picnic.

Reports claimed that LSU head coach Paul Dietzel personally chose Clemson as an easy opponent for his Chinese Bandits.

Others said that Dietzel knew if Clemson were chosen that there was no way they'd sell the allotment of 10,000 tickets. Clemson fans not only did that, but were looking for more.

Howard said that Clemson people would leave more money in New Orleans than the followers of LSU. "Most of those LSU people won't even spend the night in New Orleans," Howard guessed. "They just live right up the road from the Sugar Bowl. I expect they'll come into town with a $10 bill and the Ten Commandments, and won't break either one of them."

One sportswriter compared Clemson's playing of No. 1 LSU to "shooting a covey of quail on the ground."

And as the game neared, the negative publicity didn't abate; it got worse, if anything.

The Clemson sports information office kept a clip file of all the negative articles. The office subscribed to all of the major newspapers in Mississippi and Louisiana, and each day the clippings would be pasted into a newspaper-size scrapbook.

By the time the team left for its final training at Biloxi, Miss., the scrapbook was an inch thick.

Two days before the game, the scrapbook was shown to the players and coaches, and it was then placed in the main dining room of the motel where the team was staying.

Howard added to the psychological war by having North Carolina coach Jim Tatum call players on the eve of the game and give each one he talked to "a little pep talk" on what this game meant to them personally, to the Clemson team and to the university, as well as to the ACC.

Coach "Peahead" Walker, another of Howard's friendly punching bags, had already done his share, by saying that Clemson would have no trouble with the Chinese Bandits because the Tigers "had a

Doug Cline, George Usry, Harry Pavilack, Lon Cordileone.

Mongolian idiot coaching up there for 20 years."

Had it not been for one major mistake, the two teams might have played till dark in a scoreless tie. LSU won 7–0, but not by the two to four touchdown margin some had predicted. As Furman Bisher wrote in the *Atlanta Journal* after the game: "LSU gained the victory, Clemson won friends, glory and money and the Sugar Bowl people were vindicated in their matchmaking."

The 25th-anniversary Sugar Bowl packed in 82,000 people, and up until 1982 was the largest crowd ever to see Clemson play a football game. That record has been broken eight times, five of them by Clemson home crowds.

The Bayou Bengals scored in the third period after getting the ball at Clemson's 12-yard line.

Clemson was in punt formation, and the snap from center Paul Snyder went to the up-man, Doug Cline, who was not expecting the ball. Duane Leopard recovered for LSU.

Snyder said after the game that he grabbed some grass when he gripped the ball, which caused him to snap it badly.

Three rushing plays got LSU only three yards. Then All-American Billy Cannon started to his right on what looked like another run, but he stopped and threw a pass to end Mickey Mangham for the game's only touchdown. Cannon then kicked the PAT.

"Even though our boys played a creditable game, we still had zero points and they had seven," Howard said, "and that's the way it will always stand. Many people congratulated me, the other coaches and the boys after the game, but I don't like for people to be satisfied with a loss. When you start being content to just play a good game, and at the same time not winning,

then it's time to give up coaching."

Howard has always felt that way. In 1962, when the 60,000-acre Lake Hartwell backed up around the campus, someone asked Howard: "With all of that water around now, are you going to sponsor a rowing (crew) team?"

His answer was short and to the point: "I don't believe in any sport where you have to sit on your ass and go backwards to win."

That pretty much set school policy. Clemson still doesn't have crew.

Sugar Bowl, 1959.

George Usry stretches to receive Harvey White pass.

S. 19	20-18	W	A	N. Carolina
S. 26	47-0	W	A	Virginia
O. 3	6-16	L	A	Ga. Tech
O. 10	23-0	W	H	N.C. State
O. 22	27-0	W	A*	S. Carolina
O. 31	19-0	W	A	‡Rice
N. 7	6-0	W	H	Duke
N. 14	25-28	L	H	Maryland
N. 21	33-31	W	H	Wake Forest
N. 28	56-3	W	A	Furman
D. 19	23-7	W	†N1	TCU

N1 at Bluebonnet Bowl, Houston,
*Last Big Thursday game
†Clemson's 300th win

1959: THE DEATH OF BIG THURSDAY

The 1959 season would begin with one of the toughest opening games ever and end with Clemson's 300th collegiate victory, but it was a game in between that many fans will long remember — the last Big Thursday.

The South Carolina game at the State Fair in Columbia would be the last mid-season meeting of the two arch rivals.

The teams began a home-and-home series, played on Saturdays, beginning in 1960.

Howard remembers a note he got from Bill Murray, head coach at Duke: "I got a letter from Preacher (Howard's nickname for Murray) the other day saying how unfair it was [for Duke] to have to play South Carolina four years in a row in Columbia. I wrote back and told him to quit griping until he's played them there 58 years in a row like we have."

The death of Big Thursday was big news across the state and, of course, the people who objected most were South Carolina fans and business owners in Columbia who would suffer financially.

But Clemson fans, who had traveled to Columbia since 1896 and sat on the sunny side of the stadium every year, were overjoyed that the one-way street was closing. The Clemson athletic department would also begin to get its share of program sales and concessions.

Harvey White had one of the finest games of his career that Thursday, passing for 162 yards and two touchdowns, leading the Tigers to a 27–0 win.

Dan Foster, writing in the *Greenville Piedmont*, said: "Frank Howard, who engineered the death of Big Thursday as an institution, brazenly seized upon its gasping last-day fling for one of the grandest of all his hours as coach.

"There have been immortal Big Thursdays before, but Clemson partisans the world over are likely to acclaim 1959 as the year that housed the most treasure of them all. Not in 20 years had the Tigers been as decisive in the famed Carolina Stadium battleground as they were in the 27–0 pummeling of the Gamecocks of South Carolina."

Whitey Kelley in the *Charlotte Observer* wrote: "They held final rites on Big Thursday in Columbia and 47,000 persons saw Frank Howard preach a fine funeral."

Another, Johnny Hendrix in the *Augusta Chronicle*, had this lead on his story: "The final production of Big Thursday, that unique football holiday in the Palmetto State, was a Clemson extravaganza with

Harvey White, the son of Greenwood County's sheriff, claiming the Oscar for his performances."

And Smith Barrier of the *Greensboro Daily News* put another name on the game when he wrote: "Harvey White made it 'Black Thursday' for South Carolina's outplayed Gamecocks, and the Clemson quarterback was never better."

The State, Columbia's morning newspaper, had Howard go up in the stands after the game and the photographer took a picture of Howard blowing Big Thursday a goodbye kiss. This is still one of Howard's favorite pictures and he keeps a supply in his office and occasionally autographs one for somebody who remembers that game over three decades ago.

The first two opponents in '59 were the same as a year earlier, but North Carolina would be the first game instead of Virginia.

The trip to Chapel Hill would be a tough one for Howard. Just a few weeks before the season opened, his long-time friend Jim Tatum had died.

Jim Hickey was named to replace Tatum at North Carolina. On the Friday afternoon before the game, when Clemson went to Kenan Stadium to work out, Howard walked into the North Carolina coaches' dressing room where Hickey and his staff were dressing after the Tar Heel final run-through.

Howard started opening and closing all of the metal lockers. Finally, after six or seven lockers were slammed, Hickey asked Howard: "What in the world are you trying to do, Howard?"

"I'm looking for Tatum's ghost," Howard replied. "I know you got him in here somewhere and I don't want him to come out on the field tomorrow afternoon and haunt me and my team about the time we get ready to score."

When he was told the crowd for the game would be nearly a sellout of 44,000, Howard came back with: "It better be a sellout. I don't like the idea of packing up my Sugar Bowl team and playing before empty seats. We can't always get cranked up unless there's a full house like we have at home."

The full house must have materialized because Clemson got cranked up early. They scored early in the first quarter, went up 14–0 in the second quarter and led 14–6 at halftime.

Howard said after the game that it was "the best first quarter one of my teams ever played." The Tar Heels only had the ball for six offensive plays during the first 15 minutes.

Clemson took the second-half kickoff, started at its own 33 and didn't give the ball back for nine minutes and five seconds.

There was not a pass attempted in the entire drive—17 rushing plays with Doug Cline gaining 33 yards, "Pogo" Usry 20 and Bill Mathis 14. Mathis scored from the two, and the Tigers took at 20–6 lead.

The Tar Heels scored two more times, but missed both attempts at the two-point conversions.

Howard pretty well summed up the game. "We made three touchdowns and they made three touchdowns. We got an extra point and they didn't. That was it."

The Tigers had little trouble with the Cavaliers in Charlottesville. Clemson scored 14 points in the first quarter and 27 in the third to win going away.

Clemson's annual trek to Atlanta for the Georgia Tech game was the first loss (16–6) for the Tigers. Several of the players were hit by the flu the week of the game and were not released from the infirmary until Friday.

But Mathis did establish a modern-day record for a kickoff return when he went 99 yards.

Quarterback White sustains injury during '59 season.

Against N. C. State the next week at home, Gary Barnes scored his first collegiate points on a 26-yard pass from Lowndes Shingler, Lon Armstrong kicked a 28-yard field goal and Ron Scrudato intercepted a pass and went 60 yards to score. Barnes, Armstrong and Scrudato were all sophomores.

After the Big Thursday victory, the Tigers went to Houston next to play the luckless (0–3–2) Rice Owls, and their luck didn't improve much against Clemson. Of the three touchdowns the Tigers scored, one came on an 18-yard pass interception by Paul Snyder and another when Bill Mathis recovered a fumble in the end zone.

The Clemson defense showed up again at the Duke game and stopped the Blue Devils in their tracks. The Tigers recorded their fourth consecutive shutout and the fifth of the season in shutting down the Duke attack 6–0. The Blue Devils didn't get into Clemson territory until the fourth quarter.

In the most disappointing loss of the year, and before a homecoming audience, Maryland defeated the Tigers 28–25. The Terps led at the end of the first three quarters, and there were four touchdowns scored in the action-packed fourth period, two by each team.

Clemson's final score came on Doug Daigneault's two-yard run, putting the Tigers up 25–21.

With about 7 minutes left, Maryland started from its 15 after the kickoff. The Terps' winning drive lasted about 4 minutes, and when Clemson got the ball back White was intercepted on first down.

It had been a wild, close game. But it was nothing compared to the following week's matchup against Wake Forest. It was like a tennis match.

When the 64th point was scored, Furman Bisher, of the *Atlanta Journal,* turned and asked: "Does anyone remember who scored the first touchdown and how?"

Actually, it was Bobby Robinson, who intercepted a Harvey White pass and sped down the sidelines for a 69-yard touchdown.

Then Daigneault scored for Clemson.

Then Norman Snead passed to Jerry Ball for another Wake touchdown.

Then Doug Cline scored for the Tigers.

Then Wake Forest kicked a field goal.

A pretty busy first half, but at 17–14 they were just warming up.

Halfway through the third period, Neil MacLean took a pass out in the flat from Snead and carried 73 yards before being brought down at the Clemson 11. This is still the longest non-scoring run after a pass in ACC history.

Before the Tigers could catch their breath, Snead had passed to Bob Allen for an 11-yard touchdown. Clemson now trailed, 24–14, but it only took the Tigers about three and a half minutes to get six of those points back when Shingler found Ed Bost for a 15-yard touchdown pass.

In the fourth period, a 1-yard score by Cline gave the Tigers their first lead, with 8:16 remaining.

Wake came right back to take a 31–27 lead.

There was still plenty of time (6:40) for the Tigers to make their move. However, on the first play following the kickoff, Cline fumbled and the Deacons fell on the ball.

Then "Pogo" Usry intercepted a pass by Chuck Reiley, who had replaced Snead, and went 73 yards to the Wake Forest 10-yard line. One play later, Usry scored the winning touchdown from the two.

Clemson pushed its record to 7–2 and

jumped five places in the national rankings to 14th, with Furman the remaining game in Greenville.

It was no contest. Furman kicked a field goal to take a 3–0 lead, then ducked for cover. The final score was 56–3.

The ACC champions accepted a bid to play in the first Bluebonnet Bowl, in Houston, against Texas Christian, co-champions of the Southwest Conference.

The game was played December 19, which would give Clemson the distinction of becoming the first school to play in two post-season bowl games in the same calendar year. The 1958 Tigers had played in the Sugar Bowl on January 1, 1959, against LSU.

The *Charlotte News* obtained the services of Douglas Clyde "Peahead" Walker to write a critique on the Clemson team.

"I am going to handle my chore from right here in my apartment in Charlotte," Walker said, the long-time friendly rival of Howard's. "It will be a distinct displeasure to follow the coaching moves of Frank Howard. I would not lower my dignity by appearing in the same stadium, even as a guest, so I'm staying home."

Howard, somewhat stunned when he heard Walker had been given his assignment, answered:

"Walker is staying home because they wouldn't let him in the stadium. We're playing the Texas Christians. They don't want a heathen like Walker in sight."

Clemson set up headquarters at the swanky Shamrock Hotel. One morning Gene Willimon, who was executive secretary of IPTAY, and another member of the Clemson traveling party were about to have breakfast in the Pine Room of the Shamrock. Willimon looked over the menu and asked the waitress if the ham listed on the menu were country ham.

"I do not know," she said, "but will find

out for you."

Momentarily she returned to the table and told Willimon, "Sir, the chef says that all ham comes from the country."

"Bacon will be all right," Willimon said with a smile.

Clemson was the only team in the ACC to go to a bowl in the season of 1959. Both the Tigers and Horned Frogs had identical 8–2 records, with TCU ranked seventh in the nation and a 7½–point favorite over 11th-ranked Clemson.

There was no scoring in the game until the second period, when Lon Armstrong's 22-yard field goal gave Clemson a 3–0 lead.

TCU had only been in Clemson territory once in the first 22 minutes of the game, but when the second units of both teams came in at the 8:27 mark, the Horned Frogs began to leap. A 19-yard pass from Donald George to Harry Moreland gave TCU a 7–3 lead.

Dodson missed a field goal with the ball on the Tiger 10 on the last play of the half.

The third quarter was much like the first. Each team had two possessions, each got in the other's territory, but nobody got closer than the other's 29.

Clemson entered the final quarter still trailing, 7–3, but took the lead for good when White hit Gary Barnes on 68-yard scoring pass.

As TCU lined up on its 29 following the kickoff, Clemson coaches in the press box were yelling to get Armstrong out of the game. He had just kicked off and was playing guard, but the coaches felt that either Dave Lynn, Dave Olson or Tommy Gue would be better suited for the defense. The word was being relayed to the ground when Armstrong intercepted a George pass and returned it to the TCU 27.

After two running plays Shingler found Tommy King open over the middle. He juggled the ball a couple of steps, but held on

in the end zone for a 23-yard score. Clemson now led, 16–7 with 7:32 left to play.

The Tigers would score again less than three minutes later when Scrudato ended a 63-yard drive with a 1-yard touchdown run. Clemson's 300th school victory was in the books.

The vaunted rushing attack of the Frogs, which had been averaging 203 yards a game, was held to 89. Jack Spikes, who led the Southwest Conference in rushing in 1959, was held to 33 yards. Clemson's total offense was 306 yards to 159 for TCU.

"I don't think I've ever seen two teams go at each other like those two today," Howard said. "Sparks were really flying off those shoulder pads out there."

Meanwhile, "Peahead" Walker was watching the game back in Charlotte, getting ready for his "TV critique."

His summation: "Howard is proclaiming himself as the greatest Southerner since Gen. Robert E. Lee. He finally won a bowl game.

"Nobody could guess how long it would take Howard to wake up and throw a pass," Walker continued. "When he did get them to go to the air, they split the Frogs open like a nervous freshman in a zoology laboratory.

"There's one factor, however, which must be faced," the critic offered. "Howard, who can't pronounce or spell the word 'humility,' will be more obnoxious than ever. When Frank gets through patting himself on the back, his listeners will think Knute Rockne was a prep school coach."

Walker said he had to be on several touchdown club programs with Howard later on and that he dreaded the thought of it.

When Howard was informed of Walker's remarks about his coaching and personal appearances, the Clemson coach said: "All one has to do is to look at his record at

Wake Forest, as an assistant at Yale and as head coach at Montreal. It didn't take people long to catch on to him. Sometimes he had to move before the rent came due.

"As far as us appearing together at some of these touchdown clubs, I offered to let him be on the program with me to supplement that paltry salary he gets for his so-called scouting," Howard said. "If I wasn't on the program with him, the audience would see how quick Peahead would fall on his face.

"Most of the time, I don't pay any attention to anything unless I step in it," Howard offered. "And that's the way I'm going to treat Peahead for that uncalled for verbal attack on my good character and coaching wizardry."

Clemson at the first annual Bluebonnet Bowl, December 19, 1959.

1959: THE DEATH OF BIG THURSDAY

S. 10	14-21	L	H	Maryland
S. 17	7-6	W	A	Georgia
S. 24	31-14	W	A	Ga. Tech
O. 1	31-13	W	A	Va. Tech
O. 8	31-0	W	H	Virginia
O. 15	17-11	W	A	Duke
O. 22	7-3	W	H	N.C. State
O. 29	26-0	W	H	Wake Forest
N. 5	13-13	T	A	N. Carolina
N. 12	17-21	L	H	Notre Dame
N. 19	31-27	W	A	S. Carolina
D. 30	3-34	L	N1	‡Pittsburgh

N1 at Gator Bowl at Jacksonville, FL

1977: ENDING THE 18-YEAR DROUGHT

When Charley Pell took over as Clemson football coach after the 1976 season, he inherited a team full of talented juniors, and wasted no time turning them into winners. He took the 1977 team to the Gator Bowl.

For Tiger fans, a bowl trip was a new play-pretty. Clemson had been to seven post-season games, but had not played in one for 18 years. And these Tigers were ready to go!

Clemson, which had more than 50,000 orders for tickets, received 25,000 from the Gator Bowl. The school tried to get more from its opponent, the University of Pittsburgh, but couldn't. When IPTAY members heard there was going to be a ticket shortage, they started looking elsewhere — Pittsburgh, joining the Gator Bowl Association — anything . . . just get two or four or six anywhere.

There were a lot of disappointed fans, but there was also a lot of orange in the Gator Bowl that night.

Pittsburgh, led by quarterback Matt Cavanaugh, dominated the Tigers 34–3, Clemson's worst bowl defeat to date.

About the only things the Tigers could take pride in were helping set a new attendance record (72,289) and Obed Ariri kick-

ing the longest field goal (49 yards) in Gator Bowl history.

But the season put Clemson back in the national football limelight. The Tigers would post an 8–3–1 record for the year and all three losses came against teams ranked 10th or higher nationally.

And Clemson had its stars.

Offensive guard Joe Bostic was All-American, quarterback Steve Fuller was an academic All-American (and he later had his Clemson jersey number retired).

Fuller was selected as the ACC Player of the Year, Pell was chosen ACC Coach of the Year.

Fuller was named the top back in the South by the Atlanta Touchdown Club; Bostic received the Jacobs Blocking Trophy for both the state of South Carolina and the ACC; Fuller was awarded the National Football Foundation and Hall of Fame Scholar Athlete Award; and Fuller and Bostic along with Jonathan Brooks, Lacy Brumley, Jerry Butler, Steve Ryan and Randy Scott were named to the All-ACC team.

The Tigers started the season in an unusual way — they played Maryland at home and lost. The Terps held a No. 10 pre-season national ranking.

But then came seven consecutive victo-

Steve Fuller, Clemson's star quarterback.

ries, the first time that had been accomplished in a season since the undefeated team of 1948.

The biggest game of the streak probably was against Georgia. No Clemson team had won in Athens since 1914.

More than 55,000 people turned out for the game, played mostly in the rain.

After a scoreless first half, David Sims punted on Clemson's first possession of the third period, but Billy Woods fumbled and Jeff Soowal fell on the ball for Clemson at the 'Dog 48.

Clemson used ten plays before Lester "Rubber Duck" Brown scored from the two.

Two big pass plays by quarterback Fuller kept the drive going. He connected with Jerry Butler on a 15-yarder and then came back with a crucial third-down strike to Dwight Clark for 17 yards and a first down at the Georgia six. Jimmy Russell's PAT after Brown's touchdown would prove to be the difference in the game.

Two Clemson interceptions, one by Randy Scott and another by freshman Eddie Geathers, stopped Georgia drives, but with six seconds left in the game Bulldogs' quarterback Jeff Pyburn hit Ulysses Norris with an 8-yard touchdown pass.

Georgia went for the win, but Pyburn's pass was high as the Clemson defensive line chased him out of the pocket.

Pell started a tradition after that game that is still carried on today. As the Clemson team buses came back through Commerce, Ga., Pell stopped and sent managers into a drug store to buy a couple of boxes of cigars for the players. Each head coach who succeeded Pell has passed out cigars in the dressing room following a victory.

Although the drought hadn't been quite as severe in Atlanta as it had been in Athens, the Tigers had beaten Georgia Tech only four times (with one tie) since 1908. Of all that string of games, only one had been played in Clemson, that being in 1976 when the Tigers won 21–17.

Clemson was going to win this day by the widest margin since the Tigers won 73–

0 under John Heisman in 1903.

The Tigers got a field goal on their first possession, and got the ball back five plays later when Tech fumbled.

The 50,000-plus fans got to see something Clemson fans had become accustomed to—Fuller passing to Butler.

On the first play after the fumble recovery, Butler caught Fuller's pass in full stride and didn't slow up until 66 yards later in the Yellow Jacket end zone.

The Tigers score two more touchdowns to lead 24–0 in the second period, but Tech scored before the quarter ended to cut Clemson's lead to 24–7 at half time.

Tech scored again in the third period, but Fuller and Butler went back to work in the fourth period for Clemson's final score. The Tigers only took two giant steps to go 66 yards. One was a 46-yard Fuller-to-Butler pass, the other was Lester Brown's 20-yard score.

Clemson had little trouble with Virginia Tech in Blacksburg and Virginia at home. When the Cavaliers rolled into town for what would be their 17th consecutive loss to Clemson, the Tigers scored 31 points for the third consecutive week.

The next two weeks would find the Tigers playing a pair of Tobacco Road cronies, the first being Duke in Durham. Only three points were scored in the first half, that coming on a 31-yard Duke field goal. The Tigers lost three crucial fumbles, two in the opening half.

Fuller directed three scoring drives—two in the Tigers' first two possessions of the second half—and Clemson never trailed after going ahead on a two-yard Fuller scoring run with just over three minutes gone in the third quarter.

Plenty of fireworks were expected the next Saturday and over 50,000 fans showed up to watch.

N. C. State was leading the ACC in total offense with over 400 yards a game and a 24.4 points a game scoring average. Clemson was piling up 338 yards and nearly 22 points per game.

But instead of an offensive show, the fans were treated to one of the best defensive struggles of the season. When the first two quarters were complete, the 'Pack had 155 yards for their effort and the Tigers has just 95.

Jay Sherrill kicked a 39-yard field goal on State's first possession of the third period, and that would end the Wolfpacks' scoring for the day.

Willie Jordan took an N. C. State punt at the Clemson goal line and ran it back 75 yards to spark the Tigers in the fourth period. On third down, Fuller hit Butler on a 19-yard touchdown pass. Obed Ariri's PAT made it 7–3, and that would end the Tigers' scoring for the day.

Clemson took care of Wake Forest rather handily at home the next weekend, then went to Chapel Hill for a game against North Carolina that ended in a 13–13 tie.

Dan Devine brought his fifth-ranked

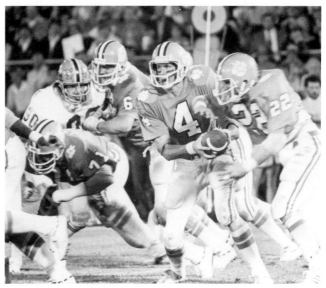

Tigers get scratched in the '77 Gator Bowl.

Notre Dame to Clemson the next Saturday, and representatives from eight bowls came to get a good look at the Irish and a peek at the Tigers. Late in the third quarter, the bowl reps were looking a lot more closely at Clemson. The Tigers held a 17–7 lead and were driving on the Irish once again.

Just when it appeared that the Tigers were ready to go in for another score, they fumbled, and the Irish took over at their 16-yard line.

Here, a guy named Joe Montana took over.

He took Notre Dame on a 15-play drive that had to overcome two 15-yard penalties. On the first play of the fourth quarter, Montana sneaked in from the two to cut Clemson's lead to three.

The Tigers lost another fumble at their 46 with 9:24 left in the game, and Montana took the Irish on the winning touchdown drive.

Montana went the final yard with 7:11 to play.

Clemson ended its season in Columbia against South Carolina, in what many say was the most exciting game ever between the two schools.

The Tigers led 24–0 midway through the third period, only to see the Gamecocks explode for 27 points to take a 27–24 lead with only 1:48 remaining.

Steve Fuller found a way to move the Tigers 67 yards in those last 108 seconds, with the winning touchdown coming on "The Catch"—Fuller to Butler.

Jim Ade, president of the Gator Bowl, was on hand to extend an invitation to the Tigers to play in Jacksonville against the defending national champion Panthers.

Invitation accepted.

Dwight Clark, future All-Pro, sidelined with injury in '77.

"The Catch" by Jerry Butler to beat the Gamecocks.

S. 16	58-3	W	H	*The Citadel
S. 23	0-12	L	A	Georgia
S. 30	31-0	W	H	Villanova
O. 7	38-7	W	H	Va. Tech
O. 14	30-14	W	A	Virginia
O. 21	28-8	W	H	Duke
O. 28	33-10	W	A	N.C. State
N. 4	51-6	W	A	Wake Forest
N. 11	13-9	W	H	N. Carolina
N. 18	28-24	W	A	Maryland
N. 25	41-23	W	H	S. Carolina
D. 30	17-15	W	N1	‡Ohio State

N1 at Gator Bowl at Jacksonville, FL
*Clemson's 100th win in Death Valley

1978: OF PELL.. AND THE PUNCH

The 1978 season had been grand. Clemson finished the regular season with a 10–1 record, including a win over South Carolina, and accepted a bid to play Ohio State in the Gator Bowl.

Charley Pell's two seasons had produced 18 wins, 4 losses and a tie, and now two straight bowl appearances.

This was fun.

But suddenly, the University of Florida became interested in Pell and BOOM, before you could say Death Valley, Pell was headed to Gainesville.

The whole deal took just a few hours — from the time he met with the Florida president at the Greenville-Spartanburg Airport until he informed Clemson president Robert C. Edwards that he was resigning as head coach.

This happened Monday, December 4th. Pell left immediately to fulfill a speaking engagement at the Jacksonville Beach Quarterback Club.

Pell remained in Florida the remainder of the week, returning to Clemson that Saturday.

The day after Pell's resignation the Student Affairs Committee of the university's Board of Trustees met to start the mechanics of naming a new head coach.

With a petition signed by nearly every football player, a group of players met with the committee asking for consideration of Danny Ford to be Pell's successor. Pell had hired Ford to be offensive line coach and assistant head coach. The two, both Alabama graduates, had served together as assistant coaches on the Virginia Tech staff.

The committee gave a unanimous recommendation to the full board that Ford be named Clemson's new head coach. The board approved, and a press conference was called to make the announcement.

The assumption was that Pell would come back from Florida long enough to prepare the Tigers for the Gator Bowl, and then take over at his new school after the bowl game.

However, after his return from Florida, another press conference was called for Sunday night. Pell announced that he was relinquishing all of his duties for the Gator Bowl game to Ford and his staff. Pell said he would be in Daytona Beach, Clemson's pre-game practice site, periodically "to help Danny at his request on some organization and probably some planning."

So Ford was tossed in the fire, to put it mildly. Clemson was ranked 7th, and the Buckeyes were 20th. But with his stripped staff (Pell had taken two of his assistant coaches with him to Florida), Ford had 19 days in which to prepare his team to meet one of the grizzled veterans of the trade — Woody Hayes.

Hayes had been coaching longer than Ford had been living. Ford, at age 30, became the youngest head coach in Division 1 with his appointment.

The pre-game buildup, aside from Clemson's coaching change, was the young Ford and his senior quarterback (Fuller) against the veteran Hayes and his freshman quarterback (Art Schlichter).

Clemson stopped two Ohio State drives on fourth downs in the first quarter before the Buckeyes went ahead 3–0 on a field goal.

Gaining possession at his 20, Fuller directed the Tigers to five consecutive first downs. He had one third-down and one fourth-down conversion during the drive. The Tigers were clicking in front of another 72,000-plus Gator Bowl crowd. In this drive, Fuller passed just twice, both times

Quarterback Fuller led the Tigers to a superlative 10–1 record in '78, including a 17–15 win over Ohio State in the Gator Bowl.

to Butler, once for six yards and another for 13. With a second and goal at the Buckeyes' four, Fuller circled left end for the score and Obed Ariri made it 7–3.

Schlichter brought the Buckeyes right back with a 78-yard touchdown drive. The quarterback scored on a 4-yard run, but the PAT was blocked, leaving Clemson down by two.

With time running out in the half, Fuller completed three passes in a drive that got to the Ohio State 37, where Ariri's field goal gave the Tigers a 10–7 halftime lead.

The second half was slow until Clemson began a 19-play, 84-yard drive that took seven minutes. There were five successful third-down conversions and, again, Fuller, Sims and Ratchford did most of the running. Two freshmen helped out—halfback Cliff Austin and wide receiver Perry Tuttle. On back-to-back plays Tuttle caught a 15-yard pass for a first down and Austin got nine yards rushing. Austin later went up the middle for a yard to score and Ariri tacked on the extra point.

Ohio State moved 87 yards on 12 plays early in the fourth quarter for a score, with Schlichter either running or passing on nine of the plays, including a 1-yard touchdown run that got the Buckeyes within two points.

Schlichter tried to circle left end for the two-point conversion, but Jim Stuckey stopped him short of the goal.

Ohio State recovered a bad pitch by Fuller after Clemson had moved to the Buckeye 36. The OSU drive started at the Tiger 44. On a third and five at the Clemson 24, Schlichter's pass was intercepted by Charlie Bauman and returned 12 yards.

As Bauman went out of bounds in front of the Ohio State bench he was punched by Woody Hayes. It would become one of the most talked about plays in the history of college football.

The Buckeyes were penalized 15 yards for unsportsmanlike conduct. There was 1:59 left in the game. Two first downs enabled Clemson to bring the clock to zero.

Because the game had not started until shortly after 9 p.m., Ford had already agreed to hold a post-game press conference at 10 a.m. Saturday, win, lose or draw.

Ford was looking forward to basking in the glory after winning his first game—a bowl game—as a head coach. But 30 minutes before Ford was to start his news conference, Ohio State officials announced that Hayes had been fired.

The game, and Ford's first victory, became yesterday's news.

At the coaches' luncheon the Thursday before the game, Ford had been given a gag gift of a king-sized jar of Rolaids because his team was such a big underdog. And because of Hayes' previous sideline outbursts toward chain crews, newspapermen, TV cameramen and others, Hayes' gag gift was a pair of orange boxing gloves.

Two games stand out in the 1978 regular season—playing Maryland for the ACC title, and the annual battle against South Carolina.

The Tigers and Terps entered the game 5–0 in the ACC. Clemson was ranked 12th nationally; Maryland was 11th. This turned out to be undoubtedly one of the most exciting games ever played in the then 25-year-old ACC.

There were 757 yards of total offense by both teams, three scoring plays were for 62 yards or better, and defensive plays were highlighted by a blocked punt by Maryland which was recovered for a touchdown with just 12 seconds left in the first half. That gave the Terps a 14–7 lead.

The excitement really started in the last half of the third quarter.

Clemson was at its own 2-yard line after

a downed punt. On the fifth play, Fuller saw Butler split three Terp backs and he threaded the needle on a reception that covered 87 yards and pulled the Tigers even again.

Maryland's Steve Atkins fielded the kickoff but fumbled out of bounds at the three. But he would soon make amends for his mistake.

It was in the Gator Bowl that Charlie Bauman was socked by Buckeye coach Woody Hayes.

After Atkins gained one, the Terps were penalized to the two for illegal procedure. Atkins was called on again, and although two Tigers put hands on him behind the line of scrimmage, he came out on the right sideline, cut across the field and went for the touchdown. That run of 98 yards is still a Maryland and ACC record. It is also

Obed Ariri kicks field goal to beat North Carolina.

the longest run ever (by 14 yards) against Clemson and is the second longest scoring play against the Tigers. Only a 100-yard touchdown run on a kickoff is longer.

Clemson started in the hole again, this time at the 11, and Fuller lost a yard on the first play. The Tigers made two first downs but faced a third and nine at the 38. This time Fuller found Dwight Clark, open over the middle, and similar to the Butler catch earlier, Clark went 62 yards for a touchdown. Ariri brought the Tigers even again, and this time it was Clemson scoring just before the end of a quarter. Fifty-five seconds were left in the third. Everything was all even going into the final period.

Gaining possession at his own 30 about four minutes into the quarter, Fuller began to move his team down the field. Between Fuller, Brown and Sims it took just a little more than three and a half minutes to go the distance. Sims carried just twice, but each time he had first-down runs. It was a pitch right to Brown that brought the six points from five yards out. Ariri was again true on the PAT. The Tigers had traveled 70 yards in 10 plays to take the lead.

Maryland kicked a field goal on its next drive, and couldn't get the ball back before time ran out.

Maryland coach Jerry Claiborne visited the jubilant Tiger dressing room following the game to offer his sincere congratulations.

John Lanaham, Gator Bowl selection committee chairman, extended a bid to Pell and his team members in the dressing room.

Pell said that "the story of this game is more than what happened in 60 minutes. We're talking about something that's been happening a long time — over a period of two years. We've tried to learn how to win and learn how to come from behind."

Although the Tigers still had South Carolina to face the following Saturday, the ACC championship was theirs to enjoy — and that they did.

A closed-circuit telecast of the game had been set up on a big screen in Littlejohn Coliseum, and several thousand fans who could not get to College Park were cheering the Tigers on just like they were sitting in Byrd Stadium. Seldom had the noise been any louder for basketball.

When the Clemson charter touched down at Greenville-Spartanburg Airport, a crowd estimated at 8,000 was on hand to greet the new champions, the school's sixth ACC title, including a co-championship. Cars were parked on both sides of the road leading to the airport all the way to I-85, a distance of over a mile.

The Greenville Airport Commission had never seen such a crush of people, and little could be done except let them worship their heroes for the few minutes as they walked from the plane to awaiting buses. The commission did make one request to Clemson next week — please do not announce on the radio network at what time to expect future charters to land. By the time South Carolina arrived in town, with George Rogers as its leading offensive threat, the Tigers had climbed to 10th in the nation.

Hardly before either coaching staff had time to adjust its head sets, Clemson was ahead 14–0, and the Gamecocks had not run an offensive play. Before the first quarter was over, Clemson had scored again.

South Carolina scored on a 41-yard pass play on the second play of the second quarter, then, after Clemson missed a field goal attempt, took the ball at its 20 and began to march again.

In 13 plays, the Gamecocks had seven more points on the board and the 21–0 lead had shrunk to 21–14.

Clemson started its next drive at its seven. Tracy Perry or Fuller had a hand in gaining every inch of a 93-yard drive for the score.

Perry rushed for 30 yards on six carries, his longest being the seven-yard TD run. Fuller had 45 yards rushing, one run for 21 yards and another for 15, and he used only one pass — a 14-yarder to Butler. The lead was back to 14, and it would stretch to 17 when Ariri kicked a 49-yard field goal just before the half.

The teams traded field goals in the third quarter and touchdowns in the fourth. The 41–23 victory was the Tigers' ninth straight of the year.

There were plenty of surprises left for this team in the days ahead.

The Tigers would change coaches, see a legendary coach self-destruct, and win the school's first bowl game in 19 years.

Six players on this Clemson team would be National Football League first-round draft picks.

The Buffalo Bills took Jerry Butler as the fifth player chosen and the Kansas City Chiefs grabbed Steve Fuller as the 23rd overall selection.

The next year the San Francisco 49ers picked Jim Stuckey as the 20th player chosen.

The Seattle Seahawks made Jeff Bryant the sixth player taken in 1982 and the Bills selected Perry Tuttle as the 19th player drawn.

Terry Kinard played early in '78 before being granted a medical hardship. He was the 10th man taken in 1983 by the New York Giants.

But maybe the one player who came out best was Dwight Clark.

When 49er coach Bill Walsh came to Clemson to test out Fuller's arm, he told the quarterback to bring someone to catch his passes. He brought his roommate, Clark, whom Walsh drafted in the 10th round.

Lester "Rubber Duck" Brown doing his end zone dance.

```
S.  8  21-0   W   H   Furman
S. 15   0-19  L   H   Maryland
S. 22  12-7   W   H*  Georgia
O.  6  17-7   W   H   Virginia
O. 13  21-0   W   A   Va. Tech
O. 20  28-10  W   A   Duke
O. 27  13-16  L   H   N.C. State
N.  3  31-0   W   H   Wake Forest
N. 10  19-10  W   A   N. Carolina
N. 17  16-10  W   A   Notre Dame
N. 24   9-13  L   A   S. Carolina
D. 31  18-24  L   N1  Baylor
N1 at Peach Bowl at Atlanta, GA
*Clemson's 400th victory
```

1979: EVERYTHING'S PEACHY FOR FORD

The 1979 season brought a new dawn for Danny Ford—his team . . . his coaches . . . his headaches . . . his joys.

Clemson's first four games were at home, and the Tigers opened against a 1-AA team. Not a bad way for a new coach to start.

Furman went down easily. Lester "Rubber Duck" Brown scored two touchdowns and ran for 101 yards on 12 carries in the first half. He was also running a fever, and team doctors recommended that he not play the second half.

Another 100-yard first-half performance came about the following week. But this time it was Maryland's Charlie Wysocki, who had 125 yards on 17 carries in the first 30 minutes. But unlike Brown, Wysocki felt fine in the second half and wound up with 178 yards, although he did not score.

The Tigers held the Terps to one touchdown, but Dale Castro booted field goals of 43, 18, 37 and 33 yards.

Ford returned to Virginia Tech for the fifth game of the season, making his first head coaching appearance there since leaving the Hokie staff to come to Clemson in 1977. He had arrived at Clemson 13 months after Charley Pell, who was also on the Virginia Tech staff of Jimmy Sharpe.

One of the classic newspaper typos appeared in the *Atlanta Journal-Constitution* after the '77 Tech-Clemson game, which the Tigers won, 31–13.

This is quoted from George Cunningham's story:

"Perhaps in recognition of the bitter feelings that exist between Pell and VPI coach Jimmy Sharpe, the Clemson team presented its head coach with the game ball. Pell and Sharpe were Alabama teammates, and the trouble started right here (Blacksburg) when Pell was Sharpe's assistant.

"Some say the situation was aggravated when Pell took highly retarded coach Danny Ford away from him."

Of course, that was supposed to read "highly regarded." Each Sunday night during the season, the staff wives would bring supper down to the Jervey Athletic Center, and the football coaches and their wives, along with the head trainer and sports information director and their wives, would stop to have supper together.

Just before the meal started after the Virginia Tech game in '77, the *Atlanta Journal-Constitution* story was read aloud to the group.

Ford's first question was, "Can I sue?"

Someone told him he would have to prove the paper was wrong.

Perry Tuttle catches TD pass against Georgia in '79.

In the sixth game of the '79 season, the Tigers went to Duke where freshman Chuck McSwain, playing for the injured Brown, ran for 120 yards and scored two touchdowns.

More than 61,000 were on hand for the N. C. State game. Clemson came in at 5–1 and the 'Pack at 5–2.

The Wolfpack, coached by Bo Rein, were pre-season favorites to win the conference title, but the 'Pack suffered a 35–21 setback to North Carolina the week before and were 3–1 in the ACC to Clemson's 2–1.

The Tigers trailed 13–3 at halftime, but Obed Ariri's 38-yard field goal and McSwain's 18-yard touchdown run brought Clemson back even at the end of three.

A 53-yard punt return by Woodrow Wilson set up the winning State field goal with 9 minutes left in the fourth quarter.

With just over three minutes left, Clemson drove to the N. C. State two. In fact, the Tigers had a first down at the four. Perry tried the line four consecutive times, but Bubba Green stopped the senior fullback on the last three attempts, and State took over on its own one.

Wake Forest, sporting one of its best teams in years, came to The Valley next with a 7–1 record and ranked 14th in the nation. Included in those victories were wins over Georgia, Virginia Tech, North Carolina, Maryland and Auburn.

But something happened after the flip of the coin, which Wake Forest won. Clemson's first drive resulted in a 47-yard Ariri field goal.

On the first play after the kickoff, Jay Venuto attempted a pass to James McDougald, but Bubba Brown deflected the throw and fellow linebacker Jeff Davis grabbed the ball and scored from 18 yards out. The Tigers had scored ten points in 16 seconds.

After a Wake Forest field-goal attempt failed, Clemson scored again, McSwain going the final 10 yards to score. In less than 12 minutes, Clemson was up 17–0.

Another Venuto interception, this time by Terry Kinard, and his return of 32 yards, put the Tigers in business at the Wake 13. Sims ran for three before Lott threw to Tuttle for 10 yards and the score.

This gave the Tigers a 24–0 halftime cushion.

McSwain scored with nine seconds left in the third period with the score again being set up on a Venuto interception. Eddie Geathers got this one, with a return of 43 yards to the Wake Forest one. It took the

Stuckey sticks it to the Gamecocks in 1979.

Tigers three plays to make the end zone.

Clemson bounced back into the national rankings (18th) after the Wake Forest win, but looming ahead for the Tigers were games at North Carolina, at Notre Dame and at South Carolina.

Obed Ariri's three field goals gave the Tigers a 9–3 lead over the Tar Heels in the first half, and he added another in the third quarter before Amos Lawrence scored on a 43-yard pass play from Matt Kupec to cut the Clemson lead to two.

Clemson got a final touchdown in the fourth quarter to put the game away. Lott scored on a quarterback sneak.

The game the Tigers had been waiting for—Notre Dame at South Bend—was next. All of the Clemson juniors and seniors remembered losing to the Irish two years earlier at home when Joe Montana scored two fourth-quarter touchdowns.

Notre Dame had a 10–0 lead at halftime, and this time it was Clemson that made the comeback.

Ariri kicked two field goals in the third quarter to cut the lead to 10–6, and Billy Lott ran 26 yards on an option play for the go-ahead score.

Clemson kept the ball for 7:32, including the last 1:02 of the third period, in driving for a fourth-period field goal, which Ariri kicked from 37 yards with 8:30 to play.

Would the Irish have another miracle finish? Nope. From the Clemson 25, Rusty Lisch's pass was deflected and intercepted by Terry Kinard.

On the next Irish possession, Kinard intercepted an end-around option pass from Pete Holohan and returned 40 yards to the Notre Dame 19. Lott's fumble was recovered by Notre Dame at the 16, but on the next play Steve Durham threw Lisch for a 14-yard loss, and on fourth and 11 from his own 15, Lisch had his pass broken up by Hall.

"We let Notre Dame take the momentum in the first half," Ford admitted after the game. "But then, we came out and played very well."

Ford announced on the plane coming back from South Bend that the Tigers had voted to accept an invitation to play in the Peach Bowl New Year's Eve against Baylor of the Southwest Conference. The bid was not contingent on the outcome of the South Carolina game.

The Gamecocks doused the Tigers, 13–9, with 15 of the 22 points coming on field goals. South Carolina took the lead for good with four seconds left in the first half when Ben Cornett caught a two-yard touchdown pass from Garry Harper.

The Tigers ended the regular season at 8–3, the same as the Gamecocks.

The weather in Atlanta for the Peach Bowl was not exactly what the Chamber of Commerce ordered. A cold, windy blustery day greeted something over 57,000 fans, not quite half of them in orange. The temperature was officially 43° but the chill factor was 20° below that.

Trailing 24–10 in the fourth quarter, Clemson drove to the Baylor 24 where an interception stopped a surge; and then to the 19 where Lott was thrown for an 11-yard loss.

But some excitement was ahead for Tiger fans, even if the game was all but lost.

Bandit end Andy Headen broke through and blocked a Baylor punt and James Robinson recovered for the Tigers at the one with 22 seconds showing. Chuck McSwain scored on the next play and Lott passed complete to Jeff McCall for a two-point conversion to bring the Tigers to within six.

Ariri's short kickoff was recovered by Headen at the Clemson 47. Lott passed complete to Tuttle for 30 yards to the Bear 23, but the Tigers got a delay penalty before the next play. Lott's next pass for Tuttle was intercepted.

This group of seniors ended with a 30–14–3 record and three consecutive postseason bowl appearances.

"We've had good senior leadership all year long," Ford said, recalling the season. "We weren't supposed to have that much. But when you get a bunch of people who believe in themselves, they'll surprise you sometimes. And that's exactly what this group and this team did this year."

Danny Ford staring down the Baylor Bear at the '79 Peach Bowl in Atlanta.

S. 5	45-10	W	H	Wofford
S. 12	13-5	W	A	‡Tulane
S. 19	13-3	W	H	Georgia
O. 3	21-3	W	A	Kentucky
O. 10	27-0	W	H	Virginia
O. 17	38-10	W	A	Duke
O. 24	17-7	W	H	N.C. State
O. 31	82-24	W	H	Wake Forest
N. 7	10-8	W	A	N. Carolina
N. 14	21-7	W	H	Maryland
N. 21	29-13	W	A	S. Carolina
J. 1	22-15	W	N1	‡Nebraska

N1 at Orange Bowl at Miami, FL

1981: NATIONAL CHAMPIONS

Danny Ford's second season, in 1980, ended with two straight losses and a 6–5 record.

There were published rumors that players were considering quitting, that the players did not like the coaches, that the coaches did not like the players.

"This summer (1981) brought some soul searching on the part of players and coaches alike," Ford said, "and when fall practice opened, the atmosphere was totally positive.

"I think I've learned a lot the last two seasons," Ford admitted. "I think I've got a lot more experience in handling a football team, in reacting to people and reacting to the press. I was extremely wrong in the way I handled those rumors a year ago. I started worrying more about them than I did coaching. They'll really get to you if you don't watch it. I've learned not to worry about that stuff anymore."

With that self-evaluation, Ford was within a couple of weeks of taking on an unlikely opponent—Wofford.

Wofford was one of three teams Clemson played in its first year of football competition in 1896, but had not played the Terriers since 1940. It was a fluke that the two teams were playing in 1981.

Clemson had Villanova scheduled for the third game but the Wildcats decided in April of 1981 that they would no longer field a football team. Clemson athletic director Bill McLellan attempted to replace Villanova with a team off the Wildcats' schedule but had no luck. Wofford was one game short of its schedule and agreed to play the Tigers.

Clemson would start the season unranked and unnoticed, and the 45–10 victory over Wofford did not stir many of the national pollsters.

No one paid much attention the following week, either, when the Tigers beat Tulane 13–5 in New Orleans.

The Georgia Bulldogs, the defending national champions, came into Death Valley the following Saturday—but the champs played like chumps.

The Bulldogs turned the ball over nine times, yes, nine times. Buck Belue threw five interceptions and the Tigers recovered four of five Georgia fumbles.

That's a Clemson record, but the 1981 team also holds the record for the most forced turnovers in a season (41) and the most per game (3.42). So Georgia wasn't the only one to feel the claws of Tigers that year.

Herschel Walker was the star for the

Dawgs that day, gaining 111 of his team's 122 yards rushing. But he was unable to score. He fumbled once at the Clemson 13 in the first quarter, and lost another fumble in the second quarter. Walker, like George Rogers of South Carolina—both Heisman Trophy winners—never scored against Clemson in their college careers.

Belue's second interception of the second quarter came deep in Georgia territory and led to a Clemson score. Belue passed from his 15 and Tim Childers intercepted and returned to the Georgia 18. Two runs by Kevin Mack and one by Homer Jordan got a first down at the eight. Jordan then passed to Perry Tuttle, who was veering out of the end zone. Tuttle's feet stayed in bounds, although most of his body was off the playing field.

William "The Refrigerator" Perry pounced on a Walker fumble at the Georgia 34 with only 29 seconds left in the half. Donald Igwebuike kicked a 39-yard field goal with 11 seconds showing and gave the Tigers a 10–0 halftime lead.

At the start of the second half, Belue moved his team on its best drive of the afternoon, going from his own 20 to the Clemson 16 before being dropped for an eight-yard loss. Kevin Butler came in and put Georgia on the board with a 40-yard field goal.

Late in the third quarter, Clemson gained possession following a punt at the Georgia 45 and Jordan passed to Tuttle twice for first downs before the drive bogged down at the Bulldog 12. The game was three plays into the fourth quarter when Igwebuike was successful on a 29-yard field goal to give the Tigers their final points.

Clemson moved into the national rankings, at No. 14, before going to Kentucky. Perry Tuttle called this "the hump game of the season. We weren't playing Clemson football (trailing 3–0) in the first half. We came out with fire and enthusiasm in the second half."

The Tigers made only four first downs in the first half against the Wildcats and had only 65 yards of total offense (on 27 plays).

As Tuttle said, the smoke started in the third quarter. On their first possession the Tigers went 83 yards in 13 plays. There were four consecutive first downs, and never a fourth down. Ford always said that the most crucial time in a football game is the first five minutes of the third quarter. The drive lasted six minutes.

Kevin Mack had the honor of putting the Tigers on top for good with a six-yard burst off left tackle.

The drive on the next possession was not as long because of Andy Headen's recovery of a fumble at the Wildcat 21. Six rushing plays is all it took before Jordan went around left end on a reverse from three yards out.

Other than one drive in the fourth quarter, when the Wildcats made five first downs as they moved from their own 14 to the Clemson 14, Kentucky didn't make even a threat.

So dominant were the Tigers in the second half that their total offense was 213 yards to 97 for the Wildcats.

"Their defense is equally as good as Alabama," said Kentucky coach Fran Curci. "Their front four is the best I've seen."

Ford told his players in the dressing room: "You and I both know how good you can be when you play with emotion. We've beaten everybody we were playing in the SEC. Now is the time to start thinking about getting your ACC championship rings."

Clemson moved up five notches in the national rankings to No. 9 after defeating Kentucky.

Virginia was next, and the Cavaliers fell for the 21st consecutive time to the Tigers. And because of action elsewhere in the

Homer Jordan, quarterback of the 1981 national champs, was said to be able to eat his weight in peanut butter and jelly sandwiches.

nation, Clemson was ready to take another big leap in the polls.

Two teams ahead of the Tigers lost that Saturday—No. 1 Southern Cal and BYU, while Alabama, also ahead of Clemson, was tied by Southern Miss.

Clemson moved up three spots to No. 6.

At Durham, Clemson lit into Duke for 24 first-half points, got 14 more in the third period and coasted to a 38–10 victory. Cliff Austin ran for 178 yards and scored twice.

Voters in the Associated Press poll moved the Tigers to No. 4 in the nation, the first time Clemson had ever been ranked that high by a wire service.

As always, N. C. State would prove to be a tough hombre for Clemson. Although having a 347 to 201 total yards advantage (including a 304 to 87 yard edge in rushing), the Tigers were their own worst enemy. The 'Pack picked off three Clemson passes and recovered two of three fumbles.

After State scored in the first quarter off a Clemson fumble, the Tigers got a 39-yard field goal from Igwebuike and a one-yard touchdown from Austin with 13 seconds left in the half.

It wasn't until midway through the fourth quarter that the Tigers got a bit of breathing room. Jeff McCall scored on a 15-yard run.

With their 7–0 record, the Tigers climbed to No. 3 in the country.

Appropriately, it would turn out, Wake Forest came to town on Halloween. It was a strange game, full of surprises, and there is no question the Demon Deacons left town a bit spooked.

It's true that the Deacons scored more points (24) on Clemson that afternoon than anyone else the entire season. But seldom has there ever been a game where more things went right for one team than it did for Clemson.

The Tigers scored 84 points—35 in the second quarter; 81 players saw action; there were 756 yards of total offense.

When all the archives had been checked, there were 10 school records set, three others were tied. There was one individual career mark reached. Four conference records were set and three new standards for Memorial Stadium were established.

The score at the end of the first quarter was 14–7, Clemson. The Tigers scored their third touchdown two seconds deep into the second period. It took 6:46 to score the next one, 2:05 for the next, 1:27 for another and 2:17 for the final score of the quarter.

"One of the last things I told one of our coaches coming into the game was I was concerned whether we would ever be able to stop them," said Wake coach Al Groh. "I guess I was correct in that prediction."

The record-breaking show against the Deacons moved Clemson into second place in the nation behind Pittsburgh in the AP poll and third behind Pitt and Southern Cal in the United Press International voting.

Two of the last three games (North Carolina and South Carolina) were on the road. Maryland was sandwiched in between, but anyone who has paid attention knows that Maryland is the only school of the original eight ACC teams that has a won/loss edge on the Tigers.

A crowd of 53,611 came out to see these the Tigers and the Tar Heels, a record for Kenan Stadium. There was only one loss between them—North Carolina had lost to Oklahoma the week before.

On the first play of the second quarter, North Carolina quarterback Rod Elkins connected with Larry Griffin on a 30-yard pass play. This would be the longest play from scrimmage against the Tigers during the season.

After a North Carolina field goal the Tigers put together a 14-play, 81-yard drive that ended with a 7-yard score by Jeff McCall.

Just before the half, the Tar Heels used their last time out (0:19) when Clemson set up to punt from its 19. When Dale Hatcher got a high pass from center, Danny Barlow rushed and blocked the punt out of the end zone, which meant a safety and a 7–5 score.

Both teams put together long drives that used up most of the third period. Each got a field goal for its work.

Probably the biggest defensive play of the day came when UNC quarterback Scott Stankavage passed incomplete to Alan Burrus. When there was no incomplete signal given by referee Robert Wood, Jeff Bryant fell on the ball for Clemson. The pass was ruled a lateral—a free ball—and Clemson took over on the North Carolina 35 with 57 seconds to play.

The Tigers ran out the clock and clinched at least a tie for the conference title.

This year, the Terps weren't so tough.

Clemson more than tripled the yardage on Maryland in the first half—308 to 101—and 214 of that came on a 15 for 18 passing performance by Jordan.

Jordan threw two touchdown passes to Tuttle in the first half and another to Jerry Gaillard. The final score came after a three-play, 55-yard drive that took just 46 sec-

onds. The three plays were passes by Tuttle, and the Tigers had a 21–0 lead.

Maryland's only score came in the early minutes of the fourth quarter when Jordan fumbled at the Clemson seven. Charlie Wysocki circled left end and scored.

And that was it . . . Clemson's eighth ACC football title.

South Carolina started out like "there'll be no perfect season in the foothills this year" as the Tigers were three downs and out and the Gamecocks drove 51 yards in slightly less than four minutes to score.

Next time, the Tigers were three downs and out, and South Carolina was the same. But on fourth down, Rod McSwain broke through and blocked the Carolina punt, and Johnny Rembert fell on the ball in the end zone for a Clemson touchdown.

Although Bob Paulling missed his first career extra point and the Tigers trailed by one, it was like a bolt of lightning had come through the team. Before the first quarter was over, Clemson was on its way to the go-ahead touchdown and would stay there the rest of the afternoon.

A Paulling field goal and Jordan's touchdown, with a missed two-point conversion try, gave Clemson a 15–7 halftime advantage.

South Carolina drove for a touchdown after the second-half kickoff, but also missed the two-point conversion for a tie. Clemson followed with a drive of its own on the ensuing kickoff, taking 20 plays and nearly six minutes to travel the 86 yards. Chuck McSwain carried the last yard. McSwain also scored Clemson's fourth-quarter touchdown giving the Tigers a 29–13 lead with nine and a half minutes to go.

The Gamecocks made only two first downs the rest of the game.

Steve Hudson, the Orange Bowl president, phoned the Clemson dressing room immediately after the game to invite the

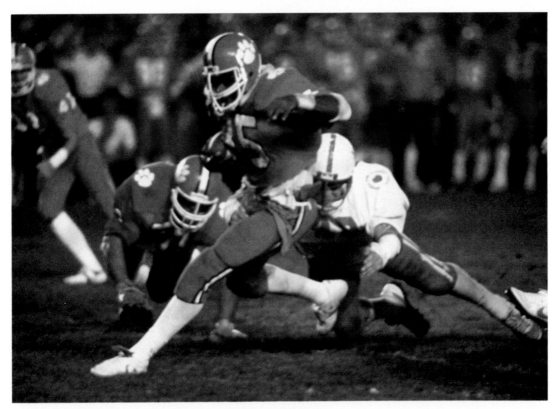

Fullback Chuck McSwain breaks for yardage in the 1982 Orange Bowl.

Donald Igwebuike kicked three field goals versus Nebraska in the Orange Bowl.

Tigers to Miami to play Big Eight champion Nebraska. Clemson President Bill Atchley accepted on behalf of the school.

The following Saturday, November 28, Penn State put a thumping on No. 1 Pittsburgh, and when the polls were announced the next Monday, Clemson, the only major undefeated team in the nation, was voted the top team in the nation in both polls. The honors came rolling in.

Ford was named coach of the year by several national groups.

A record 10 players were named to the All-ACC team.

Joe Bostic and Jerry Butler were first team All-Americans, and Fuller was a third teamer.

Altogether, seven groups and/or organizations gave Clemson their No. 1 ranking.

"We know we have one more thing to do," Ford said. "I'm just like everybody else—I want to see how good Clemson is. We've proved already that we're a great football team—the only thing that stands in our way now is Nebraska.

"Georgia can't do nothing. Alabama can't do nothing. And Penn State can't do nothing. That's the way it ought to be. This team has done its own business all year long. They just went ahead and did it all themselves. Now, they have a chance to do it again."

And they did.

As the headline read: "Pawsitively, The Best!"

Ford became the youngest coach ever to win the national championship, beating Bud Wilkinson of Oklahoma by some four months.

There was hardly a dry eye in the Clemson dressing room. They were stunned, they were jubilant.

There was one thing for certain: the scoreboard showed two things that would not change—time remaining 0:00 and final score Clemson 22, Nebraska 15.

Possibly William "The Refrigerator" Perry summed up the attitude of the entire team: "When Nebraska tried to come back, we had a little talk. We had come too far, worked too hard and had too many people cheering for us. When we went out there in the fourth quarter, we just took it to them. There was too much riding on this for us to blow it."

Homer Jordan was so dehydrated after the game that he was unable to meet the press. He might have had the biggest play of the night. Late in the game, facing a third and four at his own 37, Jordan weaved a masterpiece of a run—23 yards—to give the Tigers a first down at the Nebraska 40.

Nebraska was forced to take its final time out with 1:43 showing and didn't get the ball back until there were just six seconds left on the clock. There was time for one "Hail, Mary" pass, and that was knocked down at the 15 by Andy Headen.

So, yell it from the mountain top. The Tigers are No. 1.

Danny Ford aloft after clinching national title.

S. 14	20-17	W	A	Virginia Tech
S. 21	13-20	L	H	Georgia
S. 28	3-14	L	H	Georgia Tech
O. 5	7-26	L	A	‡Kentucky
O. 12	27-24	W	H	Virginia
O. 19	21-9	W	A	Duke
O. 26	39-10	W	H	N.C. State
N. 2	26-10	W	H	Wake Forest
N. 9	20-21	L	A	N. Carolina
N. 16	31-34	L	H	Maryland
N. 23	24-17	W	A	S. Carolina
D. 21	13-20	L	N1	‡Minnesota

N1 at Independence Bowl in Shreveport, LA

1985: BACK TO THE BOWLS

Clemson was placed on probation for two years by the National Collegiate Athletic Association beginning November 22, 1982, as a result of violations occurring in the conduct of the institution's intercollegiate football program. The penalty also prohibited Clemson's football team from participating in any post-season bowl games following the 1982 and 1983 seasons, or from appearing on any live football telecast during the 1983 and 1984 seasons.

The school was further penalized by the Atlantic Coast Conference for one more year from going to a bowl game or sharing in bowl receipts.

What this meant was that when the Tigers came off NCAA probation November 21, 1984, if the '84 team's record merited it (the record was 7–4), a bowl bid could not be accepted, and that should there be any other teams in the conference playing in bowls (and there would be two), Clemson could not share in any of the bowl receipts from these appearances.

Technically, Clemson came off conference probation January 2, 1985, which caused the Tigers to miss all the bowl action and to be cut out of any receipts from Maryland's appearance in the Sun Bowl and Virginia's going to the Peach Bowl.

Here's how the 1985 season started:

When the Clemson Athletic Department held its annual Fan Appreciation Day in Jervey Meadows, the official team photograph had to be moved inside because of a threat of rain.

The last time the Clemson team photo was taken indoors had been in 1981 — the national championship year.

A good omen? Well, things didn't work out quite that well. The Tigers would go 6–5 and accept an invitation to play in the Independence Bowl, where Minnesota beat the Tigers 23–13.

After the bowl game, Clemson offensive tackle John Watson had this to say:

"This game was typical of the whole season — start slow, get good and get to the point where you can play with anybody, just like we did at times during this season, and then fall short at the end."

And that's the way it was.

Danny Ford had good reason to be uncertain as the season began.

Clemson returned just 12 seniors, only five of whom had started in a collegiate game. The Tigers had lost their two best players due to graduation. William Perry was a first-round draft pick of the Chicago

David Treadwell kicked several game-winners during his illustrious career.

to Blacksburg, 24 were freshmen, the most first-year players Danny Ford had taken on a trip since 1981. The roster also included 13 sophomores and 28 juniors.

It took a field goal as time expired to win the game for the Tigers, and that came on a second chance.

The game-winning kick culminated a 17-point Tiger fourth quarter.

The Gobblers appeared to be in good shape with a 10–3 lead heading into the final period, but Clemson pulled even on a 45-yard drive capped by a two-yard sweep around left end by tailback Kenny Flowers. An improvised pass play between quarterback Randy Anderson and wide receiver Ray Williams resulted in a 46-yard score, which gave the Tigers a lead of 17–10 with 8:14 remaining.

Tech took advantage of a Clemson fumble and tied the score at 17 on a 21-yard pass play with 5:48 left. The Gobblers' chances to regain the lead with 2:39 to play failed as a 43-yard field goal attempt sailed wide.

David Treadwell, a walk-on placekicker from Jacksonville, Florida, was just another name in a questionable group of place-kickers—a group being counted on for little, except to avoid a kicking-game disaster.

Athletic departments of Division 1 schools spend thousands of dollars each year on brochures, posters and video tapes to sell the football or basketball teams to prospective student-athletes.

But Treadwell never saw a Clemson football recruiting film or brochure, or even a press guide.

"I came to Clemson for its engineering program," said Treadwell. "I did not play high school football, I played high school soccer. When I did not get a soccer scholarship offer at a major school, I opted for the school with the best engineering program, and that was Clemson."

Bears, and quarterback Mike Eppley was enrolled in graduate school.

As his team flew to its season opener, Ford read in the *Columbia Record* newspaper:

"Come Saturday, Clemson begins its 'After Probation' era by traveling to Blacksburg, Va., to square off against Virginia Tech.

"Although Ford will depend on two redshirt freshmen to carry the load at quarterback, the Tigers appear to have another deep and talented team. And without the psychological bonds of probation, Clemson should really be ready to return to the world of Top 10 rankings and bowl bids."

Ford could only shake his head.

Clemson's youth and inexperience were obvious as the players deplaned that afternoon. Of the 77 players who made the trip

Treadwell's only other football experience prior to the Virginia Tech game took place during Pee Wee football in Jacksonville.

"I will say I might not have gone with him if I had known that he had never played in high school," said Ford. "I did not know that until I read it in the paper on Sunday. He does not have the longest leg in the world, but he kicks it straight."

Treadwell made a 31-yarder in the first half for Clemson's first points of the 1985 season. He wasn't called on again until the closing seconds, with the score tied and the Tigers 41 yards away from the Virginia Tech goal.

His kick fell a few yards short, but defensive end Morgan Roane ran into Treadwell after the kick and the officials called a roughing penalty on the Hokies.

"I was jumping up and down going, 'He hit me, he hit me,'" said Treadwell. "I was going crazy, but then when I got up, I realized the flag was underneath the guy that hit me."

With no time on the clock, Treadwell tried again. His second kick was almost identical to his first. But the five-yard penalty made the difference, as the ball cleared the crossbar by what looked like inches to give the Tigers their 20–17 victory.

When Ford and his Tigers hopped back on the plane that evening for the trip home, they were a changed team. First of all, quite a few of the younger players had done well in their first opportunity to improve themselves. And, more importantly, the name Treadwell was no longer unknown among the Tiger faithful.

CBS Sports producer Ric LaCivita arrived in Clemson the following Tuesday to begin work for the first ever nationally televised football game from Death Valley. While the production people spent the week setting up cameras at various locations throughout the stadium, LaCivita spent the afternoons on the practice fields with Ford.

"Having CBS here for a game gives us a chance for us to show off Clemson University and we are glad to be part of it," said Ford. "I just wish we could show up and when Georgia comes into the stadium, we all just set down and have a big barbecue and not play football. There ain't too many people on God's green earth that think we can win the football game and they might be right."

From his observation tower high atop the Clemson practice fields, Ford familiarized LaCivita with a few of the Tigers' tendencies. As LaCivita took notes, he tried to convince Ford that he would make a great color commentator for college football. Ford replied, "Yeah, let's trade jobs this Saturday. You coach the team, and I'll produce the game for television. Now, wouldn't that be something to see."

Before the national television audience and the fourth largest crowd (80,473) ever at Clemson, the Tigers fell 20–13 to the Bulldogs. The win was Georgia's first in Death Valley since 1976.

The statistics left little doubt of Georgia's fourth-quarter superiority. Aided by two interceptions, the Bulldogs kept the ball away from Clemson for most of the final period. Georgia held the ball for more than 11 minutes and the Bulldogs offense did its part by converting six of seven third-down situations in the final 15 minutes.

Georgia's fourth-quarter surge created just the third time in Danny Ford's career that the Tigers had lost a game after leading at the end of three periods.

The following week—and for the third week in a row—Clemson's running game failed (101 yards) and the Tigers fumbled their way to a 14–3 setback against Georgia Tech. It was the first time ever the Tigers had lost to the Yellow Jackets outside of

Atlanta, and the 1–2 start for Clemson was the slowest one for the Tigers since 1975.

It was also the third consecutive defeat at home, counting the previous season's setback to South Carolina.

The Tigers' only score, a 25-yard field goal by David Treadwell with 2:14 left in the first half, marked the 69th consecutive game that Clemson had scored, but the three points were the fewest since Maryland blanked the Tigers 19–0 Sept. 15, 1979, in a game played at Clemson.

"I don't think we can even challenge this football team at this point," Ford said following the game. "I think that we have to go back and first learn to play football. I saw no improvement from the previous week and that is the one thing that we wanted to do as a football team. We jumped up a step last week, but we dropped back two today."

At Ford's weekly press conference the head coach commented, "It's not too late for us to be a good football team. We just don't have . . . ," Ford paused searching for the right word. "Chemistry—no, that's not it. I don't like that word. I'm not sure I know what it means."

"Cohesiveness," offered Jim Phillips, voice of the Tigers.

"No that's not it either. I can't even pronounce that," said Ford. "We're just not clicking—clickness is the word I'm looking for. Is that a word? Well, if it's not, it is now."

Clemson continued to have problems holding onto the ball the following week, and as a result the Tigers suffered a 26–7 defeat to the Kentucky Wildcats.

It was the first time in coach Ford's career that he had lost three straight games.

The Wildcats profited from seven Clemson turnovers, and the Sunday morning headline in the *Lexington Herald-Leader* played on the Tigers' punting troubles as they summed up the night's results: "Cats Kick Clumsy Clemson."

Up until that Saturday, Clemson's overall kicking game had been solid. But against Kentucky, the bottom fell out.

The Tigers roughed up a Kentucky punt returner who was calling for a fair catch; they fumbled punts twice when the punt returner was bumped by another Clemson player; and they allowed a Wildcat punt returner to score.

Brian Williams returned a punt 57 yards for a touchdown, which marked the first time that had been done against the Tigers since Scott Woerner of Georgia returned a punt 67 yards at Athens in 1980.

Following the seven turnovers at Kentucky, the Clemson Sports Information Office made a call to the NCAA to find out where the Tigers were ranked. In four games, Clemson had committed 18 turnovers to their opponents' seven. The call revealed that the Tigers were worst in the country.

If that wasn't bad enough, the *Washington Times* newspaper released a poll of the Bottom 10 football teams in the country, and the Tigers, with a 1–3 record, were ranked ninth.

So Danny Ford went looking for advice before the Virginia game.

From a high school coach in Georgia he was reminded of an important principle—don't throw away what's been good to you.

And from a legend—former Tiger coach Frank Howard, he and the team received a Thursday pep talk.

Ford took the first piece of advice and simplified Clemson's plan of attack, throwing away elements of the Tigers' early-season offensive scheme which had clicked only occasionally in the first four games.

"Coach Howard was Coach Howard," said Ford. "He loosened everybody up a little by joking around with us on Thursday.

We invited him to come talk to us—but then we have been inviting everybody, preachers, pro players, and anybody else we could find.

"I think Coach Howard was just what the doctor ordered."

The Tigers snapped a three-game losing streak and scored 27 points—more than in their three previous games combined—and defeated Virginia 27–24.

The most obvious difference in Clemson's offense was the way in which the Tigers held onto the football. The elimination of fumbles helped, of course, but just as impressive was the way the Tigers sustained their attack. After having the ball 16 minutes less than Kentucky the week before, the Tigers turned the stat around against the Cavs and for the first time all season, held the ball longer than did an opponent—32:52 to 27:08.

The next week, the Tigers punched the ball into the end zone three times in the first half to beat the Duke Blue Devils 21–9 for their third win in six games. Kenny Flowers scored on 46- and 50-yard runs, and Terrence Flagler had a 27-yard touchdown run to give the Tigers a 21–0 lead early in the second quarter.

After giving up 34 points in the fourth quarter in the first four games, Clemson had now allowed zero points to be scored in the final period over the last two games.

Then, playing near flawless ball on both offense and defense, the Tigers moved above the .500 mark to 4–3 overall, with a 39–10 whipping of N. C. State in the annual Textile Bowl at Memorial Stadium.

The Clemson defense manhandled State's backfield and recorded eight sacks on their quarterbacks, a total just two shy of the school record of ten established against Maryland in 1979. The defense also had four interceptions. Kenny Flowers scored three touchdowns and Stacey Driver sprint-

Rodney Williams sprints out, looks for receiver.

ed for a 29-yard score.

Former Tiger defensive standout William Perry was in the national spotlight the week following the N. C. State game. He was a smashing success as a "plowback" during the Chicago Bears' 23–7 Monday night victory over the Green Bay Packers. Perry cleared the way for two touchdowns by Walter Payton and scored once himself on a bellyflop to give the Bears a 21–7 halftime lead.

Perry's performance drew national attention for himself and for Clemson University when he was featured on many major news and sports telecasts.

Although the Tigers did not have the national media hounding them, the team quietly picked up its fourth consecutive win with a 26–10 victory over Wake Forest.

Defensive tackle Steve Berlin went down with a season-ending knee injury on the game's first play. At that time Berlin was the team's top down lineman. Berlin's injury came on the day when the Clemson Sports

Fleet running back Stacey Driver motors for yardage during '85 season.

Information Office launched a post-season honors campaign for the Bethel Park, Pennsylvania, native. A full-color poster featuring "Clemson's Berlin Wall" was distributed in the press box prior to the game, citing Berlin's career accomplishments.

Led by Kenny Flowers and Stacey Driver, the Tigers ground out 306 rushing yards against Wake Forest. It was the second time in the year two running backs had gained more than 100 yards rushing—Flowers had 141 and Driver had 114.

The victory set the stage for another important game in "Orange County" against ACC rival North Carolina.

After tailback Driver threw a 57-yard pass to receiver Terrance Roulhac to give Clemson a 17–7 lead over the Tar Heels early in the fourth quarter, the Tigers needed only to hang on to that lead in order to achieve what they'd been aiming for since August—an ACC title showdown with Maryland.

But the Tar Heels scored on an 80-yard drive, and the Tigers got a 30-yard field goal by Treadwell to take a 20–14 lead.

Clemson's four-game win streak ended with just ten seconds remaining in the game when tailback William Humes scored from the one and Lee Gliarmis kicked the extra point. It was the first UNC victory at Clemson since 1971.

So, how do you get the team up for the Maryland game?

The team assembled in the squad room in Jervey Athletic Center awaiting the scouting report on the Terrapins. The defensive assistant coaches gave their presentation, and then everyone looked around for the offensive coaches.

Suddenly the room was filled with the sounds of a funeral march, and the offensive coaches emerged from a door at the front of the room, wheeling in a "Tiger Paw" casket.

As Nelson Stokely, Lawson Holland, Larry Van Der Heyden and Steve Shaughnessey positioned the casket, tight end coach Woody McCorvey delivered the eulogy. "Friends of the Tiger Football family. We are gathered here today to pay our respects to the Clemson Tigers, who died on Saturday, November 9, 1985, in a careless, thoughtless accident in Chapel Hill.

"Let's now pay our respects as we say goodbye to the 1985 Clemson Tigers."

As McCorvey completed the eulogy, Chuck Reedy, running back coach, arose from the coffin in a football jersey and helmet and said, "Hey Maryland, we ain't dead yet!"

As the Clemson football team entered the locker room for the Maryland game, they were met by a surprise visitor—former teammate Carlon Box.

But the pre-game spirit wasn't enough to carry the Tigers. Box, confined to a wheelchair because of a severe car accident, watched his teammates from the sideline as they led the Terps 24–17 at the half. But for the second week in a row, Clemson lost in the final ten seconds as Maryland's Dan Plocki booted a 20-yard field goal with three seconds left to give the Terrapins a 34–31 win.

To much of the country, it was one of the most exciting and dramatic television shows of the season. To Maryland, it meant a third straight ACC championship. To Clemson, it was perhaps one of the most bitter and frustrating losses of the Danny Ford era.

It was a game that had everything: raging controversy, offensive explosions, point-producing defensive plays, conference titles, bowl bid drama, and poised, determined effort by both teams.

Clemson got off to a quick start when Donnell Woolford blocked Maryland punter Darryl Wright's kick and Terence Mack tipped the ball to Perry Williams, who ran 30 yards for the score.

Following a Treadwell field goal, the Terps came back with an 80-yard drive in just eight plays for a touchdown. Then Terrapin quarterback Stan Gelbaugh, who for the game was 23 of 35 for 361 yards and three touchdowns, fired a 50-yard strike to wide receiver Eric Holder with 12:27 left in the half to make it 14–10.

Clemson responded with another score as Kenny Flowers, who rushed for 120 yards on 22 carries, scooted in from five yards out to give Clemson a 17–14 advantage. Flowers became the only Clemson player to reach the 2,000-yard plateau as a junior with his performance in this game.

Clemson's next score was set up by another blocked punt. Gene Beasley got his hand on the ball.

Maryland pulled even at 24-all early in the fourth quarter on a 20-yard pass play

with 13:48 to play. The Tigers' final lead came with 5:33 remaining when fullback Tracy Johnson capped an 80-yard drive with a five-yard run.

Normally in a game involving so many big plays, lead changes and momentum shifts, it would be difficult to point to a single play as an undisputed turning point.

Not so with this game.

It boiled down to a third-down play from the Clemson two-yard line with 1:18 left on the clock. The Tigers led 31–24 and had twice stopped the Terps on plays from inside the three.

As Maryland lined up for its third-down play, the 25-second clock ticked down—inside five seconds as the Terps set their formation, and then to zero before quarterback Stan Gelbaugh took the snap from center.

With Danny Ford already screaming at the officials, Gelbaugh dropped back and floated a pass to tight end Ferrell Edmunds in the left-hand corner of the end zone. Edmunds had the ball momentarily and then dropped it.

The officials on the spot signaled a touchdown, and as Ford and the Tigers protested the Terps lined up for the game-tying PAT.

The CBS-TV replays left little doubt that Edmunds did not have proper possession of the pass.

Ford was enraged—primarily because of the officials' failure to penalize the Terps five yards for the 25-second violation. He stormed onto the field and made his case to at least three officials as well as a large regional television audience. But, as usual, nothing would come of it.

The Tigers tried a double-lateral on Maryland's final kickoff. Tracy Johnson fielded the low, bouncing kick and pitched to Rodney Quick, who then pitched the ball to Terrance Roulhac. Roulhac ran out of room

Keith Jennings hurtles would-be tackler.

on the sideline in front of the Clemson bench and was tackled by Maryland's Lewis Askew.

At that point trouble broke out.

According to the description in the *Greenville News and Piedmont:* "Tape replays show Askew being surrounded by at least five Tigers players. The replay showed Askew being struck by nine blows as he was pinned on the Clemson sidelines. Players and coaches from both teams swarmed the scene. Fans rushed onto the field, and the replay shows Clemson defensive tackle Raymond Chavous, outside linebacker Terence Mack and David Bennet, a Clemson graduate assistant, trying to protect Askew. The three of them and a uniformed security guard finally pulled Askew out and escorted him from the area.''

For their actions five Tiger players involved in the incident were suspended for Clemson's game against South Carolina and were placed on probation by the university.

Ford received an official reprimand by Clemson University for his behavior at the conclusion of the game. He was also placed on one-year probation by Clemson and he would not be allowed on the sidelines for the 1986 Clemson-Maryland game in College Park. His coaching activities would be limited to the press box.

After the Terps tied the game at 31–31 on the controversial touchdown which brought about Ford's reprimand, Clemson was forced to punt on its next possession. Andy Newell's 37-yard punt was fair-caught by Al Covington at the Maryland 25. There were 44 seconds left in the game. Gelbaugh then went to work.

He threw 12 yards complete to Eric Holder, threw incomplete to Azizuddin Abdur-Ra'oof, hit Alvin Blount with another 12-yarder coming out of the backfield, and then connected on a bomb of 44 yards to Ferrell Edmunds that carried to the Clemson seven-yard line. Blount ran the ball for four to the three and in line for Dan Plocki's 20-yard field goal attempt which was good and a 34-31 Maryland win.

The following Saturday, Clemson and South Carolina entered the game with 5–5 records. The matchup was billed "The Battle for Independence," as both teams sought a bid to the Independence Bowl. It was the 83rd meeting between the intrastate rivals, and the game was played before a Williams-Brice Stadium record crowd 75,026.

The Tigers rallied from a 14–3 deficit in the second quarter to capture their 49th win in the series.

Running back Kenny Flowers became only the fourth Clemson back to gain more than 1,000 yards in a season when he rushed for 136 yards against the Gamecocks, giving him 1,052 for the year.

The Tigers accepted a bid to the Independence Bowl, the 12th bowl invitation in Clemson history.

Clemson met a Big 10 school for only the second time when it faced Minnesota in the Independence Bowl. It was an interesting matchup of teams that enjoyed moving the ball on the ground.

Both teams gained more than 200 rushing yards, but the Golden Gophers got a few more as they churned out a 20–13 victory.

The first three times the Tigers had the ball they turned it over—two fumbles and an interception. The saving grace in the first quarter was that Minnesota converted three turnovers into just three points.

Clemson held a 13–10 lead going into the fourth quarter, but for the fifth time in the last 13 games, the Tigers could not hold the lead. Valdez Baylor scored on a one-yard run with 4:56 left to give Minnesota its final points.

Clemson mounted a final drive in the last few minutes and advanced to the Minnesota 31, but a fourth-down pass for Ray Williams was overthrown.

Kenny Flowers had another outstanding day for the Tigers with a career-high 148 yards. It was his seventh 100-yard day of the year.

And so, the season ended much like it started. As John Watson said, the Tigers had gotten to the point where they could play with anybody, but had fallen short in the end.

Kenny Flowers breaks away for a long gain.

1985: BACK TO THE BOWLS

S. 13	14-20	L	H	Virginia Tech
S. 20	31-28	W	A	Georgia
S. 27	27-3	W	A	Georgia Tech
O. 4	24-0	W	H	Citadel
O. 11	31-17	W	A	#Virginia
O. 18	35-3	W	H	Duke
O. 25	3-27	L	A	N.C. State
N. 1	28-20	W	A	Wake Forest
N. 8	38-10	W	H	North Carolina
N. 15	17-17	T	N1	Maryland
N. 22	21-21	T	H	S. Carolina
D. 27	27-21	W	N2	Stanford

N1 at Baltimore, MD
N2 at Gator Bowl in Jacksonville, FL

1986: WHAT A DIFFERENCE A YEAR MAKES

As the effects of probation faded, the Clemson football team was ready to begin again with a new purpose and enthusiasm.

Along with the new purpose, there were new faces, both on the coaching staff and in the cast of principal players. But prior to the season, Danny Ford viewed the 1986 Tigers as a question mark.

But behind the questions were some potentially pleasing answers. While nobody would be settled until the first snap, there had been some signs of progress, particularly on the defense, due to a major change. Not only had Ford brought in a new defensive coordinator in Bill Oliver, but Oliver brought with him an exciting brand of defense.

In terms of X's and O's, the most significant change was the use of three down linemen, with a pair of outside linebackers replacing the "bandit" and "rush" ends.

Former "bandit" Terence Mack—an outside linebacker under the new system— hinted about those changes in an interview with the *Greenville Piedmont* newspaper.

"If a team comes here expecting us to line up and play the same type of game, they're in for a big surprise," said Mack. "We'll run blitzes and stunts . . . and sometimes line up all 11 guys on the line of scrimmage, just to give an opponent a different look."

The Tigers also anticipated a different look in another aspect of the game. Heading into the pre-season, the Tigers did not have a punter, so Ford even went as far as to place an advertisement in the campus newspaper for the vacant spot on the Clemson football team.

"We are concerned about our punting situation," said Ford. "I think we need to put an ad in the school paper. If there is a student reading this who can punt, please call me. We aren't looking for any (Dale) Hatchers, just someone who can average about 40 yards with a four-second hang time."

Twenty-six students applied for the job.

"I don't know any of their names yet," coach Ford said. "One of them was wearing Jams out there and no shirt, but he kicked pretty good. . . . We'll just put them all in uniform and have 11 guys run at them and then see how they kick it. Then we will probably find a punter."

Ford picked Bill Spiers, the shortstop on the Clemson baseball team. He is currently the starting shortstop for the American League Milwaukee Brewers.

So Clemson fans were indeed witnessing

Bill Spiers, current Milwaukee shortstop, answered Coach Ford's want ad for a punter in the campus paper.

a new look for the football program, and the look wasn't very pleasing when the Tigers stumbled in the first game out.

The Virginia Tech Hokies ended Clemson's 32-year domination over teams from Virginia by spoiling the Tigers' season-opener with a 20–14 upset win at Tigertown.

While the Tigers' many breakdowns added up to defeat, Clemson's performance wasn't without bright spots. The young defensive unit generally stopped Virginia Tech's running game, limiting the Gobblers to 82 net yards rushing.

The final statistics reflected a relatively even game, with Clemson holding the edge in many categories. Clemson's greatest failures, however, came in efforts to put together a sustained offense and in not getting points from scoring opportunities.

Led by the passing of Erik Chapman, who riddled Clemson's defense for 242 yards on 13 of 23 pass completions, the Hokies snapped a nine-game losing streak to the Tigers in picking up their first win since 1954.

Virginia Tech opened the scoring when Victor Jones blocked a punt by Spiers ("Bill Shortstop" as Coach Ford called him) and Mitch Dove recovered in the end zone. It marked the first time since the opening game against Georgia in 1982 that Clemson had a punt blocked.

A rough beginning for the "new look."

Things looked better the following Saturday, when the Tigers ended an era of frustration by upsetting the No. 14 Georgia Bulldogs 31–28 on David Treadwell's second career game-winning field goal as time expired.

Never before had Georgia lost in a game in which it had scored 28 points or more.

Clemson's 18 seniors had never beaten Georgia, and only once in the last 17 tries had a Tiger team left Sanford Stadium victorious, that a 7–6 win by the 1977 Gator Bowl Clemson team.

Before a regional television audience on ABC, the Tigers had to rally three times for a 21–21 halftime tie. As it turned out, the game ended as the highest scoring in series history, breaking a 66-year-old record.

Kenny Flowers carried the ball six times for 72 yards, but an ankle sprain kept him out of the second half.

Flowers' departure marked the emergence of senior tailback Terrence Flagler. He began his All-America journey in this game by carrying 10 times for 90 yards. He was also Clemson's leading pass receiver, as he grabbed three for 58 yards. One went for a touchdown, while another—a diving, fingertip catch—rescued the Tigers from their own end zone in the final period and provided field position which eventually led to Treadwell's game-winner.

In short, Clemson's 31–28 victory, between the legendary hedges, couldn't have happened without him. For Flagler, Clemson's post-game celebration was a moment of personal satisfaction.

"I feel like I did my job," he said. "My

career has been frustrating at times, but I've had some good people around me, and when I've gotten down they've picked me up and told me to keep working—that someday it would pay off.

"Today, it paid off, and hopefully it is going to mean something big to the whole team."

Former *Columbia Record* sportswriter Doug Nye described the final seconds of the Clemson-Georgia battle this way:

"As the final seconds of the thriller between Clemson and Georgia were ticking away, many observers in the stands began to question aloud the wisdom of Ford's strategy. It was obvious the Tiger coach had instructed his team to work the ball into position for a field-goal attempt. With four seconds left and the ball on Georgia's 30-yard line, Clemson called timeout and Treadwell trotted onto the field with hopes of breaking the 28–28 tie. Considering that Treadwell had missed a 39-yard attempt a few minutes earlier, the chances of him making what was now a 40-yard effort seemed remote.

"Maybe Ford would have been wiser to have his team put the ball in the air a couple of times in an attempt to at least get the ball closer for Treadwell. After Georgia called timeout, hoping to shake up Treadwell, he calmly stepped up to the ball and sent it sailing through the uprights to give the Tigers a gasping 31–28 victory. Not surprisingly, that field goal set off a wild midfield celebration by the Tigers and their fans. Understandable. It was the biggest victory for Clemson since the Tigers defeated Nebraska in the Orange Bowl five years previously to win the national title.

"Thirty minutes later, Danny Ford, his orange shirt soaked with sweat from the heat of the day and the game, sat in a little room adjacent to the noisy Tiger locker room. Most of the newspaper writers and television reporters had gone, but Ford was still there, ready to talk to anyone about one of his sweetest wins ever.

"Told that his strategy had been questioned, Ford just smiled, 'Well, you fellows were wrong today and sometimes I'm wrong on other days. Really, I thought David had just had some tough luck on that first one he missed. I was just confident he could make it. Before the game he and Rusty (Seyle) were kicking 'em through from 50 yards out.'"

Following a week of celebration, the Clemson football team continued its winning ways as the Tiger caravan headed back into the state of Georgia, but this time to Atlanta. And just as they had done in Athens, Tiger fans had plenty to cheer about. Only this time, the Tiger victory was a little more convincing.

"We own Georgia! We own Georgia!" was the chant heard in the North Stands of Grant Field as the Tigers beat Georgia Tech 27–3. For only the third time in the 17 seasons in which Clemson had to play Georgia and Georgia Tech on the road, the Tigers swept the two clubs.

Before a sellout crowd of 46,062 and its third straight television audience, Clemson snapped a two-game losing streak to the Yellow Jackets.

Playing ball-control offense, the defense and special teams dominated Tech. Clemson had the ball 21:58 longer than the Yellow Jackets as Ford upped his "no letdown" record to 11–1 (games played the week after a Ford-coached squad has tied or defeated a top 20 team).

Terrance Roulhac took the opening kickoff four yards deep in the end zone and decided to run it out. He streaked down the right sideline and was finally knocked out of bounds at the Tech 19.

The Tigers had the kick start they were looking for. From that point on, the Clemson offense used five plays and 2:17 to score the first touchdown.

Whereas the tailbacks stole the show at Georgia, Clemson's fullback Chris Lancaster and Tracy Johnson combined for 118 yards and three scores at Tech. Johnson gave Clemson 14 points in the first half on a pair of one-yard scores, David Treadwell added field goals in the middle two quarters, and Lancaster got the final score in the fourth on a 10-yard run, his first career touchdown.

Walk-on punter Bill Spiers nailed a pair of coffin-corner punts and posted a 41-yard average.

The Citadel, next on Clemson's schedule, came into Death Valley to show off quarterback Kip Allen's arm. He threw 57 times, more than anyone had ever thrown against a Clemson team.

But the Tiger defense responded by helping Clemson to its first shutout victory in 25 games and the 20th in 34 meetings with The Citadel. The victory over the Bulldogs gave the Tigers a 3–1 record and they cracked the Associated Press Top 20 poll for the first time since November 12, 1984.

Next came Virginia, and the Cavalier student paper asked the question "Will the Clemson Jinx Ever End?"

The answer: Not This Year.

For the 26th time in 26 tries, the Tigers beat Virginia 31–17 at Scott Stadium before a Parents' Day crowd of more than 40,000. As a result of Clemson's four consecutive victories, the Tigers moved three notches to 17th in the AP's poll.

Not even an extraordinary performance by Cavalier backup quarterback Scott Secules, who completed a school record 30 passes for 298 yards, was enough to keep the Cavaliers in contention past the opening minutes of the third quarter. Once again, tailback Terrence Flagler stepped into the spotlight. He snapped his week-old personal best performance with 210 yards on 30 carries—the third largest one-game rushing total in Clemson history.

After four consecutive wins, many of the media covering Clemson thought a letdown would be in order when the Tigers played Duke. But this was not the case as Duke quarterback Steve Slayden confirmed after the game.

"They physically beat the hell out of the offensive line," said Slayden. And he should know. He spent most of the afternoon running from the Clemson blitz.

The Tigers spent most of the day stunting their linebackers and assorted linemen and playing man-to-man coverage in the secondary. It was a defensive game plan which Duke could not contend with.

For the third straight game Clemson's defense withstood a potent passing attack—allowing 26 completions on 47 attempts—but did not allow a passing or rushing touchdown. In fact, the Tiger defense had 14 tackles for losses, one off the school record and sacked Duke quarterbacks five times.

Kenny Flowers, who said he was almost back to 100 percent after the ankle injury suffered at Georgia, broke the Clemson career rushing record on a 12-yard gain midway through the third quarter. The gain pushed Flowers' career total to 2,577 yards, eclipsing the old mark of 2,571 set by Buddy Gore in 1966-68.

There was some confusion on the play because the Tigers were flagged for a 10-yard holding penalty. But after the ball was marked, Atlantic Coast Conference referee Dayle Phillips picked up the ball and took it to the Clemson huddle to present it to Flowers. Flowers did not accept the ball because he was not sure he had broken the record. The ball was then tossed to the Clemson sideline for safekeeping.

"It meant a lot to me when the official

handed me the ball, but I was not sure that I had made it," said Flowers. He had, though. The penalty had occurred far enough downfield for Flowers to get credit for the entire 12 yards.

With Flowers finally back to 100 percent and Flagler rushing toward an unexpected All-America season, the Tiger fans were excited about the challenge of going into Raleigh and attempting to beat up on the Wolfpack. But the letdown that Clemson hoped would never come came at Carter-Finley Stadium that rainy afternoon.

Playing before a television audience for the fourth time, the 16th ranked Tigers' five-game win streak was halted by 20th-ranked N. C. State 27–3. The loss dropped Clemson to 5–2 overall and 3–1 in the ACC.

A pre-game blueprint for the one-sided Wolfpack victory would have included most of the elements found in the post-game statistics. State wanted to establish its rushing game against a Clemson defense which was ranked fourth in the nation against the run. The Wolfpack did just that — rushing 57 times for 253 yards (more than half of what Clemson had given up on the ground in the previous six games).

Defensively, any effective plan to dim Clemson's chances of victory would center around stopping the Tiger rushing game. Again, the Wolfpack came up with exactly what it needed — snapping Clemson's string of 14 consecutive 200-yard rushing games.

After such a dismal performance, the following week's game against Wake Forest seemed even more important.

Terrence Flagler set a Clemson single-game, all-purpose rushing record with 274 yards, and the Tigers came back and raised their record to 6–2 overall and 4–1 in the ACC with a 28–20 victory over the Deacons.

Flagler became the first Clemson player since 1950 to score four times in a game. He scored all of the Tigers' points, ripping

Terrance Roulhac returns opening kickoff from the minus-four-yard line to the Georgia Tech 19.

off runs of 88 and 50 yards and catching two touchdown passes from quarterback Rodney Williams from 39 and 21 yards. For the day, Flagler ran for 209 yards in becoming the first player in school history to have two 200-yard rushing games in one season. Without Flagler, an otherwise poor production of a first half might have landed the Tigers in serious trouble. Instead, Clemson went to the dressing room at intermission with a one-point lead, while the Deacons shook their heads over many lost opportunities.

The all-purpose rushing record had been held by Cliff Austin, who had 260 yards. The amazing fact about Austin's day was that all the yardage was on the ground against Duke in 1982.

"If Kenny Flowers is a candidate for the Heisman Trophy," said Wake coach Al Groh, "then Flagler is a candidate for Mister Universe."

Ford said he still was not sure how to read his team from week to week.

"This football team is awfully hard to understand," the coach said. "We seem to have an A-team and a B-team. Sometimes we bring the A-team and sometimes we bring the B-team. Today, we brought both and we had them playing at different times."

With the victory over the Deacons, Clemson returned home the following week to host ACC rival North Carolina with an opportunity to move one step closer to capturing the ACC crown.

With the Tigers giving their finest all-around performance of the year, according to Ford, Clemson pounced on North Carolina 38–10, moving to 5–1 in the league and securing at least a share of the 1986 ACC title.

When Clemson entered its locker room to prepare for the game, the Tigers had a choice of pants to wear for the game. They chose orange.

"When you put on orange, there is only one thing that can happen—you're going to win," said Ray Williams. "We couldn't let ourselves lose in orange pants."

The game took place in front of 80,000 fans for Spirit Blitz 1986, a CBS regional television audience and numerous bowls' scouts at a muggy, cloudy, rain-soaked Death Valley. With Williams guiding the offense, Clemson rushed for 326 yards and compiled 434 yards in total offense, while Terrence Flagler led the Tiger ground attack with 114 yards and two touchdowns. Early in the second quarter, Flagler became the fifth Clemson back to rush for more than 1,000 yards in a single season and the first to reach that mark in his ninth game.

North Carolina head coach Dick Crum found it just as hard to get around in Death Valley as his offense did. Crum was forced to use a golf cart at the game due to a leg injury suffered in an earlier North Carolina game. The team could have used the cart against the hard hitting Clemson defense.

The week following the North Carolina

game, former Tiger coach Frank Howard joked with Danny Ford, after Ford asked Howard to be on the sidelines for the upcoming game against Maryland at Baltimore.

Howard said he'd fill in for Ford—who was banned from the sidelines as a disciplinary measure for the incident which took place at the end of last year's Tiger-Terp game—but only for adequate compensation.

"I've got to talk to my agent and see how much they pay before I can commit myself," Howard said. "You know I never got any of that big money when I was coaching. If Ford won't give me about a week's worth of his salary, I reckon he can coach himself."

Ford countered by saying that Howard is "a wonderful coach and a great man, but I can afford him (only) if he'll coach for what he first coached for. I believe we'll offer him the same contract he started with."

"I quit selling papers for about 25 cents a day, which is about what I got paid when I was coaching," Howard said. "I want that big money."

Howard said he's also interested in a few "perks."

"I want me some highway patrolmen for protection on the sidelines, like Bear Bryant used to have," Howard said. "I believe I'd like a limousine like Reagan has, too. If they can do all that, I'll consider it."

Maryland coach Bobby Ross joined Ford in the press box for the game as a penalty for his conduct following Maryland's 32–30 loss to North Carolina the previous week. Ross received an official reprimand from the school and the conference and was banned from the field for the Clemson game.

Without Ford or Howard or Ross on the sidelines, Clemson's late-game performer came through once more. With two seconds remaining on the scoreboard clock, David Treadwell kicked a 21-yard field goal to tie Maryland 17–17, giving the Tigers their first outright ACC Championship since 1982 and ninth overall.

Trailing 17–14 and starting from their own eight-yard line with 7:01 left to play, the Tigers marched to the Maryland two, but Rodney Williams' third-down pass with ten seconds left was too low for Terrance Roulhac to handle, so the Tigers went with Treadwell's leg.

"As I told the team, we don't play for ties, and I am not happy that we tied," said Ford after the game. "The only time we'd ever play for a tie is if it would help our football program—and I think we helped our football program today by winning the conference championship."

The following week, 82,500 people—the largest crowd ever to watch a sporting event in the state of South Carolina—filled the stands in Death Valley for a wild Tigers-Gamecocks game that ended . . . in another tie.

It marked the first time since 1919 that a Clemson team had ties in consecutive games, and the 21–21 game was just the fourth tie in the long series between the Tigers and the Gamecocks.

"I guess we feel like the people in the stands at this point," Ford explained. "It was a frozen stadium at the end of the football game. Everybody just sat there and looked at each other and did not know whether to jump up, holler or start crying. That's kind of the way it is like in our dressing room.

"It might have been a good day for a playoff," said Ford. "I think everybody would have liked an overtime today."

The other head coach agreed.

"It's been a funny football season all year long for us," said USC's Joe Morrison. "No one is happy with a tie."

While David Treadwell's field goal enabled Clemson to avoid a loss, South Carolina's Scott Hagler missed a 41-yard field goal with 25 seconds left that would have given Carolina the victory.

All but three of the game's 42 points were scored in the first half as both teams did what they did best, with the Gamecocks utilizing their passing game and the Tigers relying on the run.

Immediately following the game, the 7–2–2 Tigers accepted a bid to play Stanford in the Gator Bowl. After a brilliant first half display of offense and defense, Clemson managed to hold off a second-half Stanford rally and go on to defeat the 17th-ranked Cardinal, 27–21 before a crowd of 80,104. The Tigers scored 27 points in the first half and appeared to be on the way to a rout. But the second half was a different ball game as Stanford came out strong and put up 21 points of its own.

Gator Bowl MVP Rodney Williams completed eight of 11 passes in the first half for the Tigers. After punting on their first possession, the Tigers scored on their next five. But the Cardinal came back from the break a different team. Kodak All-America Brad Muster rushed for a touchdown and caught two scoring passes, while the Clemson offense came to a standstill. But the Clemson defense held in the end.

As the memories of the Gator Bowl victory started to slowly fade, the Tigers' coaching staff and fans began talking about the upcoming season. Clemson would return 50 lettermen from the 1986 squad, including 17 starters. Going into the 1987 season, Clemson would be especially deep and talented in the offensive and defensive lines.

Coach Ford would certainly start the 1987 season with fewer questions . . . maybe he could even get himself a scholarship punter.

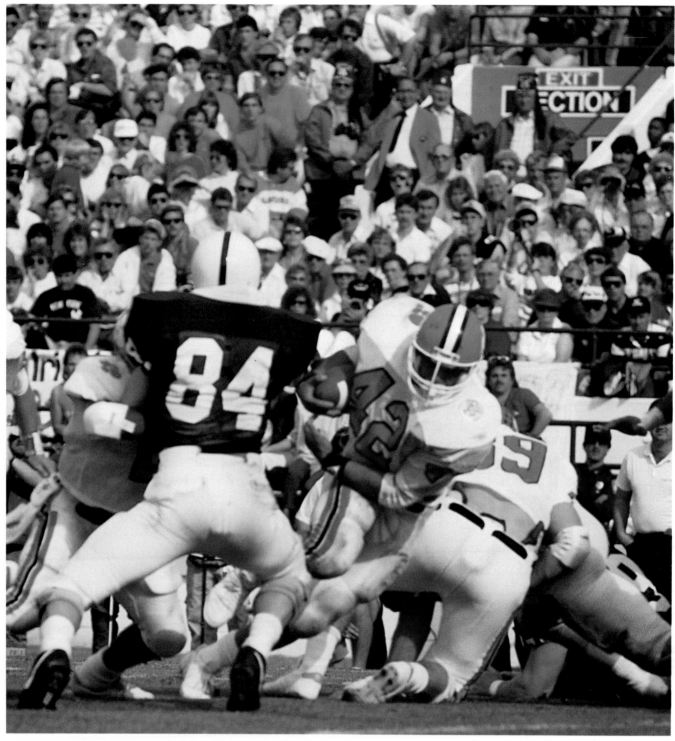

Tracy Johnson bursts through against Penn State in the '88 Citrus Bowl.

1987: RUN, RUN, RUN – TO THE CITRUS BOWL

Coming off an 8–2–2 season with an ACC championship and a Gator Bowl victory and 17 starters returning, two words kept popping up in newspaper articles, sports talk shows and IPTAY gatherings: national championship.

North Carolina State and South Carolina would end that talk later in the season, but along the way David Treadwell would continue his habit for winning football games in the last seconds, the Tigers would get their first kickoff return for a touchdown since 1962 and their first punt return for a score since 1970 — both in the same game — and Rodney Williams would be named MVP of a bowl game for the second straight year.

All in all, it was a fine year, especially if you were one of the lucky few to get tickets to the bowl game . . .

Tiger fans were licking their wounds after the loss to South Carolina in the final regular-season game.

Still they were more than ready to follow Clemson to Orlando for the Citrus Bowl game against Penn State, the defending national champions.

After two straight years of having a plentiful supply of bowl tickets, Clemson's athletic ticket office was not able to meet the demand for the Citrus Bowl. The Tigers were allotted 10,400 tickets, which was far less than anticipated requests.

As a result, athletic officials had to revert to the bowl ticket priority system established in the late '70s.

Although many fans could make the trip, everything went the Tigers' way in sunny Florida when Clemson soundly defeated Joe Paterno's team, 35–10.

Rodney Williams was selected as the Citrus Bowl's Most Valuable Player after leading the Tigers' brilliant passing attack that took the Nittany Lions by surprise.

In the month leading up to the bowl game, Danny Ford used his routine lines about establishing the run. But Rodney Williams was anything but routine as he connected on 15 of 24 passes for 214 yards.

Fullback Tracy Johnson rushed for 88 yards and three touchdowns and the Clemson defense made one key play in each half to stop the Lions.

"Clemson played a great football game and just kicked our rears," said Paterno. "There was not any key. I just think Clemson played extremely well in every area."

The win was Danny Ford's fourth bowl victory in nine seasons as Clemson's head coach. It also marked Rodney Williams' second bowl victory in his three-year playing career at Clemson and the second consecutive year that he was named the MVP.

The one constant with Clemson football in '87 was that Williams was the target of weekly criticism from the media and the fans. The most often heard line about Williams was that he couldn't throw and he couldn't run.

All he could do was win. Against Penn State, he proved that again.

"Our game plan coming into the game was to throw the ball on first down to keep Penn State off balance because they were so good against the run," said Williams. "We decided we were going to come in and throw the ball a lot more than we did in the regular season."

Clemson's final touchdown drive started with 5:26 to play and the offensive starters still in the game. With 3:21 remaining, Ford took out the offensive starters, including Williams, who exited to the joyful chant of "Rodney, Rodney" from the Clemson cheering section.

He had been booed in October and questioned all year. There were no boos in Orlando, and, if anyone had a question, Williams had all the answers.

The Tigers had started the season ranked No. 9 in the country, and on a dismal, rainy day pounded the Western Carolina Catamounts. It was the first shutout for Clemson since 1984, when they defeated the Virginia Cavaliers 55–0.

The Tigers were led by the rushing of three tailbacks who had never carried the ball in a college game before that day. Joe Henderson was the leading rusher with 80 yards and one touchdown. Terry Allen added 75 yards and two touchdowns, while Wesley McFadden ran for 63 yards and two touchdowns.

Although the opening-day victory brightened Clemson's hopes for a championship season, the rain continued to haunt the Tigers as they moved into the second game.

It was a rain bowl in Blacksburg, Virginia, as the Tigers sloshed their way to victory against the Virginia Tech Hokies 22–10. Heavy rain and bad field conditions did not stop the powerful Clemson offense that rushed for over 300 yards, or a defense that held Virginia Tech to only 60 yards in total offense.

The Tigers' only first-half scores came off of three David Treadwell field goals.

The second half became the Wesley McFadden highlight film as he ran for two touchdowns and brought his rushing total for the day to 226 yards, the third highest for an individual in a single game in Clemson history.

Michael Dean Perry had eight tackles for the day—four for losses—and three sacks.

"Our goal defensively was to dominate the game," said linebacker James Earle. "That's what we believe we're capable of, and that's what we go for every time we take the field. We take a lot of pride in this type of defense. Some things happened down home last year against them and we all remembered that. When we came down the hill in Death Valley, they were waving at us. Then after they beat us, they made some interesting comments.
"You remember things like that—especially when it happens on your field."

Remembering is something Georgia fans were to do a great deal of the following week as a very familiar name came back to beat them again: Treadwell.

For the second year in a row, a foot was the difference between victory and defeat for the Tigers against the Bulldogs; David Treadwell's foot that is. With only two seconds remaining in the game, Treadwell kicked a 21-yard field goal and gave the Tigers their first consecutive wins against Georgia since 1905-06.

Both teams kicked two field goals and scored a touchdown in the first half, tying the score at 13–13.

Midway through the third quarter, Ford watched his Tigers squander a touchdown opportunity with a motion penalty and take an unnecessary timeout. With the timeout wasted, Ford called Clemson's entire offensive unit over to the sidelines and went jaw-to-jaw with the group for several intense seconds.

"He pretty much let us have it," remembered offensive guard John Phillips. "It wasn't so much what he said, but the fact that he did it in front of 80,000 people and national TV."

"He wanted to know if we were putting it on the line and whether we were going to do everything possible to win the game," said fullback Tracy Johnson. "It was like a challenge."

But the Tigers could only manage a Treadwell chip shot.

With 8:59 remaining in the fourth period, Rodney Hampton scored a touchdown for the Bulldogs, putting them up 20–16. It was the first touchdown the Clemson defense had given up all year, but it was a costly one.

The Tigers got the football and managed two first downs before the Bulldog defense held. At that point, several Clemson players said they had doubts they'd be able to manage a touchdown and wipe out the Bulldogs' lead.

They got a boost from an unexpected source—the punting team.

On what Ford called the most important play of the game, punter Rusty Seyle's kick hit inside the 10 and bounced high, allowing the coverage team to run under it. Chinedu Ohan kept the ball in the field by tipping it as he ran into the end zone, and John Johnson caught the ball at the one-yard line.

Rodney Williams showing that he *can* throw.

James Lott and Gene Beasley tackled Georgia quarterback James Jackson in the end zone for a safety, and the Tigers took the ensuing free kick and moved the ball 53 yards to set up Treadwell's dramatic last-second field goal.

With fourth-and-two at the five, Treadwell came on to attempt the game-winner. But the situation was anything but routine.

Having used all three of their timeouts, the Tigers had no way to stop the clock. The time moved under 20 seconds as the Clemson kicking unit huddled on the left side, while Treadwell and holder Greg Bailey prepared for the kick.

With single digits showing on the scoreboard clock, the Tigers settled into position, and Treadwell punched home the winning kick with just two seconds to spare.

"I couldn't believe it when our guys went out and huddled up," said Ford. "I could just see us—in front of 80,000 people and TV—letting the clock run down and not get the kick off.

"We practice running on the field with-

Treadwell beats Georgia for the second year in a row.

out a huddle in those situations, but we must not have practiced it too well last week."

Treadwell took it all in stride.

"My grandmother gave me something to say this year that she wrote in a letter this summer before our first game," the kicker said. "The phrase was, 'If you throw your heart over the bar, the ball will follow.' I take a deep breath and say that every time before I kick. It helps me relax."

The Tigers unveiled new satin-like orange pants against the Bulldogs. Ford introduced the pants during a meeting with the Clemson seniors earlier in the week. He held up a pair of the Tigers' old orange pants and asked if the players wanted to wear them against Georgia.

After a unanimous "Yes," Ford discarded the pants and said, "We're not going to

wear them." Then Ford removed his own warm-up pants to reveal a pair of new shiny orange football pants.

"We're wearing these."

Georgia also got into the pants changing act, emerging from the locker room in red pants for just the second time since going to silver britches in 1980 when the Bulldogs won the national title.

The last time Georgia wore red pants was in 1985, when the Bulldogs beat the Tigers at Death Valley.

Just as last season, the Tigers would play Georgia Tech following the Georgia game, but this time the Jackets had to step into Death Valley.

Georgia Tech came to Clemson the following week and got a history lesson along with a 33–12 defeat.

The win marked the first time since 1902-03 that Clemson had defeated both Georgia and Georgia Tech in consecutive seasons.

It was also the first time since 1906-07 that Clemson had defeated Georgia Tech in consecutive seasons.

And for the first time in school history, the Tigers also returned both a kickoff and a punt for touchdowns in the same game.

Donnell Woolford's 78-yard punt return for a touchdown was the first for a Clemson player in 17 years, 185 games and 450 punts. Prior to Woolford's return, the last Clemson player to return a punt for a touchdown was Don Kelly, who went 85 yards against Maryland on October 31, 1970.

The Tigers' next shock hit Tech early in the fourth quarter after the Jackets had scored their first points. Joe Henderson came up to take the kickoff at the Clemson 5-yard line. But the ball bounced off his shoulder pads and rolled in front of him. With Tech's coverage bearing down, Henderson scrambled to pick up the ball, and he and Wesley McFadden bumped into each other.

It was ugly.

But Henderson avoided a tackle, sprinted behind a wall of orange blockers and headed down the left sideline. Around midfield, he got one final block when James Coley cut down a defender who was closing in on the wedge from behind. The rest of the way was smooth sailing and Clemson had broken another streak.

Henderson's kickoff return was the first for the Tigers since Hal Davis went 98 yards against Georgia on October 13, 1962 at Clemson.

But perhaps the most positive thing to come out of the Clemson win was the solidification of Rodney Williams as the Tigers' quarterback.

The week before the Tech game, it seemed almost everyone was questioning the effectiveness of Williams as Clemson's quarterback. He entered the game as the eighth-rated passer in the ACC and was in the midst of an early-season slump.

But against the Jackets Williams completed eight of 16 passes for 165 yards and one touchdown — a 52-yarder to Gary Cooper with 4:23 remaining in the third quarter.

The Tiger defense held the Yellow Jackets to only 73 yards as Michael Dean Perry once again led the way, moving into second place on the all-time ACC career sack list.

After four games, the Tigers had their strategy down for the season: run, run and run again.

Clemson stuck to that plan the following week when it ran over the Virginia Cavaliers with 403 yards rushing in a 38–21 Homecoming victory. Clemson, ranked seventh in the UPI poll and eighth in the AP, brought its season record to a perfect 5–0, and lengthened its streak of consecutive victories against Virginia to 27.

The Tiger tailbacks rushed for 331 yards against the Cavaliers, the second highest total from the position in school history. Terry Allen rushed for 183 yards, while teammate Wesley McFadden ran for 119 yards.

"Earlier in the year, we had been relying on our defense too much, and I think everybody on the offense knew that," Williams said. "Today the defense was a little flat and we realized that we were going to have to set the tempo. We saw from the start that we could move the ball against Virginia, and with the fine offense that Virginia has, we knew we had to score more points.

"We had put the defense into some bad situations in the first four games, and they've given us the ball in great field position time and time again. Today it was our turn. We were able to help our defense by keeping UVA's offense off the field."

Donnell Woolford's punt return for a TD versus Georgia Tech.

Duke was next on Clemson's '87 schedule and the Blue Devils gave the Tigers a scare as Anthony Dilweg put on an air show, passing for over 300 yards to keep the game tied until the fourth quarter.

But in the final period it was Clemson's ground attack, led by fullback Tracy Johnson, that put the Tigers up to stay and helped them hang on to their No. 7 spot in the AP rankings.

After Duke tied the score in the third period, Johnson got the call and ran for 60 yards on the Tigers' 90-yard drive, scoring a touchdown to put the Tigers up to stay, 17–10. Johnson's total yardage of 93 was a career high for the fullback at the time.

"Hopefully, we learned a lesson," said Ford. "We just were not very intelligent in knowing what we had at stake today. We went out there like it was a Saturday-morning scrimmage, where it doesn't count, and it counted, a whole lot.

"I wish we were a little more mature as coaches and players, and not think we're just going to show up and play good and that other people are going to roll over and play dead."

But following Clemson's poor showing against Duke, the Tigers had to face nemesis N. C. State. And if the Tigers had hopes of beating N. C. State, some changes had to be made. But the changes did not come in time as Clemson's unbeaten streak ended at 11 and the Wolfpack upset the seventh-ranked Tigers 30–28. The Tigers' last loss had been to the Wolfpack in 1986.

It was a weird day in Death Valley.

The most brilliant performance of Clemson's season thus far was dimmed by defeat as N. C. State withstood an impressive Tiger rally and escaped Memorial Stadium with a victory.

Led by a career-high 271-yard passing performance by Rodney Williams — the third highest total in Clemson history — the

Tigers rallied with three fourth-quarter touchdowns and then got the ball back for a final, unbelievable chance at victory.

But when Williams and fullback Tracy Johnson failed to connect on a pair of identical pass patterns, hopes for a miracle and the dream of a national championship passed them by.

The Wolfpack did all of its scoring in the first half with 252 yards in total offense. The Tigers had only one first down in the entire half, this coming late in the second quarter. The 30–0 half-time score was the largest deficit a Danny Ford Clemson team had ever faced.

The Tigers rallied in the second half behind Williams, who set an NCAA record for most passes attempted in a half with 46. Williams' total of 52 attempts was a new record for the most attempts in a game at Clemson. His 21 completions were also a personal best for the quarterback and third highest in Clemson history.

Keith Jennings was Williams' prime target with six receptions for 84 yards, while Terry Allen was the Tigers' top rusher with only 68 yards.

To try and shake his team from the October blahs, coach Ford used two of his time-honored techniques — butting heads and the orange pants.

Clad in all orange, the Tigers rekindled their ACC Championship hopes the following week against conference rival Wake Forest. The Tigers overcame a half-time deficit and went on to soundly defeat the Demon Deacons 31–17.

Rodney Williams did not start the game, due to a knee problem suffered in practice. Chris Morocco ran the Clemson offense in the first half, and Williams took over in the second.

Joe Henderson, who had a career high 131 yards rushing and two touchdowns, was the leading runner for the Tigers.

"I beat them down all I could, and they responded very well," Ford said about the week of preparation for Wake. "We had some heavy contact this week that helped us."

Clemson also broke the school's all-time mark for total attendance in a season against Wake Forest. A total of 536,042 fans had witnessed the Tigers play over the first seven home games. The previous high was 521,898 over seven games in 1983.

North Carolina got into the changing-uniform routine the following week in Chapel Hill when the Tar Heels warmed up in white pants and left the field early to change to their light blue pants.

As the Heels came running out to the field through a tunnel of balloons, the team breezed by its bench area and went to the student section for a brief pep rally. "Blue Heaven" erupted in a show of enthusiasm.

This excitement was fueled by the fact that Kenan Stadium was anything but blue a few days prior to the game. Someone—presumably Clemson supporters—scaled the stadium's fence the Thursday night before the game and administered a coat of orange paint to everything in site . . . the field, the scoreboard, the press box and even the Tar Heel victory bell. But by game time on Saturday all the evidence had been washed away and "Blue Heaven" was back to normal.

The incident was the talk of the town—a Durham newspaper printed a story covered by orange Tiger tracks across the top of its page, UNC officials called the act "immature" and students urged the team to take revenge by "going out there and kicking Clemson's butt."

The Tar Heels played with enthusiasm and passion, but the balloons burst with 32 seconds left in the game, when David Treadwell broke a 10–10 tie with a 30-yard field goal.

Clemson drove 67 yards in 18 plays for 7:13 to the winning field goal, as fullback Tracy Johnson had 37 yards on the drive.

The Tigers clinched no worse than a tie for the league championship with their victory over the Tar Heels, giving the team an opportunity to wrap up its second consecutive ACC title with a home victory over Maryland.

As the seniors played in front of the packed Death Valley crowd for their final time, the Tigers won their 11th ACC title (including one tie) by defeating the Terrapins 45–16 in Danny Ford's 75th career victory. It was the first time Clemson had beaten Maryland since 1983. Clemson, 9–1 overall and 6–1 in the ACC, put on its best performance of the season in front of a Spirit Blitz crowd of 78,000.

The ninth-ranked Tigers used a combination of option pitches, timely long passes and strong defense to crush the Terps and earn the bid to the Florida Citrus Bowl.

Terry Allen led the way for the Tigers with 103 yards rushing and two touchdowns. Wesley McFadden followed with 101 yards rushing and one touchdown. Gary Cooper also had two touchdowns, both on passes from Rodney Williams.

"We just got our butts whipped," said Maryland coach Joe Krivak. "It was a good, old-fashioned knock-down, drag-out whipping. They were by far the best team on the field today, and they just whipped us."

Although the Tiger faithful were excited about spending New Year's in sunny Florida, they were eagerly anticipating the game against South Carolina.

As Saturday approached, "The Game" gained intensity. For only the second time in series history, Clemson and South Carolina were both ranked in the top 20 in the AP poll. But even though the Tigers went into the game with the higher ranking and the better record, the South Carolina Gamecocks won the in-state rivalry and the year's bragging rights by a score of 20–7.

Before a record crowd of 75,043 in Columbia's Williams-Brice Stadium and a national television audience (ESPN), South Carolina's nationally ranked "Fire Ant" defense held the Tigers to only 166 total net yards.

One bright spot for the Tigers was that defensive lineman Michael Dean Perry broke the all-time ACC record for career tackles for losses. Michael's brother William ("The Refrigerator") Perry had held the record with 60 tackles.

The Citrus Bowl victory over Penn State was the final appearance for 13 Clemson seniors. That group had four straight winning seasons, three bowl appearances and two ACC championships.

S. 3	40-7	W	H	Virginia Tech
S. 10	23-3	W	H	Furman
S. 17	21-24	L	H	Florida State
S. 24	30-13	W	A	Georgia Tech
O. 8	10-7	W	A	Virginia
O. 15	49-17	W	H	Duke
O. 22	3-10	L	A	N.C. State
O. 29	38-21	W	A	Wake Forest
N. 5	37-14	W	H	N. Carolina
N. 12	49-25	W	A	Maryland
N. 19	29-10	W	H	S. Carolina
J. 2	13-6	W	N1	Oklahoma

N1 at Florida Citrus Bowl in Orlando, FL

1988: FOILED BY THE "PUNTROOSKI"

Optimistic? You bet.

Clemson returned 18 starters, evenly divided on offense and defense, from the 10–2 season of '87.

The Associated Press thought enough of the Tigers to give them a No. 4 ranking in the pre-season voting.

"People are excited about Clemson football," Ford said. "It is nice to be considered among the elite of college football. But last year we were rated too high before the season started and our team and fans got a false idea of how good we were.

"We lost three first team All-Americans from last year (John Phillips, Michael Dean Perry and David Treadwell)," Ford said, "and the schedule is very challenging because we have to play five conference games on the road. Plus our non-conference games include Florida State, Georgia and South Carolina."

Clemson lost one of its leaders in Chris Lancaster before the season opened. The senior had a neck injury, with a possibility of some spinal damage. He sat out the entire year and served as a student assistant coach.

"I don't know of anyone on this team who loves the game more than Chris Lancaster," said Ford. "This is as big an injury loss as I've had at Clemson. He is a team leader who has done more for Clemson than he has received in return. He is one of the hardest workers I've ever coached and one of the most respected."

Lancaster's injury brought Henry Carter out of retirement. Carter, who had not played fullback since 1984, was a fifth-year senior who did not figure to play much in '88 and had dropped off the team but remained in school working on his degree. Without hesitating an iota, Carter came back and checked out his uniform again.

The Tigers would play their first three games at home.

They overwhelmed Virginia Tech in the opener. Then Furman, destined to be the Division 1-AA national champions, was back on the Clemson schedule for the first time since 1979.

Had it not been for a deflected pitchout which the Tigers recovered inside the Paladin five and converted into a touchdown, things might have been a little tighter for Clemson. The Tigers held just a 13-3 halftime lead but ended up winning 23-3.

Game No. 3 received one of the biggest buildups in Clemson history ... Florida State ... pre-season No. 1 ... not a ticket available for months ... everybody was

Clemson quarterbacks Rodney Williams and Chris Morocco.

"We have a chance to prove ourselves at Clemson," Ferguson continued. "They are a very good team, and with our loss to Miami we have to show the country we belong among the best teams."

It was quite evident that the Miami game was still very much on the minds of Seminole players. "We have to erase the shame of the Miami game," said starting defensive back Leroy Butler. "We erased 60 percent of it in the Southern Miss game (a 49–13 FSU win seven days earlier) and now we must get the other 40 percent with a win at Clemson."

This would be a game for the ages.

One of Florida State's touchdowns came on a 76-yard punt return by Deion Sanders, which tied the score at 14. It would turn out to be the only punt return for a score against kicker Chris Gardocki in his three years at Clemson.

A 19-yard dash by Clemson's Tracy Johnson tied the game again at 21 with just 2:32 to go.

The Clemson defense took the field, and the largest crowd in Death Valley history (84,576) was in a frenzy. A quick stop and the Tigers could have a chance at a game-winning field goal.

On third down Vince Taylor just missed an interception at the FSU 20. The ball trickled through his hands, which brought up fourth down . . . and a punt.

Or so everyone thought . . .

With a fourth and four at his own 21, Bowden made what turned out to be one of the gutsiest calls of his gutsy career. The decision by Bowden will go down in history as "the puntrooski."

All week Clemson coaches had told the team about Florida State's abilities to fake off a punt formation. However, who would figure (except Bowden) that the Seminoles would go for it in a tie game from their own 21?

heading for Tigertown to make it the state's second largest city that day.

This was supposed to be a game between two of the nation's top four teams. With a 2–0 record Clemson had jumped to No. 3, but the Seminoles, because of a 31–0 loss at Miami had skidded to No. 10.

With CBS in town and many national print media present, the Florida State loss to the Hurricanes did not diminish the impact of this game.

"This is really a big game for me and my team," said Chip Ferguson, the Florida State quarterback, who lives in Spartanburg, some 60 miles from the Clemson campus. "I was recruited by both schools, and two years ago I thought about transferring to Clemson when things were not going very well at Florida State.

The Seminoles aligned in a normal punt formation, with three blocking backs. Two players, Alphonso Williams and LeRoy Butler, flanked the center. Dayne Williams was two steps behind Butler. Tim Corlew was the punter and was in his normal position.

The snap came directly to Dayne Williams. He moved a couple of steps forward and tucked the ball between Butler's legs. Butler remained in a crouched position.

Meanwhile, Corlew leaped as if the ball had been snapped over his head, turned and began chasing the imaginary football to the right side. Both Dayne Williams and Alphonso Williams raced to the right as if to block for Corlew, as did the rest of the Seminole blocking flow.

That left Butler all by himself on the left side.

Gary Cooper and Chip Davis celebrate a TD early in the '88 season.

Asked later if he had butterflies in his stomach as the play developed, Butler said, "No, they were more like pterodactyls. I was supposed to count to four before I could begin running to the left, but I took off after two."

Butler was 20 yards down field before anyone, including the CBS cameramen, knew he had the ball. Donnell Woolford was deep in punt formation on the play and he came all the way across the field and tackled Butler at the one-yard line.

The 78-yard run by Butler made him the leading rusher in the game, and the leading rusher for the first three games of the season for FSU.

"We knew Florida State had fakes off punting situations and we knew something would be up when Butler was in the game," said Woolford afterward. "It was just a great call, but we should have been more alert."

"You can't fault our people," Ford pleaded after the game. "I wish now I could go back and call timeout and alert our people for the fake. We knew they had a fake and we had talked about it. We wanted to save our timeouts for our drive for a winning field goal."

When Ford said the Tigers were aware of the fake punt, he was not kidding. A former Ford player who lives in Florida had learned of the exact play the week of the game and had diagramed the formation for Ford.

The dead giveaway was Butler taking the up-back position.

Clemson even practiced its defense for the play. But Butler ran onto the field late, and those who saw him could not communicate to the Clemson players.

Dayne Williams scored from a yard out, but the touchdown was disallowed. With no timeouts remaining, Bowden did not want to take a chance with another running play, and Richie Andrews kicked the winning field goal with 32 seconds left.

"If that play didn't work, Clemson was going to kick a field goal and beat us," Bowden said in his post-game press conference. "I just wanted someone to win the game. A tie was unacceptable in our minds because we already have a loss and we would be out of the national championship picture.

"I saw Jerry Claiborne run that play a couple of times in the 1960s," the Florida State coach continued, "but we got the specifics from Arkansas State. We have a graduate assistant who was there in 1987, and he made a copy of the tape for us.

"In the second half our coaches decided to use it at some point. This was the perfect situation."

The Seminoles did not win the national title that season, but finished with an 11–1 record and third in the polls behind Notre Dame and Miami.

Clemson sophomore John Johnson about summed up the feeling of the team at the time. "I saw the play develop from the sideline and watched Butler run down the field carrying all of our season's goals with him."

But there was still much to play for.

One might have thought it would be impossible to come back from such a shocking loss, especially having to go on the road to Georgia Tech, where the Tigers had only won four times in 43 years.

But the prime goal of Week Four was a win over the Yellow Jackets as a start to a third straight conference championship.

Clemson got out of Atlanta with a 30–13 win. Linebacker Doug Brewster turned the game in Clemson's favor with a 68-yard interception return for a score. James Lott batted away a pass intended for Jerry Mays and the ball popped into Brewster's hands. It was his first and only touchdown as a Tiger.

This was one case where it paid off to be a swift skinny inside linebacker.

The Tigers next headed for Virginia to face the improved Cavaliers. A big, strong quarterback named Shawn Moore was a Virginia sophomore with outstanding abilities. Clemson would rest its hopes on senior Rodney Williams.

Both teams' defenses dominated the first half and it ended in a scoreless tie, the first scoreless first half in a Clemson game in nine years. Chris Gardocki kicked a field goal late in the third period, but Virginia came back with a 14-yard scoring pass from Shawn Moore to Herman Moore.

Clemson was down 7–3 with five minutes left against a school that, in 27 games, had never beaten the Tigers.

The Wahoo fans were in hysterics. They were actually loosening their blue ties from their starched white collars, and some were even shedding their blue blazers.

In 1965, when the Tigers went to Charlottesville and came out onto Scott Field to work out Friday afternoon, one of those old, staid FFV's (and Frank Howard said that didn't stand for First Families of Virginia) was up in the stands with his wool cap and scarf and crooked-stemmed pipe and he yelled down at Howard: "Frank, we're going to get you tomorrow."

Howard looked up at the old-timer and said: "Yeah, that's what your grandaddy said, too."

But even Howard would admit that this October Saturday in Charlottesville was no laughing matter.

But Rodney Williams had been in this situation before. Fourth-quarter comebacks were his specialty. Ten times in his Clemson career he brought Clemson back from a fourth-quarter deficit to win or tie a game.

Down by four and needing a touchdown, Clemson faced a third and two at the Cavalier 14. Now third and two means the option play at Clemson. If you can't bowl over your opponent on third and two you don't deserve to win. At least, that was always Ford's attitude.

As Clemson lined up for the play, Chip Davis was flanked to the left, and as Williams approached the line of scrimmage he noticed that no Virginia defensive back came up to defend against Davis.

Williams nearly bobbled the snap, then calmly tossed the ball to Davis, who went untouched into the end zone for a 10–7 Tiger lead.

The play was a complete surprise to Danny Ford, who said he was watching the Virginia defensive alignment on the right side of the formation and never noticed Davis alone.

"I was looking for the fake to the right and watching Virginia's end to see what he would do," Ford said. "At first I thought Rodney had fumbled the ball and was going to throw it away. I didn't know what the heck was happening."

Williams, Clemson's career leader in passing yardage, said: "This is actually the second time that has happened. I figured it was a once-in-a-lifetime situation when it came at North Carolina last year. But here it was again. Ironically, it happened with the same formation and exactly the same play called."

The play the year before enabled Clemson to beat the Tar Heels 10–7 late in the game.

Clemson returned to the friendly confines of Death Valley for Homecoming against Duke and quarterback Anthony Dilweg. He was the nation's leading passer and ranked high in total offense. But Dilweg, who would go on to play for the Green Bay Packers, had not faced a secondary with Clemson's level of proficiency.

Heading into the season Clemson's secondary was cited by John Hadley in *The Sporting News* as the best in the nation.

Dilweg soon found out that this was a

talented, veteran group. He completed 22 of 51 passes and was intercepted four times.

The secondary featured Donnell Woolford, who was named a finalist for the Thorpe Award (nation's best defensive back), was named All-American and was a first-round draft pick of the Chicago Bears.

James Lott would be drafted by the Bears a year later.

Jerome Henderson, a second-round pick of the 1991 NFL draft, was a backup cornerback.

Gene Beasley was a three-year starter

Eager fan wants a piece of Gary Cooper.

and Richard Smith had been the free safety for two years.

But the Duke game was a coming out party for a true freshman. Dexter Davis made his first college start and broke up four passes. He actually broke up six passes, which would have set an all-time Clemson record for a single game, but two of the plays were nullified by penalties.

Clemson went on to a 49–7 victory over Duke and a nationwide ESPN audience.

The Tigers climbed back into the Top 10 (No. 9) in the next poll, and would ride into Raleigh to face old nemesis N. C. State.

The Wolfpack turned a high snap over the punter's head into a touchdown and went on to defeat Clemson 10–3. This was the third consecutive season N. C. State had beaten the Tigers.

The conference loss rekindled Clemson's desire to win its third consecutive ACC title. The offense got its act together and over the last four weeks of the regular season averaged 38.3 points and 469 yards of total offense per game.

Williams always seemed to come on strong the last few weeks of the season and he did so this time. Over the last four games he connected on 35 of 65 passes for 520 yards and two scores with just one interception.

He scored twice himself the week after the loss to N. C. State as the Tigers beat Wake Forest by 17 points.

The spread against North Carolina the next Saturday at home was even more — 37–14.

So once again the ACC title would be decided by the Clemson-Maryland game and the winner would get a spot in Orlando's Florida Citrus Bowl.

The Tigers would win their third straight title with a victory over the Terps. A win would bring Clemson's conference record to 6–1 while all of the other teams would have

at least two losses.

A Maryland win could create as much as a four-team tie.

The Tigers grabbed the championship with a fourth-quarter blitz. Leading by four points after three periods, Clemson scored four more touchdowns to win 49–25.

Levon Kirkland went on to a celebrated career at Clemson, but he had his first great game at College Park in 1988.

The Lamar, S. C., native had 13 tackles, one sack, three tackles for losses and an interception. For his efforts, he was named ACC Player-of-the-Week.

"I guess I'm as proud of this football team as any we've ever had," said Ford, who tied Frank Howard's record for out-right ACC championships with five. "It's been a tough year. We were picked to be a very fine team, but we got beat twice early and had to fight and scratch for everything all season.

"I honestly didn't know if we would respond in the second half (against Maryland) or not, but our seniors showed great leadership. I can't tell you how proud I am of this group of seniors. To win three straight ACC titles is something no group of seniors has done before."

The victory sent Clemson to the Citrus Bowl because of the tie-in with the ACC and the bowl. Ford had been critical at first of the ACC's bowl contract because he thought it might prohibit Clemson from playing for the national championship again.

He was quoted as saying, "Why should you buy a Buick when you have a chance to get a Cadillac?"

But the final contract contained escape clauses for teams in contention for the national title.

"It's a Cadillac of a bowl" Ford said with a grin after accepting the bid.

The largest crowd in Memorial Stadium

history, 84,687, showed up for the regular-season finale against the Gamecocks. This was 291 more people than saw the Florida State game earlier in the season.

The South Carolina game turned out to be a showcase for the seniors, in particular Rodney Williams.

Williams connected on 13 of 26 passes for 192 yards and picked up another 38 on the ground for a season best of 230 yards in total offense.

What a difference a year and a location can make. In 1987 South Carolina fans in Columbia had chanted "R-o-o-o-d ney ... R-o-o-o-d ney," throughout the game, mocking the Clemson quarterback. But in 1988 the Clemson fans retaliated with a different emphasis ... "ROD-ney, ROD-ney."

"That chant felt a lot better this year," said Williams, who directed Clemson to 32 victories in his career. "Our fans were great today and I think that was the biggest difference in the game."

Another senior, Jesse Hatcher, had a major impact on the game. Hatcher caused a fumble on each of South Carolina's first two possessions. On the Gamecocks' second possession Hatcher drilled quarterback Todd Ellis, causing a fumble. It was the hit of the year for Clemson.

"The hit felt great," Hatcher said. "That's the kind of hit I had been dreaming of all week. I didn't know he (Ellis) had fumbled. I felt so good about the hit, I just stayed there for awhile to enjoy it."

All that remained of the '88 season was the Citrus Bowl and a date with Barry Switzer and the University of Oklahoma. "We are excited about playing Oklahoma," Ford said as he prepared his team to meet the Sooners. "We think we have made significant strides in recent years with our program. This game will be a test. Can we play with the teams that have been among

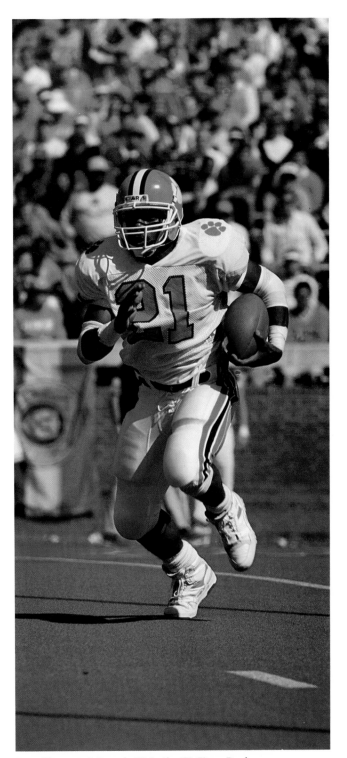

Terry Allen scored the only TD in the '89 Citrus Bowl.

the elite year after year? Are our boys as big and strong, as fast? You can look at film, but you just never know until you go up against a team like Oklahoma."

This was a matchup of two of the winningest active coaches in the nation. Switzer ranked first in the nation and Ford was fifth. Switzer's mark was 157–28–4 and Ford's was 85–27–4.

Once the two teams got to Orlando, the Sooners got all headlines, most of them negative.

There were reports the NCAA was investigating Switzer and his program. (Within the next five months, Oklahoma would be on NCAA probation. There also would be a rape in the athletic dorm, a shooting of one player by a teammate and the drug-related arrest of Charles Thompson. Additionally, former Sooner All-American Brian Bosworth would publish a book that was extremely critical of the Oklahoma program.)

There were other reports that Oklahoma players trashed an entire floor at their hotel and that some assistant coaches did some damage at a local country club.

The game itself was a thriller, in doubt until the final play.

Two field goals by Chris Gardocki staked Clemson to a 6–3 halftime lead. But a Tiger fumble late in the third quarter led to a Sooners' field goal that tied the score.

Clemson took the kickoff and drove 80 yards in 15 plays. The drive took nearly seven minutes before Terry Allen took the pitch from Rodney Williams and went the last four yards for the game's only touchdown, and a 13–6 Tiger lead.

But there were still better than ten minutes left in the game.

Clemson had two more possessions before the game ended, got nowhere either time. After the last Gardocki punt, quarterback Jamelle Holieway started to move the Sooners.

The play that put some steam into the drive came on a fourth and 10 from the Oklahoma 20, when Holieway kept for a gain of 11 and a first down. That was the last rushing attempt in the drive. Holieway completed seven passes, and in 40 seconds had moved to the Tiger 14. His last three passes were all incomplete.

On the last play of the game Holieway was rushed by Jesse Hatcher, but got the ball away just before he hit the ground. As the ball floated into the end zone toward receiver Carl Cabbiness, Dexter Davis leaped to knock the ball to the ground.

Clemson had its 10th victory of the season and its third bowl triumph in a row.

Switzer found it difficult to compliment Clemson after the Tiger victory, the first loss by Oklahoma to an ACC team after 16 straight wins. "Clemson would have to win 71 consecutive games and lose one to tie what we have accomplished the last 16 years," said Switzer in his post-game interview.

Oklahoma linebacker Kurt Kaspar told *USA Today* that he "wasn't impressed with Clemson at all. Clemson had some players who were supposed to be All-Americans, but we treated them like rag dolls."

Sooner tight end Adrian Cooper said, "Clemson knows they can't compete with us . . . I don't think they have anybody we would recruit."

The Tigers saw things a bit differently, of course.

"I think the program is definitely on the way," said Rodney Williams. "We won the national championship in 1981, but a lot of people think that was a fluke. The last three years we have proved ourselves by beating some very good football teams.

"Clemson is gaining respect and what happened today will help," Williams continued. "People will take notice, not just because we beat Oklahoma, but because we beat them without doing anything fancy. We beat them doing what we always do . . . running the ball."

S. 2	30-0	W	H	Furman
S. 9	34-23	W	A	#Florida St.
S. 16	27-7	W	A	#Virginia Tech
S. 23	31-7	W	H	Maryland
S. 30	17-21	L	A	Duke
O. 7	34-20	W	H	Virginia
O. 14	14-30	L	H	Georgia Tech
O. 21	30-10	W	H	N.C. State
O. 28	44-10	W	H	W. Forest
N. 4	35-3	W	A	N. Carolina
N. 18	45-0	W	A	#S. Carolina
D. 30	27-7	W	N1	#W. Virginia

N1 at Gator Bowl in Jacksonville, FL

1989: ROCKY ROAD TO THE GATOR BOWL

Many of Clemson's faithful figured the Tigers would be high in the national rankings in 1989, especially with back-to-back 10–2 seasons and consecutive bowl victories over two of the nation's best known football powers, Penn State and Oklahoma.

The big question in coach Danny Ford's mind was who would replace Rodney Williams at quarterback.

Williams' replacement took up much of the spring and summer discussions among the media, as well as the fans on the IPTAY circuit. Would it be Chris Morocco, who had been in on just 199 career plays heading into 1989; or would it be DeChane Cameron, a freshman who had shown talent in limited playing time?

The people's choice was a redshirt freshman from Amite, La. Michael Carr had been a *Parade* All-American, who reportedly could run a 4.4 in the 40-yard dash and could throw the football through a tire from 40 yards.

While Carr did not make many headlines during the pre-season because of his playing abilities, he still got more attention than the rest of the team.

The *Atlanta Constitution* broke a story August 16, 1989, that Clemson was about to receive a preliminary letter of inquiry from the NCAA. The headlines said Clemson could get the "death penalty" if put on probation, because it had been on probation between 1982 and 1984.

Clemson eventually did not receive any penalties from the NCAA, but going through the investigation was not easy.

Michael Carr was at the center of the storm. There were reports that Carr had received his Toyota Supra illegally. Carr compounded the problem when he decided to quit the team after a poor showing in a scrimmage. Feeling he was destined to be a third-team quarterback, he caught a 5:30 a.m train from Clemson the morning the story of the preliminary letter of inquiry appeared.

It seemed he had departed because he was the central figure in the NCAA investigation. Carr simply left because of his poor play on the field. The car he was driving was owned by his brother, who was just loaning the car to Michael in between trips home.

The following May (1990) when the NCAA rendered its final decision and announced its minimal violations, there was no mention of any problem with any automobile for any player. Carr's only involvement was a minor violation. His

Chris Morocco led Tigers to a third straight 10–2 record in '89.

host, a member of the Clemson team, had bought him a Clemson cap when Carr was on campus for his official visit. That is illegal under NCAA rules.

The entire scenario did not do much for Michael Carr's football career. In fact, he later transferred to the University of Texas-El Paso (UTEP) in the spring of 1990. Morocco and Cameron continued their competition for the first-string quarterback job. The Tuesday before the opening game with Furman, Ford said he would name his starting quarterback when Clemson had its first possession.

When the time came, he called on Chris Morocco.

Ford said later that he picked Morocco because "he was the first one I saw after we ran down the hill." It might have been the truth. Ford was known to make decisions by hunches on occasion.

Both the defense and offense had a good day against Furman, shutting down the Paladins 30–0. The defending NCAA Division 1-AA champions gained just 58 yards of total offense, the low for the entire nation over the first six weeks of the '89 season. This marked the first time Furman had been shut out in 76 games.

Although no Clemson coach or player would say so, the Florida State game was a revenge game for everyone associated with the 1988 Tiger-Seminole contest in Death Valley.

FSU coach Bobby Bowden had beaten the Tigers in the fourth quarter with his famous "puntrooski" play.

The Seminole fans certainly hadn't forgotten about the play. When the Tiger baseball team played in Tallahassee eight months after the football game, FSU students were still having fun about it.

When there was a change of Clemson pitchers, a group of students on the first-base side stood up and yelled: "Hey, Clem-son, did you ever find the football?"

The Tigers did not let the 1989 game come down to a fourth-quarter punt. They scored three quick touchdowns—one on a 73-yard interception return by precocious freshman linebacker Wayne Simmons.

After the Seminoles scored to close the gap to 21–7, Terry Allen, who had two of the earlier touchdowns, was at it again, this time with a 73-yard run with just 1:16 to go in the half.

Clemson's 28 points at the half were the most yielded by Florida State in a half since 1965.

Although Florida State made a slight comeback in the second half, Clemson was never in serious danger. The Seminoles scored with just five seconds left in the game to get within 11 at the end.

Morocco was masterful, hitting eight of nine passes for 134 yards. Rodney Fletcher, who had not caught a pass the entire season a year ago, snagged four for 92 yards.

Stacy Long became an All-American that night, or at least took a giant step in that direction. He was named ACC Player-of-the-Week as he had ten knockdown blocks against Odell Haggins, a player who went on to be a first-round NFL draft pick the next April.

The victory gave Danny Ford a 6–0 record in the State of Florida and it broke a 10-game home winning streak for Florida State. This was just the 10th home loss in 10 seasons.

"I wasn't surprised that we played that well," Ford said, "but I am surprised that it came as early as it did in the season against that kind of football team. We beat a quality team at their place. This is a great win for our team, it should give us plenty of confidence the rest of the season. I just hope we don't get overconfident."

Ford would prove to be a prophet.

One of Clemson's touchdowns the next

week in a 27–7 victory over Virginia Tech was a 47-yard interception return by Levon Kirkland. This marked the third interception return for a touchdown by a Tiger linebacker in the last 12 games.

Heading into the 1990 season *The Sporting News* rated Clemson's corps of linebackers as the best in the nation. The first few games of the 1989 season led to that ranking because Kirkland, John Johnson, Wayne Simmons, Vince Taylor and Doug Brewster had been truly dominant.

Only FSU had been able to score a touchdown against Clemson's defense, and the Seminoles ended the season ranked third in the nation.

All these players had unique personalities that Clemson coaches were able to blend together into a cohesive unit. With the exception of Taylor, they played together for the 1989 and 1990 seasons, years in which Clemson ranked in the top five in the nation in total defense.

Brewster and Johnson were roommates for three years, then separated in 1990 when Brewster got married. They were both highly recruited players from Georgia, and were significant parts of Clemson's defensive machine since their freshman seasons.

Johnson was a team leader and prankster who kept everyone loose at the right time. At one practice the bald Johnson wore a 1960-style Afro wig. On a hot day when Clemson was not working in pads, he took off his jersey and taped his number 12 to his chest and back.

Brewster, at 205 pounds, was the lightest inside linebacker at Clemson in over a decade, while outside backer Johnson, at 225 sopping wet, was the lightest player at that position in seven years.

They tried to gain weight. In the summer before the 1989 season, they used to set their alarms for 3 a.m. They would then raid the fridge and devour peanut butter and jelly sandwiches.

Kirkland and Simmons also have outgoing personalities, and they both showed relentless pressure on quarterbacks, combining for 11 sacks and over 30 quarterback pressures for the season.

The summer prior to the 1989 season they worked at the local Piggly Wiggly grocery store as ... you guessed it ... "sackers."

Taylor was the only senior of the group in '89. At 5–11 and 235, the native of Clearwater, Florida, had the most impressive biceps on the team. And he had the highest bench press on the team at 465 pounds. Vince was a free spirit and his favorite summer pasttime when he was home was surfing ... in tropical storms. "I just love those challenging waves," he said.

There were over 4,000 no shows at the Maryland game at Clemson on a sunny Saturday afternoon, but those who weren't there had good reason. In fact, there was talk of possible postponement of the game.

Hurricane Hugo had devastated the coast of South Carolina, as well as many miles inland, forcing inhabitants to evacuate.

The disaster hit close to home for some of the Tigers. Wayne Simmons, for instance, did not hear from his mom for 48 hours while she was stranded at her home near Hilton Head Island. Clemson fans on hand for the game raised over $50,000 in contributions at the stadium during the game.

Clemson defeated the Terps 31–7, and two of the scores came from Wesley McFadden. Both ended in "McFadden's Touchdown Corner." Every time McFadden, the all-time leading rusher in South Carolina high school history, scored a touchdown in Death Valley he ran to the hill on the Clemson sideline where he exchanged high fives

Wesley McFadden exchanging high-fives with fans in his "touchdown corner."

with his fans. He even did it when he scored a touchdown in a scrimmage game and feigned high fives with imaginary fans.

After his second touchdown against the Terps, the celebration got out of hand. A section of the three-foot-high fence came down, and fans who had been leaning on it spilled into the end zone. For those who knew him, this affection for McFadden was no surprise.

Danny Ford made no bones about the fact that McFadden was one of his all-time favorites, if not the favorite of his 11-year Clemson career. He was the consummate team leader, earned his undergraduate degree after the 1989 season and then entered graduate school at Clemson.

The next Monday the pollsters elevated Clemson to No. 7 in the nation, and improvement was expected the next week

when the Tigers would invade Durham to meet a 1–3 Duke team.

Clemson had not lost at Duke since 1980, Ford's second full season.

Ford was his normal cautious self in what he said about Duke before the game. He's famous for poor-mouthing, but this time everyone should have listened. Apparently his team did not.

The worst thing that could have happened to the Tigers was to take an early lead. Two touchdowns by Terry Allen in the first half gave Clemson a comfortable 14–0 advantage.

The Tigers appeared to be running through Duke with ease. Wesley McFadden was leading the blocking. He had a record 19 knockdown blocks for the day.

Clemson had several chances to put the game away, but twice the Tigers fumbled interception returns. They had five interceptions on the day, two by freshman Robert O'Neal.

But the Blue Devils kept plugging away and Clemson ended up on the short end of a 21–17 score.

The Duke students, long legendary for their zany exploits in basketball, stormed the field and tore down the goal posts after the victory, a triumph that propelled the Blue Devils to a seven-game winning streak to close the regular season.

Clemson got back on the winning track with its 29th consecutive victory over Virginia at home the next week. The win brought the Tigers up one notch in the polls to 14th after they fell from seventh to 15th following the Duke loss.

The main success against the Cavaliers can be credited to the offensive line. Eric Harmon, Hank Phillips and Jeb Flesch all had knockdown blocks in the double figures that day.

Few people ever criticized Danny Ford when it came to his coaching record. He retired from the Tigers as the fourth winningest coach in college football. He won five ACC titles and had seven Top 20 teams during his years at Clemson.

He had 16 wins over Top 20 teams during his career.

His ability to get his team up for a nationally renowned opponent was well documented. Ohio State, Notre Dame, Nebraska, Penn State, Oklahoma, Georgia, Florida State . . . the list goes on.

So how does this 1989 team lose to Duke? How could that same team beat Florida State in Tallahassee and lose to a Georgia Tech team with just one win?

And that was Clemson's Homecoming game!

The '89 roller coaster ride continued when the Yellow Jackets blitzed the 14th ranked Tigers 30–14. It really wasn't that close. Tech jumped out to a 23–6 lead at half time and dominated the Tigers in every statistic.

Trailing by 24 points, Ford went to his bull pen and brought in DeChane Cameron, who had been solid in relief appearances so far, but had never been told to go out and win the game.

He could not bring Clemson back, and it's doubtful that a Joe Montana-Dwight Clark combination could have, that day. But Cameron did complete 15 of 23 passes for 195 yards. That was important. Important for the rest of the season and for Cameron's career.

"We just got whipped," said Ford, a quote he offered after most of his 28 rare losses as a head coach. "This is the worst prepared football team I ever put on the field. You don't win games by being fundamentally unsound. You've got to block and tackle and knock people down in the four-down zone. We didn't do that all week."

As with Duke, Clemson had turned an opponent's season around. Georgia Tech

went on to a 7–4 season, winning six of its last seven. The win at Clemson was the turning point for the Yellow Jacket program. In fact, it could safely be said that their drive to the 1990 UPI national championship began in Death Valley October 14, 1989.

The loss gave Clemson a 5–2 overall mark, but more importantly just 2–2 in the ACC. Clemson had dropped out of the polls for the first time in 41 weeks. The drive to become the first ACC team to win four straight league titles was over. Suddenly a team that had been ranked seventh in the nation just three weeks previously now was wondering if seven wins and a minor bowl were realistic.

An undefeated (6–0) and ranked (12th) N. C. State team was next. The 'Pack had beaten the Tigers for the past three years.

Sunday's senior meeting following the Tech loss was interesting. Ford was at his wits' end. What was the problem with his team that not too many weeks before was a challenger for the national championship?

When the team could have gone on a slide, senior Wesley McFadden put a bug in the coach's ear. He also put the club on a course for five straight wins and another 10–2 season. In the last four regular-season games and the bowl appearance, Clemson would score 181 points while holding the opposition to just 30.

"We weren't having fun," said McFadden, a fifth-year senior. "We were playing not to lose instead of playing to win. We (the seniors) told the coaches that the ACC championship was by the boards, to let's just go out and have fun and play with reckless abandonment."

The seniors' attitude changed this team's attitude . . . and its place in the national standings. The tough task of facing an undefeated, nationally ranked team was just what the doctor ordered.

John Phillips puts a lick on the Dogs during '89 season.

The Tigers blasted the 'Pack 30–10 and probably frustrated Clemson fans even more in terms of their team's predictability. This was another victory to crow about, or as the players did . . . have fun with.

The Clemson defense yielded just 67 yards on the ground and State filled the air with 56 passes, averaging just over five yards a pass (297 total) and no touchdowns. Dexter Davis was all over the field with a career high 10 tackles and an interception.

"As the week went on, the train started moving," said Hank Phillips. "We had a lot of confidence and enthusiasm today and we got the 12th man into the game."

Ford put it this way: "When you go into a season trying for a perfect record, you probably try too hard. It's not a lack of effort, it's just a tightness and sometimes you make more mistakes than you do when you go out and have fun and just play.

"There was pressure on Clemson to win four straight ACC championships," Ford said. "We were playing to lose and you can't do that. Perhaps N. C. State was doing that today since they came in 6–0. We had nothing to lose."

The positive attitude continued over the last three weeks of the regular season. The Tigers would score 44 points on Wake Forest, 35 on North Carolina and have their highest season output (45 points) against South Carolina.

North Carolina was struggling through its second straight 1–10 season. With one of the worst offenses in the nation, the Tar Heels were going up against one of the best defenses in the nation. The result: North Carolina had minus six yards rushing, just 114 yards of total offense and five first downs for the game.

The victory over North Carolina brought Clemson back into the Top 20 (at No. 15). Moving up in the polls was one motivating factor remaining for Danny Ford's club. But the Tigers didn't need any additional motivation for the playing of South Carolina in Columbia.

The Tigers scored on their first four possessions and went on to a 45–0 victory, Clemson's second largest margin of victory in the series, the greatest since 1900. This was the first shutout of South Carolina by the Tigers since 1959.

"I can't complain about anything our team did tonight," said a jubilant Ford, whose team accepted a bid to play West Virginia in the Gator Bowl.

"Clemson played a perfect game," said South Carolina coach Sparky Woods. "I think the turning point took place when we kicked off. We just got beat throughout the entire game."

Clemson wore orange pants, a first for a Tiger team in an opponent's stadium, and raised its record to 16–2 when wearing them. That gave the team a little extra incentive, as did the presence of ESPN.

"Having the game on ESPN gave us a chance to show the country that we were as good as they saw when we beat Florida State earlier in the season," said linebacker John Johnson. "We took a hit with the losses to Duke and Georgia Tech, but we got some respect back tonight."

Terry Allen gained 97 yards in the first half and scored two touchdowns. But he reinjured his knee just before half time, and that would be his last action in a Clemson uniform. He was unable to perform in the bowl game because of the knee and decided to enter the NFL draft and give up his final year of eligibility.

He was just 137 yards away from breaking the career Clemson rushing record of Kenny Flowers.

There were some distractions in Clemson's preparation for the Gator Bowl. The NCAA was continuing its investigation and everyone knew the official letter of inquiry,

the document with specific allegations, was on the way. All involved hoped it would be after the bowl game before the specifics were released so it would not interfere with the team's concentration on the Mountaineers.

The second Saturday in December the fire was stoked when CNN's Danny Sheridan reported that Danny Ford and Notre Dame's Lou Holtz would leave their respective schools in 1990. It was not any more specific than that, but it did state both parties would make amiable separations.

Sheridan would be proven half right a month later when Ford indeed did resign.

The West Virginia game would serve as quite a natural matchup — the nimble Heisman Trophy finalist Major Harris of the Mountaineers against the quickest corps of outside linebackers in the country.

The Clemson defense was no doubt facing its toughest and sternest test of the season. "This is a big challenge for us," Levon Kirkland said the week of the game. "I haven't seen a quarterback so quick and so athletic since I have been at Clemson."

Harris had an excellent year, but it was a disappointment compared to his 1988 season when he took the Mountaineers just one game away from winning the national title. West Virginia lost to Notre Dame in the '88 Fiesta Bowl in a battle of unbeaten and untied teams.

Most of the Clemson players had seen the second half of that game after disposing of Oklahoma in the Florida Citrus Bowl. They were excited about playing against a program that played for the national title just 12 months before.

Harris came into the game ranked eighth in the nation in total offense and ninth in passing efficiency. The Clemson defense allowed him just 17 yards rushing and 119 yards in the air. Everyone contributed, but Kirkland was the ringleader with nine tackles, a five-yard sack, a caused fumble and three quarterback pressures.

Harris picked Clemson apart on his first drive and threw a 12-yard touchdown pass to James Jett, who would later become one of the top sprinters in the nation in 1991.

But a Chris Gardocki field goal and a one-yard run by Wesley McFadden gave Clemson a 10–7 half time lead. McFadden was testing his knee after missing the South Carolina game.

Clemson's relentless linebackers and linemen forced three Harris fumbles in the second half. And Chester McGlockton might have become the first Clemson player in history to sack the quarterback, cause a fumble, recover a fumble and score a touchdown all on the same play. There was 8:08 left in the game. Later on, Gardocki added another field goal as the Tigers exploded for 17 points in the final quarter.

Mountaineer coach Don Nehlen said afterward: "When we had the ball, they hunted us. We knew they were quick, but we didn't know they were that quick. They ran us down from behind and everywhere else. Clemson's very basic, but they really pound you."

Tiger quarterback Chris Morocco ended his career with a strong performance — completing five of nine passes for 57 yards and rushing 11 times for 65 yards.

Morocco suffered a mild concussion in the fourth quarter. While he was doing some post-game interviews on the field he nearly fainted twice and had to be helped to the locker room.

As usual, Ford praised his seniors in his post-game analysis. "We have gone through a lot of adversity this year and you have to give credit to our seniors. They held us together. This was their 38th win in four years. They have been a part of a great four years and a significant period in Clemson history. I am going to miss this bunch."

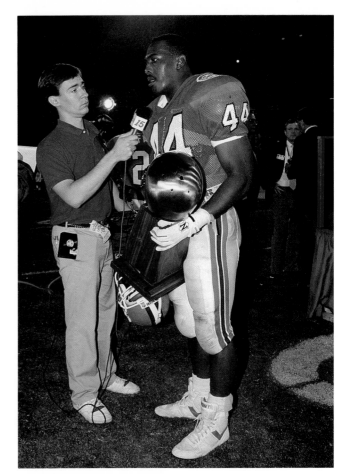

Levon Kirkland, Gator Bowl MVP.

This would be Ford's last interview as Clemson's head coach.

The victory over West Virginia brought Clemson its third straight 10–2 season, its fourth in a row with just two losses. The UPI poll rated the Tigers No. 11 in its post-bowl rundown, while they were 12th in the AP and *USA Today* polls.

It had been a season of ups and downs, landmark victories and shocking losses.

One stat no one knew about until the following May.

People wondered how much the NCAA investigation hurt this team. At 10–2 most felt they were able to put the investigation behind them and just play football.

But the only two weeks that the NCAA investigators were on campus to interview Clemson players were the weeks of the Duke and Georgia Tech games.

Chris Gardocki kicked a record-tying four field goals against UGA.

S. 1	59-0	W	H	Long Beach State
S. 8	7-20	L	A	Virginia
S. 15	18-7	W	A	Maryland
S. 22	48-0	W	H	Appalachian State
S. 29	26-7	W		Duke
O. 6	34-3	W		Georgia
O. 13	19-21	L	A	Georgia Tech
O. 20	24-17	W	A	N. C. State
O. 27	24-6	W	A	Wake Forest
N. 3	20-3		H	North Carolina
N. 17	24-15	W	H	South Carolina
J. 1	30-0	W	N1	Illinois

N1 at Hall of Fame Bowl in Tampa, FL

1990: KEN HATFIELD'S DEBUT

The 1990 football season may be revered as the year that Clemson football and the credibility of the entire athletic program took two steps forward when many thought it might take three steps backward.

The new decade brought a new era to Clemson football as Ken Hatfield replaced Danny Ford as the head coach. Ford resigned January 17 and Hatfield was the "surprise" replacement. It was a surprise because a story circulated after Ford's resignation that Hatfield had just signed a new contract at Arkansas.

The reports were erroneous, and on a cold but sunny Sunday afternoon, January 21, Clemson had gone outside its program to hire a head football coach for just the third time in 50 years.

Ford's resignation was controversial, to say the least. January 18–21 proved to be the most quixotic four days in the history of the Clemson Athletic Department. Even the day Hatfield was hired and a press conference was held, there were around 200 protestors outside the president's box at the stadium where the announcement was made.

Hatfield handled the tense atmosphere like a pro. Frank Howard had spoken to the group and then sent word inside for Hatfield to come out "and meet some of his future fans."

"I am glad you are here," Hatfield told the group. "That shows people at Clemson really care. It shows interest, enthusiasm and your concern for this purpose. I am not going to ask you or force you to accept me right away. I have to prove myself."

Hatfield and his wife, Sandy, walked to the middle of the angry crowd.

It did not take Hatfield long to prove himself.

The people who doubted his reasons for coming to Clemson and his ability to relate to the grass-roots fans saw a Ken Hatfield who spoke at every IPTAY meeting in the spring of 1990. His team won 10 of 12 games in his first season as head coach. Those who questioned his ability to recruit in this area saw him sign a Top 20 group in the signing period of 1991.

Players who questioned Hatfield changed their tune quickly. There was a threat of a boycott if Ford weren't re-hired or a member of his staff named head coach in the four-day period of Ford's leaving and Hatfield's coming.

"He was a pretty brave man to take on all those things when he first came here," said tight end Stacy Fields, one of the senior

New coach Ken Hatfield.

leaders of the 1990 team. "After seeing what the media said and our fan supporters, some of them were pretty rowdy about what had happened. For him to come in like that, I thought it took a lot of guts. He was ready for whatever anyone threw at him."

Quarterback DeChane Cameron added: "He tried to make you a responsible person. We resented him at first. But now we know he's on our side. He's preparing us for life after we leave Clemson."

Hatfield quickly instituted some team rules. No swearing, no drinking, no cutting classes and no skipping breakfast. "If a player gets up early and goes to breakfast before class, he will retain more in the classroom and he won't get behind," Hatfield said.

From a football standpoint, Clemson fans should not have noticed a change in the Tiger attack. Ken Hatfield football featured a relentless ground attack.

Ford did not leave the cupboard bare, especially on defense. Eight of the 11 starters on defense returned for '90, and that '89 defense wasn't any slouch, finishing fifth in the nation in scoring defense, total defense and rushing defense.

The offense returned just five starters, but there was not much experience at all at the skill positions. In fact, research showed that this was the youngest collection of skill-position players (fullback, halfback, wide receiver, flanker and quarterback) since 1943, a year in which Clemson was dominated by freshmen players because of World War II.

With a new coach at Clemson, one would expect that the interest from the media and fans would be at an apex when Long Beach State traveled to Clemson for the Tigers' first game in the decade of the '90's.

There were two major stories in the opener that were of national importance. *Sports Illustrated, The National* and *USA Today* had reporters at the game.

George Allen was coming out of retirement to coach the 49ers (Long Beach State variety). He was more familiar with the San Francisco 49ers, when some 14 years previously he was taking the Washington Redskins to the Super Bowl.

For the first time ever, Clemson held a press conference at the stadium the day before the game ... for the opposing coach. Doug Looney from *Sports Illustrated* followed Allen's every move. From a media standpoint, it took some of the pressure off Hatfield.

And it was reflected in the final score: Clemson 59, Long Beach State 0.

Hatfield did what he could to hold the score down against the undermanned team dominated by junior college transfers. "In the fourth quarter we had our scout-team line in there and they knew only two plays," Hatfield said.

Many Clemson fans waited for the 77-year old Allen after the game. He signed autographs, posed for a few more pictures for *Sports Illustrated*'s photographer, then boarded the bus.

Despite the fact Clemson had dealt him the worst loss of his lengthy and colorful career, regardless of the level, he exited with dignity, something he always carried with him. Allen brought that team back for a final 6–5 record.

Just five months later he died of natural causes in Los Angeles.

Next for the Tigers came Virginia in Charlottesville. And everything pointed to an upset and the end of the longest winning streak of one team over another in college football. It had to happen sometime, and this looked to be the day and time.

Clemson people who live in Charlottesville said they had never seen the town so alive for a game. Cavalier fans had never been more confident.

Another generation had come along since the Tigers won their first of 29 in a row from Virginia back in 1955.

The Cavaliers were coming off a 10–3 season in which they lost only to Notre Dame, Clemson (on the road without the services of quarterback Shawn Moore) and Illinois in the Citrus Bowl.

Shawn Moore, a bona fide Heisman Trophy candidate, was ready for Clemson this time, as was wide receiver Herman Moore and an offensive line that featured four seniors. The game was nationally televised.

After trailing 7–6 at halftime, the Cavaliers took the lead in the third period when Terry Kirby, the ACC's top rusher in 1990, scored from four yards out.

On Clemson's next possession the Tigers failed to convert on a third-down play when Doug Thomas dropped a pass near the Virginia sideline.

Jason Wallace then took Chris Gardocki's deep punt back for 79 yards to the Clemson seven. (In the 1988 Clemson game, a 10–7 Tiger victory also in Charlottesville, Wallace had missed an assignment and allowed Chip Davis to score the winning touchdown inside the last two minutes of play.)

Two plays later Shawn Moore floated an alley-oop pass to a 6–5 Herman Moore, who outleaped 5–11 Jerome Henderson. That put the Cavaliers up 20–7.

With 48 seconds left in the game, they tore down the goal posts, causing a substantial delay in completing the game.

"I'm glad we won and I'm glad this streak is over," said Cavalier head coach George Welsh. "We have been hearing about this streak all summer and now we won't have to hear about it any more."

Clemson coach Ken Hatfield won't be haunted by the streak any more either, a burden Frank Howard placed on his predecessors for 20 years. Somewhere every year, some writer would drag out Howard's quote about Virginia being "tender white meat" because he never lost to the Cavaliers. And Danny Ford would make his annual pilgrimage by Howard's office prior to the Virginia game asking, almost on his hands and knees "to lay off the white meat stuff."

If Ken Hatfield coaches at Clemson for 10, 15 or 20 successful years, he might look back on the Maryland game in Baltimore in 1990 as the most important of his career. With fans questioning the short-term future of this team after the first-ever loss to Virginia, the floodgates could have opened with a loss to the Terps.

But Doug Thomas, the senior wide receiver stopped that talk on a brilliant Saturday afternoon in Memorial Stadium.

Thomas made two of the biggest plays of the season in this game. First, with Maryland leading 7–3, he took a kickoff on a 98-yard return for a go-ahead touchdown.

Late in the fourth period, with Clemson again trailing, 17–12, Thomas caught a pass in heavy traffic over the middle. He turned this into a 37-yard gain and a vital Clemson first down.

Five plays later Cameron connected with fullback Rudy Harris with an 11-yard scoring pass. This was the first touchdown reception by a Clemson fullback in 18 years.

At the end of the season Hatfield said of the 18–17 victory over Maryland: "This was the key game of our season, there is no doubt. That win gave us confidence to go forward. We made strides in our passing game that day and showed we could win a big game away from Clemson.

"Doug Thomas' catch was the biggest single play of the season in my mind," the first-year Tiger coach continued. "DeChane threw a fine pass, but another receiver had run the wrong route so there were a lot of Maryland players in that area. Doug made the catch in traffic and turned it into a big gainer. If we had not gotten a first down right there, I don't know what would have happened."

Thomas became the talk of the Clemson campus, but he was just another well-known player in his hometown of Hamlet, North Carolina. That city may have the largest group of great athletes per capita of any town in the country.

Doug, who signed with the Seattle Seahawks, followed in the footsteps of his cousin, Mike Quick, an All-Pro wide receiver with the Philadelphia Eagles after playing at N. C. State.

Cornerback Perry Williams was a starter with the New York Giants Super Bowl champions a few years back.

The town boasts of two players in the major leagues — Ed Marshall of the New York Yankees and Franklin Stubbs of the Houston Astros.

Doug's older brother, Skeets, was in the minor leagues in 1990. The Thomases teamed up to lead the Hamlet Little League team to the World Series in 1982.

Two freshmen running backs, Ronald Williams and Derrick Witherspoon, held their coming-out party against Appalachian State. The two rushed for 306 yards on just 24 attempts and combined for four touchdowns. One run by Witherspoon went for 81 yards, the longest by a Clemson player in Death Valley in 40 years.

Williams would go on to lead the Tigers in rushing (941 yards) and in touchdowns (8), which tied a Clemson freshman record. He became the first Clemson true freshman to be named first team All-ACC on the offensive team, and he was chosen the ACC rookie-of-the-year, just the second Clemson player to be selected for that honor.

Cameron and Harris were the stars the following Saturday against Duke in the Tigers' 26–7 victory. Dexter Davis made a key play of the game in the first period with a diving interception of a Dave Brown pass. The Blue Devils were inside the Clemson 10 and had kept the ball 11:22 of the opening period until Davis ended the threat with his interception.

Nine of the previous 11 meetings between Clemson and Georgia had been decided by a touchdown or less, but the Tiger players from Georgia who had heard nothing but "Dawgs, Dawgs, Dawgs" all of their lives saw to it that this game was not close. In fact, Clemson's final 34–3 margin of victory was the largest by the Tigers in this storied rivalry since 1905.

The Bulldogs could not penetrate the Clemson 25-yard line all day long and the only score that Georgia could muster came on a minus-six yard drive that led to a field goal.

The Clemson seniors from Georgia did

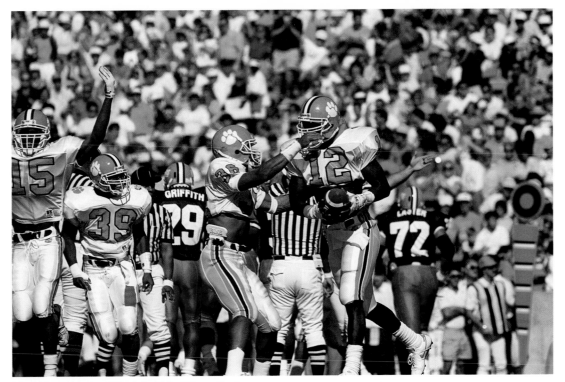

John Johnson against Illinois in Hall of Fame Bowl.

not want to lose to the Bulldogs in their final season. All-America tackle Stacy Long had six knockdown blocks as he opened holes for Clemson's runners, who picked up 341 yards.

Chris Gardocki, not a senior but a Georgia native, had a record-tying four field goals and averaged 42 yards a punt. As it turned out, this would also be Gardocki's final game against the Dawgs as he would later decide to make himself available for the pro draft at the end of his junior year.

Clemson controlled the clock for 35 out of 60 minutes and allowed Georgia just one third-down conversion in 13 attempts. The Bulldogs could muster only 81 yards rushing and eight first downs during the afternoon.

The margin of victory over Georgia gave the Tigers renewed confidence as they traveled to Atlanta for a battle of Top 20 teams. Clemson entered the mid-October game ranked 15th in the nation, while Georgia Tech, undefeated at 4-0, was ranked 18th.

The game was expected to be a defensive battle. Clemson had not allowed a touchdown at home all season and Georgia Tech had not allowed a touchdown to anyone all season, just a string of field goals to N. C. State, UT-Chattanooga, South Carolina and Maryland. Both Clemson and Georgia Tech were ranked in the top five in the nation in all four major defensive categories.

As happens many times in situations like this, the game did not go according to plan.

There were 40 points scored. The team that held the ball for 38:10, won the rushing battle 290 yards to 74 yards, and had 40 more offensive plays, lost the game.

Although Clemson had the impressive statistics, the Tigers never led in the game but were nearly successful on a 61-yard field goal which would have brought a one-point victory instead of a 21–19 loss.

Clemson lost just two games in 1990 and in both of these, a special team's play proved to be the most costly. Kevin Tisdale, a walk-on who did not even have a biographical sketch in the Georgia Tech press guide, returned the kickoff after Gardocki's fourth field goal for 87 yards to set up a five-yard touchdown run by T. J. Edwards.

The Tigers came right back and scored on a three-yard run by Cameron to bring the count to 21–19. A short punt then gave Clemson the ball near midfield with two minutes left. Clemson's last drive would net just six yards. Gardocki came on for an attempt from 60 yards out. He was about five yards short.

A second team All-American, Gardocki ranked fourth in the nation in punting and was also fourth in placekicking in '90, the second straight year he had two top five rankings. He is the only player in NCAA history to do that. He kicked 22 of 28 field goals and averaged 44.5 yards a punt.

The four-time All-ACC choice began kicking at age three. He would go to his brother Tad's soccer practice and kick the ball around on the side. At the age of ten he would pretend he was Kevin Butler, then a Georgia All-American, who attended Redan High School in Stone Mountain, Georgia, the same school Chris would attend.

In April of 1991 Gardocki was drafted by the Chicago Bears, the same team that Butler kicks for.

Clemson entered the home stretch with a 5–2 record. Hatfield's team had dropped to No. 22 in the polls and it was another make-or-break point in the season as the Tigers had to travel to N. C. State and Wake Forest on consecutive Saturdays.

"Hey, it's good to lose every once in awhile," defensive tackle Vance Hammond said before the N.C. State game. "You get refocused when you lose. This is going to be a great week of practice because we won't be lazy, we know our backs are against the wall. The last two years we have been in the same position of having to win the remaining games to get a good bowl bid and we are going to do it again."

Clemson was victorious each of the next two weeks, 24–17 in Raleigh and 24–6 in Winston-Salem, which was the 14th consecutive Tiger win over the Deacons.

A late Wolfpack fumble, forced by Hammond, gave Clemson possession deep in State territory. Howard Hall scored the game winner on a one-yard run with 3:12 remaining.

Hammond had a stellar game, recording 11 tackles, two of them for losses and another for a sack. The 6–7 defensive tackle would repeat his 1989 All-ACC honor again in '90 and would be a fifth-round choice of the Phoenix Cardinals NFL club in the April draft.

Hammond's father, John, is a highway patrolman who has worked the sidelines at Clemson and South Carolina football games for years. When Vance was ten, he accompanied his father to the Clemson-South Carolina game in Columbia. At the time, Vance had not been to many Clemson games with his dad and was partial to the Gamecocks.

In that 1977 thriller, considered by many as the most exciting game ever played between the two schools, South Carolina fell way behind (24–0), then mounted a comeback in the final quarter to take a 27–24 lead late in the game. Vance got so excited that he ran into the end zone and jumped on the pile of South Carolina players in celebration of the last touchdown. Clemson went on to a 31–27 win on Jerry Butler's famous catch.

That allegiance obviously changed over in time as Vance came to more and more Clemson games with his dad.

Clemson's victory over Wake Forest was the 500th in Tiger history. Ed McDaniel had a 10-tackle performance while Hammond was named ACC player-of-the-week for his two sacks and four tackles.

Arlington Nunn had another interception return for a touchdown, as he did in the opener against Long Beach State. "I rode with coach Hatfield on the bus over to the game," said Nunn, a senior who was academic All-ACC in 1989. "He said, 'You're due for another interception return for a touchdown. I think you are going to do it today.'"

Sure enough, on Wake Forest's first possession, Nunn intercepted a Phillip Barnhill pass and raced 26 yards to score for a 7–0 Clemson lead with just 1:16 passed in the game.

When North Carolina came to Death Valley the first Saturday in November, the Tigers had four goals in mind: Keep winning to assure a January 1st bowl game with a ranked opponent; keep winning to move up in the polls; keep winning so the seniors can reach 40 wins and become the winningest senior class in Clemson history; and keep the opponent's offense out of the end zone so the defense can continue its shutout record at home.

Mission accomplished!

North Carolina moved into the nation's top 25 teams by beating Maryland 34–10 the week before.

"We felt that North Carolina presented a challenge," said linebacker Levon Kirkland, who combined with Chester McGlockton to knock starting North Carolina quarterback Todd Burnett out of the game on the fourth play from scrimmage in the second half. "When we saw what they had done to Maryland and then heard the polls, that is all we needed. We took this very seriously to a man."

After Burnett departed, North Carolina made only one more first down. The Tar Heels had just 31 yards rushing the first half and added a mere seven more in the final 30 minutes, and only 38 yards of total offense during that same time period.

Dexter Davis intercepted a pass at the 9:06 mark of the second period and ran it back 30 yards for a touchdown. The momentum moved to Clemson's favor and the defense dominated for the rest of the afternoon.

"Dexter Davis is a great player," said North Carolina coach Mack Brown in his post-game comments. "He just made a great play and it turned the game in Clemson's favor. Clemson's defense forces you to make something happen, and that plays right into their hands. They really make a lot of big plays. And they are so quick at every position."

The South Carolina game was next as a big game for Dexter Davis and every other Tiger who claims the state of South Carolina as home. It was also going to be a big game for Ed McDaniel and Levon Kirkland, two of the top linebackers in America.

Kirkland grew up in Lamar, South Carolina. As a child, Kirkland would play football in the backyard by himself.

"I was a strange little boy," Kirkland admitted. "I would snap the ball to myself, throw it high in the air and then go catch it. Then I would also be the public address announcer and describe the touchdown, all the while spiking the ball and slapping the air with high fives. I pretended everyone in town was watching."

McDaniel also started football at an early age, and his years growing up in Batesburg, South Carolina, had a lot to do with it. When he was seven years old, his Uncle Charlie bet him a dollar he could not record a sack in his next Little League game. By the end of the game Uncle Charlie was a dollar poorer and Ed decided he liked this game of football, especially playing defense.

Uncle Charlie would have been even poorer after the South Carolina game. McDaniel was the ring leader in tackles with ten, including two for losses as the Gamecocks only recorded 85 yards rushing.

Clemson's 24–15 victory gave the senior

DeChane Cameron quarterbacked the Tigers to their fifth straight bowl victory.

class 39 wins, an ACC record for wins by a class. The triumph also made Ken Hatfield just the second Clemson coach since 1940 to beat South Carolina in his first meeting.

A jubilant Clemson locker room accepted the invitation to play in the 1991 Hall of Fame Bowl in Tampa, Florida. No person was any happier in that sweaty, steamy room than Allen Reeves. A 1951 Clemson graduate and president of Reeves Import Motorcars in Tampa, Reeves has been a member of the bowl selection committee for several years, but had never been able to woo the Tigers to the bowl.

This time Clemson officials were in agreement that the Hall of Fame Bowl had all of the ingredients they were looking for in a post-season game, and when the invitation was issued, there was no debating.

This was Clemson's sixth consecutive post-season bowl invitation and the ninth straight for Hatfield. Only Bobby Bowden at Florida State, Pat Dye of Auburn, Tom Osborne at Nebraska and Lavell Edwards at Brigham Young have been to a bowl game that many years in a row.

This would be a special bowl for Hatfield. It was rewarding enough to be playing in a bowl after a 9–2 regular season in light of the events of the previous year. It was rewarding that Clemson's program had remained in the Top 15 under his leadership.

But this game with Illinois would be particularly interesting to Hatfield because he would be going against John Mackovic, who had been a graduate assistant with Hatfield at Army 22 years earlier.

"We used to play basketball together almost every night in the summer at Army," Hatfield recalled. "Those were some great times there because there were some great coaching minds there. Bobby Knight was the basketball coach, Bill Parcells was on the football staff and even Coach K (Mike Krzyzewski of the national champion Duke Blue Devils) was a point guard on the basketball team."

The pre-game rhetoric was dominated by talk of the two defenses. "Several NFL people have told me that the greatest number of defensive stars playing collegiate football would be in our bowl game," Hatfield said. "They have a big and quick defense and we are quick and deep and led the nation (in defense) this year."

That proved to be correct as seven defensive starters in the game were drafted by the NFL the next spring.

There were some developments in the month of December that added spice to the confrontation. Clemson had a record three players chosen on the first and second team Associated Press All-America squad. Stacy Long was a first team All-American and a finalist of the Outland Trophy. Levon Kirkland was a finalist for the Butkus Award and was named second team All-American, while Chris Gardocki was the second team AP All-America placekicker and an honorable mention All-America punter by United Press International.

On the negative side, Clemson lost two starters prior to the bowl game, the center on both sides of the line of scrimmage. Middle guard Rob Bodine went down with a knee injury the second day of practice in Orlando, and center Curtis Whitley was suspended from the game for a violation of team rules.

The Tigers scored 24 points in the first 22 minutes of the game. Chris Gardocki opened with an 18-yard field goal that culminated a 71-yard drive. On Illinois' first play from scrimmage, Chester McGlockton forced a fumble which John Johnson fell on for the Tigers.

On the next play Clemson scored when Doug Thomas caught a 14-yard scoring pass from DeChane Cameron. In the second period the Tigers added a 17-yard scoring pass from Cameron to Howard Hall. When Arlington Nunn raced 34 yards with his third scoring interception return of the year, Clemson fans knew they were seeing another Clemson bowl victory.

"That interception return was a special thrill for me," said a happy Nunn. "I am from Clearwater (just a few miles from Tampa) and had played my last high school game in this stadium. Now I am playing my last college game, and who knows, it might be my last game . . . period. So to score in my last game was just awesome."

Clemson's defense and Gardocki finished off the Illini in the second half. Gardocki kicked two field goals, but he missed one in the fourth period that would have given him the Clemson career record.

John Johnson led Clemson's third shutout of the season. The senior from LaGrange, Georgia, who was playing his 48th and final game as a Tiger, had seven tackles, two sacks, a caused fumble and a recovered fumble. His performance was a key to his second-round selection in the NFL draft five months later by the San Francisco 49ers.

Cameron was the most valuable player of the game. He completed 14 of 19 passes for 141 yards and a pair of touchdowns.

The victory vaulted Clemson five spots in most polls, including a No. 9 final ranking by the Associated Press. The fifth straight bowl victory gave Clemson a 40–8 record over the last four years, the fourth best record in college football during this time and the best ever by an ACC senior class.

Clemson ended the season ranked fifth by the *New York Times;* sixth by *The National, Football News* and the *Sagarin Computer,* eighth by *Sporting News* and ninth by UPI and *USA Today.*

Mackovic, a former head coach at Wake Forest and familiar with the Clemson program, summed up the game and perhaps the entire Tiger season in his post-game interview. "Clemson is a terrific football team," he said. "I don't know if we have ever played a better defense, and certainly they are as talented as any team we have played at any time. Colorado might have been more explosive on offense, but Clemson ranks above everyone on defense.

"Ken Hatfield has done a masterful job, absolute coach-of-the-year material," Mackovic continued. "He has provided Clemson with outstanding leadership this year."

All-Time Lettermen

A

Aaron, Jack — 1961-62-63
*Abell, Frank — 1931-32
Abrams, Jimmy — 1966-67
*Adams, J.P. — 1914-15-16
Abreu, Ed — 1978
Addison, Jimmy — 1965-66-67 (Capt)
*Adkins, Gary — 1976-77-78-79
Alexander, Gary — 1973-74-75
Alford, Hugh — 1945
*Alford, J.L. — 1916
Aliffi, Vic — 1961-63
*Allen, Banks — 1906-07
Allen, Terry — 1987-88-89
Allen, Thad — 1974-75-76-77
Alley, Kendall — 1981-82-83
*Allison, J.W. (Switzer) — 1917-18-19-20
Ammons, Billy — 1966-67-68 (Capt.)
Anderson, Ben — 1970-71-72
Anderson, Jack — 1968-69-70
Anderson, Joe — 1960-61-62
Anderson, Randy — 1985-86-87
Anderson, Sam — 1958-59-60
Anderson, Tony — 1970-71-72
Anderson, Willie — 1972-73-74 (Co-Capt.)
Andreas, Karl — 1971-72-73
Andreo, Ron — 1959-60-61 (Capt.)
Ankuta, Neuf — 1954-55
Anthony, Vernie — 1981-82
Ard, Wendall — 1943-44
Ariri, Obed — 1977-78-79-80
Armstrong, F.E. (Boo) — 1918 (Acting Capt.) 1919-20 (Capt.)
*Armstrong, Hoyt — 1921
Armstrong, Junior — 1930
Armstrong, Lon — 1959-60-61
Arrington, Vandell — 1981-82-83
Arthur, Gary — 1966-67-68
Asbill, Henry — 1927-28-29
Austin, Cliff — 1978-80-81-82
*Austin, P.B. (Plowboy) — 1925-26
Avery, Wingo — 1953-54-55 (Alt. Capt.)

B

*Bailes, J.P. — 1919-20-21
*Bailes, W.B. — 1922
Bailey, Bob — 1936-37-38
Bailey, Greg — 1987
Bailey, Rick — 1982-83-84
Bak, Jeff — 1985-86-87-88
Baker, Archie — 1950-51-52
Baker, Wayne — 1969-70-71
Baldwin, Bob — 1964
Baldwin, Mike — 1974
Balles, Joe — 1961-63
*Banks, B.C. (Stumpy) — 1915-16-17-18 (Capt.) - 19 (Capt.)
Barbary, Bill — 1955-57
Barfield, Don — 1964-65-66
Barnes, Gary — 1959-60-61
Barnette, Jimmy — 1968-69
*Barnwell, T.G. — 1902

Barter, Lynn — 1971-72
Bartlet, J.H. — 1917
Barton, Tom — 1950-51-52
Basich, Rick — 1980
*Bates, Joe A. (Warhorse) — 1909-10-11
*Bates. J. Mc — 1918
Bauman, Charlie — 1977-78-79-80
Beasley, Gene — 1985-86-87-88
Beasley, Kenny — 1985
Bell, Jimmy — 1962-63-64 (Alt. Capt.)
Bell, Randy — 1967
Bell, Larry — 1969-70
Bell, Wayne — 1964-65-66
Bell, William — 1988
*Bellows, C.A. — 1900
Belton, Mitch — 1988-89
Bengel, Gordy — 1971-72-73
Benish, Dan — 1979-80-81-82
Berlin, Steve — 1983-84-85 (Capt.)
Berry, Mike — 1989
Berry, Net — 1934-35-36 (Capt.)
Berryhill, Tony — 1979-80-81
Bethea, Fitzhugh — 1983
Bethea, Frank — 1973-74-75
Beville, Scott — 1988-89
*Bissell, Paul L. — 1909-10-11 (Capt.)
Black, Carl — 1936-38-39 (Alt. Capt.)
Black, Manuel — 1934-35-36 (Alt. Capt.)
Black, Tommy — 1961
Black, Wendall — 1959-60-61
Blackwelder, Tim — 1975
Blackwell, Joe — 1963-64
*Blain, J.M. — 1896
Blakeney, Rock — 1930
*Blalock, Joe — 1939-40-41
Blanton, Bo — 1979-80
Blessing, Jim — 1939-40
Bollinger, Rich — 1976
*Blease, J.W. — 1898-1900
Bodine, Rob — 1989
Bolubasz, John — 1971-72-73
Boozer, Tom — 1972-73-74
Bosler, Bob — 1970-71-72
Bost, Ed — 1959-60-61
Bostic, Jeff — 1977-78-79
Bostic, Joe — 1975-76-77-78
Bounds, David — 1981
Bowen, Joe — 1953-55
Bowick, Ray — 1958
Bowlan, Roland — 1973-74
Bowles, H. Julian — 1923-24-25
Bowles, M.G. (Monk) — 1929-30-31
Bowman, Nick — 1979-80-81
Boyer, Shelton — 1983-84-85
Boyette, Johnny — 1962-64-65 (Capt.)
*Boykin, Bolivar — 1909
*Box, Carlon — 1984
*Bradley, L.T. (Prep) — 1925
Brady, Kevin — 1984-85
*Brandon, T.B. — 1914-15-16
Brantley, Craig — 1973-74-75
Branton, Joey — 1965-66-67
Bratton, Bruce — 1988-89
Bray, Cliff — 1976-77-78

Breedlove, Billy — 1956
*Breedon, Joe — 1901
Brewster, Doug — 1987-88-89
Brickley, Glenn — 1985
Brisacher, Art — 1971-72-73
Brisendine, Rod — 1946
*Bristol, W.H. — 1912-13-14
*Britt, Ben — 1910-11-12 (Capt.)
*Britt, D.C. (Toots) — 1907-09
*Britt, S.L. — 1910
Broadwater, Crosby — 1986-87
Brodie, Bunny — 1948-49
*Brock, W.T. — 1896-97 (Capt.)
Brooks, Jonathan — 1975-76-77-78
Brown, Dave — 1962
Brown, Gary — 1979-80-81-82
*Brown, H.W. — 1916
Brown, Ken — 1980-81-83-84
Brown, Lester — 1976-77-78-79
Brown, Lockie — 1981
Brown, Marlon (Bubba) — 1976-77-78-79 (Capt.)
Brown, Mike — 1989
Brown, Norris — 1989
Brown, Ray — 1979-81-82-83
Brown, Ricky — 1971-72-73
Brown, Roy — 1980-81-82-83
*Brown, Tom I. — 1933-34-35
*Browne, G.H. (Skeet) — 1913
Browning, Sebo — 1984
Brumley, Lacy — 1974-75-76-77
Brunson, Jack — 1948-49-50
Brunson, Lawrence — 1984-85
Bruorton, H.B. — 1954-55-56
*Bryant, Bill — 1935-36-37
Bryant, Jeff — 1978-79-80-81
Bryant, Joe — 1950-51-52
*Bryant, Shad — 1937-38-39
Buckner, Mike — 1971-72-73 (Capt.)
Bukowsky, Dick — 1969-70-71
Bullard, Wilbur — 1983
Bunton, Donnie — 1955-56-57
Bunton, Ted — 1962-63-64 (Capt.)
Burbick, Bruce — 1967
Burgess, Robert — 1973-74
Burgner, Greg — 1967-68-69
*Burnett, George — 1966-67-68
Burton, C.C. — 1921-22
Burton, Dave — 1965
Burton, Richard — 1984
Buscher, L.E. — 1934-36
Bush, Jack — 1955-56-57
Bussey, Charlie — 1954-55-56 (Capt.)
Bustle, Rickey — 1974-75-76
Butcher, Brian — 1980-81-82
Butler, Butch — 1941-42-43-45
Butler, Jerry — 1976-77-78
Butler, Richard — 1982-83-84
Buttermore, Curt — 1972-73-74
Butz, Sam — 1945
*Byers, Monty — 1942
*Byrd, Gary — 1950-51-52

C

Cagle, Bully — 1940-41-42
Cagle, John — 1966-67-68

Cagle, Mavis — 1944-45-46-47
Cain, Harold — 1974-75-76
Cain, Jack — 1978-79-80
Cain, Sammy — 1967-68-69
Caldwell, Charlie — 1969-70
Caldwell, Mark — 1980
Callahan, Sonny — 1971
Callicutt, Ken — 1973-74-75-77
Calvert, Forrest — 1950-53
Calvert, Jackie — 1948-49-50
*Calvert, Jim — 1949-50
Cameron, Dechane — 1989
*Camp, Bill — 1904
Campbell, Blake — 1988
Candler, Steedley — 1967
Cann, George — 1920-21
*Cannon, C.L. — 1907
Cannon, W.M. — 1915
Caplan, Stu — 1964-65
Carothers, Rocky — 1948-49-50
Carr, Michael — 1989
Carson, Gene — 1948-49
*Carson, Jules L. (Doc) — 1910-11-12-13
Carson, Lynn — 1973-75
*Carter, Bert — 1906
Carter, Henry — 1984-86-87-88
Carter, Oscar — 1969-70
Case, Johnny — 1961-62-63
Cassady, Sonny — 1968-69-70
Cathcart, Joe — 1933
Catoe, Jimmy — 1966-67-68 (Capt.)
Cauble, Charlie — 1969
*Caughman, F. Porter — 1907
*Caughman, Kenny — 1911-12-13
Chamberlain, Force — 1970-71-72
Chandler, Tommy — 1949
Charpia, Rusty — 1986-87-88
Chappelear, Glenn — 1984
Chappell, Henry — 1943
Charleston, Pat — 1983-84-85
Chatlin, Rabbit — 1957-58-59
Chavous, Raymond — 1985-86-87-88
Cheatham, Andy — 1982-83-84
Cheek, Randy — 1980-81
Childers, Stan — 1971
Childers, Tim — 1981-82-83
Childers, Tracy — 1962-63 (Capt.)
Childers, Wilson — 1965-66-67
*Childress, John — 1948-49-50
Chipley, Bill — 1940-41
*Chovan, Phil — 1938
*Chreitzberg, C.K. — 1898
*Chreitzberg, A.M. — 1896
Chuy, Don — 1961-62
Ciniero, Geoff — 1985-86
Clanton, Ray — 1945-46-47-48
*Clardy, Warren — 1904
Clark, Brian — 1979-80-81
Clark, Chip — 1942-45-46 (Capt.)
Clark, Dwight — 1975-76-77-78
*Clark, W.C. — 1906-07
Clayton, David — 1984
Cleveland, Olin — 1945-46
Clifford, Chris — 1975-77
Clifford, Mark — 1979

166

Cline, Doug — 1957-58-59
Cobb, Joe — 1989
Cobb, Maret — 1972-73-74
*Cochran, J.T. (Boots) — 1908-09-10
Cockfield, Barry — 1966
Coffey, Bob — 1974-75
*Cogburn, H.L. — 1903
*Colbert, W.C. (Pinky) — 1919-20-21
Coleman, Bob — 1959-60-61
Coleman, Dan — 1937-38-40
Coleman, Jim — 1954-55-56
*Coles, Marion (Pony) — 1910-11-12
*Coles, Strick — 1906-07-08 (Capt.)
Coley, James — 1985-86-87-88
*Collins, Joe — 1928
Compton, Gary — 1958-59
Cone, Fred — 1948-49-50 (Capt.)
*Connelly, Bill — 1909-10
Cook, Pete — 1950-51-52
Cooper, Gary — 1986-87-88-89
Cooper, Jay — 1964-65-66
Cooper, Richard — 1963-64
Cordileone, Lou — 1957-58-59
Cornell, Mike — 1973-74-75
Coursey, Tom — 1949
Cox, Carol — 1945-47-48-49
Cox, Cary — 1946-47 (Capt.)
Cox, Ed — 1949
Cox, Jack — 1948-59
*Cox, M.E. — 1914-15
Cox, Walter, Sr. — 1938-39
Cox, Walter, Jr. — 1961-62-63
Cox, Wyatt — 1957-58
Craig, Arthur — 1965-66-67
Craig, Bob — 1966-68-69
*Craig, Johnson — 1931-32
Craig, Marion (Hawk) — 1940-41-
42 (Alt. Capt.)
Crain, Pat — 1962-63-64
Crain, Willis — 1954
Crawford, Barclay — 1950-51-52
Crawford, Craig — 1983-84
Crawford, Eddie — 1974
Crite, Brendon — 1980-81-82
Crolley, Ronnie — 1959-60-61
Cropp, Willie — 1966-68
Crout, Sammy — 1958-59
Croxton, Bill — 1933-34-35
Cruce, Jeff — 1983-84
*Crumbie, Alton — 1944-45
Cunningham, Bennie — 1973-74-75
(Co-Capt.)
Cunningham, James — 1975
*Cummings, Pony — 1932-33-34
Curtis, Ralph — 1946
Curtis, Rodney — 1985
Cuttino, H.B. (Hop) — 1925-26

D
Daigneault, Doug — 1958-59
*Dailey, B. T. — 1915
Daniel, Ralph — 1969-70-71
Danforth, Kenny — 1983-84-85
Dantzler, Ellis — 1963-64-65
Davis, Billy — 1980-81-82-83
Davis, Chip — 1986-87-88-89
Davis, David — 1988-89
Davis, Dexter — 1988-89
Davis, Footsie — 1930-31-32
Davis, Guy — 1926-27-28
Davis, Hal — 1962-63-64
Davis, Heide — 1970-71-72
Davis, Jeff — 1978-79-80-81 (Capt.)
Davis, Jerry — 1972-73
Davis, Jud — 1944-45-47-48
*Davis, St. Clair — 1928
Davis, Tyrone — 1982-83-84
Davidson, L. S. — 1925-26

Dawson, Eric — 1985
Day, Dean — 1981
Deanhardt, Luke — 1946-47-48-49
Deanhardt, Luke, Jr. — 1971
DeBardelaben, Bob — 1958-59
Decock, Bruce — 1971-72-73
*DeCosta, E. J. (Beef) — 1901-02
Deitz, Frank — 1939-40
Deluliis, Frank — 1985-86-87-88
*DeLoach, Billy — 1949
Demery, Pete — 1981
Demps, Reggie — 1989
DePew, Bill — 1968-69
*Derrick, O. L. (Puss) — 1903-04-05-06
DeSimone, Dick — 1954-56-57
Devane, William — 1980-81-82-83
*Dickson, Laury — 1905
Diggs, Bubba — 1978-79-81-82
Dillard, Bill — 1932-33-34
DiMucci, Dan — 1949-50-51
Dixon, Bruce — 1989
Dolce, Chris — 1978-79
Donaldson, Richard — 1982-83-84
Dorn, Jim — 1969-70-71
*Dotterer, E.G. (Gilly) — 1922-23
Dotherow, Fudge — 1962
*Douthit, Claude (Pug) — 1898-99-
1900-01 (Capt.)
Dozier, Ted — 1931-32-33
Drag, Mark — 1985-86-87-88
Driver, Stacey — 1982-83-84-85
*Duckett, Graves — 1916
*Duckworth, Joe — 1898-99-1900
Ducworth, C.H. — 1974
Ducworth, George — 1968-69-70
Ducworth, Ronnie — 1966-67-68
(Capt.)
Ducworth, Thomas — 1973
Dukes, Mike — 1956-57-58
Duley, Tom — 1965
Dumas, Charlie — 1962-63-64
Duncan, John — 1984
*Dunlap, Tom — 1919-20
Dunn, K.D. — 1981-82-83-84
Durham, Steve — 1977-78-79-80
Dyer, Clint — 1945-46-48
*Dyess, Jimmy — 1929

E
Earle, James — 1984-85-86-87
*Earle, J.C. — 1900
Eberhart, Terry — 1958
Eidson, Wesley — 1967-68
Eley, Thomas — 1975
Ellenburg, Charlie — 1966-67
Ellis, Joe — 1981-83-84
*Ellison, Gill — 1904-05
Elvington, B.B. — 1968-69-70 (Capt.)
Emanuel, Emmett — 1920-21-22
(Capt.)
*Emerson, Jack — 1947
Engel, Karl — 1962
English, Tom — 1968
Enzor, Scott — 1985-86
Eppes, Roy — 1976-77
Eppley, Mike — 1982-83-84 (Capt.)
*Epps, M.H. (Pepper) — 1910
Esgro, Greg — 1984
*Eskew, H.L. (Bud) — 1925-26-27
(Capt.)
Ethridge, Brooks — 1970
Ethridge, Don — 1969-70-71
Evans, Charlie — 1962
Eyler, Rick — 1968-70
*Ezell, J.F. (Sam) — 1909-10
*Ezell, R.B. (Doc) — 1912

F
Fabers, Leon — 1972-73
Facciolo, Mike — 1964-65-66 (Capt.)
Farnham, Dave — 1969-70-71
Farr, James — 1980-81-82-83
(Capt.)
Fellers, Mark — 1972-73-74
(Co-Capt.)
Fellers, Stan — 1932-33-34
Few, Bill — 1955-56-57
Fewell, J.A. (Jake) — 1924-25
Fields, Stacy — 1987-88-89
*Finklea, Gary — 1923-24-25 (Capt.)
*Finley, States Right G. — 1916-17
Fisher, Brad — 1979-80-81
Fitzpatrick, Pat — 1978
Flagler, Terrence — 1982-84-85-86
(Capt.)
Flathman, Gene — 1936
*Fleming, F — 1907-08
Fleming, J.M. (Fatty) — 1925
*Fleming, Vic — 1930-31
Fleming, W.H. — 1929-30
Flesch, Jeb — 1988-89
Fletcher, Rodney — 1988-89
Flowers, Kenny — 1983-84-85-86
Floyd, George — 1939-40
Fogle, Lou — 1961-62-63
Folger, Mac — 1934-35-36
*Fordham, Red — 1930-31 (Capt.)
Foster, Jon — 1988
*Forsyth, J.A. (Pee Wee) — 1901-
02-03
*Forsythe, W.C. — 1898-99-1900-01
Fox, Angelo — 1987-88
Franklin, Harry — 1941-42
*Freeman, Eddis — 1943-44-45-46
*Frew, W.L. (Red) — 1918
Frierson, Bob — 1982
*Fritts, George — 1939-40-41
Fuller, Steve — 1975-76-77 (Capt.)
78 (Capt.)
Fulmer, John — 1967-68-69
Funderburk, Mike — 1968
*Furtick, Fritz — 1903-04-05-06
(Capt.)

G
Gage, Bobby — 1945-46-47-48
Gaillard, Jerry — 1978-79-80-81
Gainer, Chick — 1943-46-47-48
Galloway, G.G. — 1972-73-74-75
Galuska, Pete — 1969-70-71
*Gandy, A.P. (Hop) — 1909-11-12-
13 (Capt.)
*Gantt, Jonnie — 1902
*Gantt, W.A. — 1905
Gardocki, Chris — 1988-89
Garick, Richard — 1966-67-68
*Garrison, Bill — 1902-03
Garrison, C.C. — 1923
Garrison, Gene — 1953
Gaskin, Dreher — 1950-51-52-53
(Co-Capt.)
Gasque, Mike — 1980-81
*Gassaway, Jim — 1928-29
Gaston, Clark — 1961-62-63
*Gaston, R.T. — 1905-06-07
Geathers, Eddie — 1978-79-80
*Gee, C.F. (Little Mutt) — 1912-13-14
*Gee, J.G. (Mutt) — 1914-15-16-17
Gehret, Guy — 1972-73-74
Gemas, Kevin — 1983-84
Gennerich, Gary — 1970-71-72
*Gentry, Charlie — 1896-97-98
Gentry, Frank — 1950-51-52
*George, A.P. — 1899-1900

George, Buck — 1951-52-53-54
(Capt.)
Gerald, Henry — 1965
Gerrald, Steve — 1988
Geter, Eric — 1989
*Gettys, E.F. (Red) — 1918-19-20-21
Gibbs, Steve — 1974-76-77-78
Gibson, Cameron — 1988
Gibson, Tyrone — 1989
Gillespie, Bill — 1943
Gillespie, Dick — 1948-50
Gillespie, Frank — 1946-47-48
*Gilmer, Grover G. — 1917-19-20-21
*Gilmer, Frank — 1908-09-10
Gilstrap, Clay — 1986
Gilstrap, Earl — 1970-71
Gilstrap, Rick — 1969-70-71
Glaze, Coleman — 1960-61-62
Glenn, Joe — 1979-80-81-82
Gobble, Robert — 1958
Godfrey Steve — 1976-77 (Capt.)
Goehring, Jim — 1976-77
Goff, Johnnie Mac — 1968
Goggins, Harold — 1975-76-77-78
*Goins, Gus — 1936-37-38
Goldberg, Bob — 1977-78
*Gooding, R.F. (Fatty) — 1904
Goodloe, John — 1977
Gordon, Chuck — 1976
Gore, Buddy — 1966-67-68
Goss, Dennis — 1971-72
Graham, Bernie — 1950-51
*Graham, George — 1944
Granger, Ty — 1985-86-87-88
Gravely, Mike — 1974
*Gray, Bill — 1911
Gray, Ricky — 1980
Grdijan, John — 1955-56-57
(Co-Capt.)
*Green, Harry — 1901-02
Green, Mervin — 1988
Greene, Earle — 1955-56
Greene, Johnny — 1955
Greenwalt, Stan — 1973
Gresham, Metz — 1929
Gressette, Larry — 1951-52-53
(Co-Capt.)
Gressette, Nathan — 1951-52-53
(Co-Capt.)
Griffin, Steve — 1982-84-85-86
Griffith, Frank — 1954-55
Grigsby, Billy Luke — 1948-49-50
Grimes, Tyler — 1986-87-88
Gue, Tommy — 1959-60-61
*Gunnells, Bill — 1928-29
Gunnells, Dan — 1965-66-67
Guy, Ruben — 1932

H
Haddock, Lee — 1970-71
Hagen, Arthur — 1944
Haglan, J.D. — 1976-77-78
Hair, Billy — 1950-51-52 (Co-Capt.)
*Hair, J.C. — 1924-26-27
*Hall, Bill — 1938-39-40 (Alt. Capt.)
Hall, Delton — 1983-84-85-86
Hall, Hollis — 1979-80-81
Hall, Howard — 1989
Hall, Les — 1989
*Hall, R.M. (Fatty) — 1926-27-28
Hall, Wade — 1960-63
*Hamer, Ray — 1939-40-41
*Hamilton, R.G. — 1896 (Capt.)
*Hammett, L.O. — 1918
Hammond, Brian — 1985
Hammond, Vance — 1987-88-89
*Hane, J.K. — 1924-25
*Hane, Kit — 1928-29

Hankins, Kelvin — 1989
Hankinson, Crimmins — 1953-54
*Hankle, Witt H. — 1908-09-10 (Capt.)
Hansford, Ogden — 1974-75-78
*Hanvey, Ernest — 1913
*Hanvey, George — 1897-98
*Hanvey, Jock T. — 1896-97-1902-03
*Hardin, L.G. — 1916
Harmon, Eric — 1987-88-89
*Harmon, H.M. (Duck) — 1914-15-16
*Harmon, S.E. (Pat) — 1922-23-24
Harper, J.C. — 1985-86-87-88
Harps, Wayne — 1986-87-88-89
Harrell, Ricky — 1970-71-72
*Harris, H.S. (Lazy Bill) — 1914-15-16
*Harris, L.D. — 1919
Harris, Reggie — 1986-87-88
Hart, Chris — 1989
*Hart, Willard L. (Bub) — 1916-17
Harvey, B.C. (Chubby) — 1925-26 (Capt.)
*Harvey, Randy — 1967-68
Harvey, S.A. (Speck) — 1922
Harvin, Lionell — 1929-30-31
*Harvley, Clyde — 1931
Hatcher, Dale — 1981-82-83-84
Hatcher, Jesse — 1987-88
Hauser, Tad — 1980
*Hayden, C.J. — 1911
Hayes, Rudy — 1956-57-58 (Alt. Capt.)
Haynes, Joey — 1987
Haynes, Norman — 1985-86-87
Headen, Andy — 1979-80-81-82
Hecht, Bill — 1963-64-65 (Capt.)
*Heffner, L.B. — 1920
Hefner, Larry — 1969-70-71 (Capt.)
Heilig, Don — 1959
*Heinemann, John — 1931-32-33 (Capt.)
*Hendee, H.M. (Tick) — 1925-26
Henderson, Jerome — 1987-88-89
Henderson, Joe — 1987-88-89
Hendley, Dick — 1946-48-49-50
Hendley, Richard — 1980-81-82
*Hendricks, L.L. — 1896-97
Heniford, Mark — 1974-75-76-77
Heniford, Todd — 1984
*Henley, Cliff — 1934-35
Henry, Dale — 1969-70-71
Herlong, Doug — 1948-51
*Herlong, Henry — 1930
Hicks, Harry — 1954
Hicks, Ken — 1972
Hill, Jerome — 1974-75
Hilderbrand, Nolten — 1953
Hinson, Randy — 1933-34-35
*Holland, Joe — 1904 (Capt.)
Holland, Lawson — 1974
Holloman, Duke — 1983-84
Holohan, R.F. (Butch) — 1921-22-23 (Capt.)-24
Homonoff, Edward — 1973-74
Hook, Charlie — 1965-66-68
*Hook, Fred — 1931-32
Hooper, Ricardo — 1986-87-88
Hope, Leon — 1973-74-75
Hopkins, Stan — 1971-72
Horne, Charlie — 1956-57-58
Horton, Tate — 1933-34-35
Hostetler, Hoss — 1964-66-67
Hough, James — 1945
Howard, Jimmy — 1961-62-63
Howell, Trey — 1988
Hubert, Pooley — 1950-53
Hudson, Alex — 1980-82-83
Hudson, Billy — 1954-55-56
Hudson, Billy — 1976-77-78

Hudson, Bob — 1947-48-49-50
Hudson, J.C. — 1950-51-52
Hughes, Wade — 1971-72 (Capt.)
Hunt, Revonne — 1951
Hunter, Bill — 1942-46-47
Hunter, Hamp — 1953-54-55
*Hunter, N.M. (Buster) — 1899-1900-01
Huntley, Chuck — 1970-73
*Hydrick, Onan — 1908-09
Hynes, Dave — 1960-61-62

I
Igwebuike, Donald — 1981-82-83-84
*Inabinet, B.C. — 1953-54-55
*Inabinet, Clarence J. — 1933-34-35
Inge, Mark — 1986-87-88
Ingle, Reid — 1982-83-84
Ingram, Keith — 1987
Inman, Don — 1984
Isaacs, Mike — 1983-84-85

J
Jackson, Jack — 1969
Jackson, Jacky — 1965-66-67
Jackson, Jackie Lee — 1966-67-68
Jackson, Kenzil — 1989
Jackson, Kit — 1965-66-67
Jackson, M.E. — 1921
Jackson, Scott — 1952-53-54 (Capt.)
*Jackson, S.L. (Stonewall) — 1922-23-24
Jackson, Wister — 1938-39
James, Charlie — 1988-89
*James, M.B. (Jimmy) — 1911-12-13-14
Jameson, Hugh — 1939-40-41
Jansen, John — 1984-85-86
Jaynes, Danny — 1976-77
Jehlen, George — 1974-75-76
Jenkins, Hunter — 1983
*Jenkins, Ralph — 1943-44 (Capt.) 45 (Capt); 46 (Alt. Capt.)
*Jennings, A.T. — 1914
Jennings, Keith — 1985-86-87-88
*Jeter, J.P. — 1913
Jetton, Neal — 1973-74-75 (Co-Capt.)
Johnson, A.J. — 1984-85
Johnson, Bobby — 1970-71-72
Johnson, John — 1987-88-89
Johnson, Ricky — 1963-64-65
Johnson, Tracy — 1985-86-87-88
Jollay, Mike — 1985-86
Jolley, Bobby — 1951
*Jones, Bob — 1928-29-30
Jones, Bob — 1972-73
Jones, Jimmy — 1949
Jordan, Homer — 1980-81-82 (Capt.)
Jordan, Leonard — 1941
Jordan, Whitey — 1955-56-57
Jordan, Willie — 1975-76-77-78
Justus, Johnny — 1928-29-30 (Capt.)

K
*Kaigler, Ben — 1902
*Kaigler, J.G. — 1898-99-1900
Kaltenback, Leon — 1955-56-57 (Co-Capt.)
Kane, Mark — 1953-54 (Capt.)
*Kangeter, Jonnie — 1910-11-12
Katana, Ted — 1965-66
*Kay, L.R. — 1917-19
*Keasler, A.L. (Gus) — 1904-05
*Keel, J.W. (Rastus) — 1906
Keller, Morris — 1959
Kelley, Don — 1969-70-71
Kelley, Freddy — 1965-66-67
Kelley, Steve — 1973

Kempson, Otis — 1950-51-52
Kendrick, Tommy — 1969-70-71
Kennedy, Frank — 1950-51
Kennedy, Tony — 1988-89
Kenney, Steve — 1976-77-78
Kesack, Gary — 1974-75-76
Keys, Larry — 1965-66-67
*Keyserling, H.L. (Golden) — 1920
Kier, Brian — 1974-76-77
Killen, Pat — 1959
Kinard, Terry — 1979-80-81-82 (Capt.)
King, Anthony — 1976-77-78
King, Buddy — 1970-71-72 (Capt.)
King, Don — 1952-53-54-55 (Capt.)
King, Jack — 1968-69
King, Jimmy — 1959-60-61
*King, L.O. — 1901-02
King, Tommy — 1959-60-61
*Kinsler, J.H. — 1900
Kirkconnell, Ben — 1932
Kirkland, Levon — 1988-89
*Kissam, Roddy — 1933-34-35
Kitchens, Ronnie — 1967-68-69
Knight, Herman — 1949-51
*Klugh, W.W. — 1925-26
Knoebel, Fred — 1950-51-52
Knott, Hal — 1959
Kormanicki, Dave — 1968-69
Kreis, Kevin — 1976
Kubu, Jon — 1989

L
*Lachicotte, G.E. (Boo) — 1910
Lam, Elmo — 1960-61-62 (Capt.)
Lambert, John — 1931
LaMontagne, Joe — 1951-52-53
Lancaster, Chris — 1985-86-87-88
Langford, Charlie — 1979
Langston, J.L. — 1920
Lanzandoen, Jim — 1973
Laraway, Walt — 1953-54-55
Latimer, Al — 1978
*Latimer, Bill — 1906
*Lawrence, Bert — 1902
Lawrence, Floyd — 1956
Lawrence, Reggie — 1988-89
Lawson, Larry — 1970
Lawton, Streak — 1935-36
Lawton, Winston — 1969
Learn, Randy — 1979-80-81-82
LeBel, David — 1973-74-75
*Lee, A.C. (Bun) — 1907
Lee, Mark — 1974-75
Lee, Harry — 1934-35
Leonard, Hal — 1946-47
Leverman, Gerald — 1945
*Lewis, Alex P. — 1911-12-13
*Lewis, Gus — 1900-01
Lewis, Harold — 1935-36-37 (Capt.)
*Lewis, J.B. — 1898-99-1900
Lewis, Merritt — 1932-33-34
Lewis, Stacy — 1989
Lewter, Steve — 1969-70-71
Lhotsky, Joe — 1966-67-68
Liberatore, Frank — 1964-66-67 (Capt.)
*Lightsey, F.B. (Bull) — 1922-24-25
*Lightsey, L.M. (Yen) — 1917-18-19-20
Lindsey, Otis — 1981-82
Link, A.C. — 1926
*Littlejohn, C.E. (Mule) — 1913-14-15
*Locklair, Ed (Pop) — 1941
Locklair, Mike — 1966-67-68
Logan, Jimmy — 1966
*Logan, J.R. — 1912-13
Long, Evans — 1930
Long, Stacy — 1986-88-89

Lott, Billy — 1977-78-79 (Capt.)
Lott, James — 1986-87-88-89
Lowman, P.I. (Pi) — 1918-19
Lundeen, Danny — 1970-71
*Lykes, Powell — 1905-06
*Lynah, Jim — 1900-01
Lynn, Dave — 1958-59-60 (Capt.)
Lytton, Jeff — 1983-84-85

Mc
McBride, Dan — 1973
McCall, Jeff — 1979-80-81-82
McCanless, Jim — 1955-56-58
McCarley, Bob — 1927-28-29
McCauley, Jim — 1949
McClure, Bruce — 1963-64-65
*McConnell, H.S. — 1914-15
*McConnell, R.E. — 1925-26
McConnell, S.W. — 1934-35-36
*McConnell, T.S. — 1934-35-36
McCory, Bob — 1944
McCown, Fred — 1942
*McCown, Slick — 1933-34
*McCown, T.M. — 1918
McCullough, Richard — 1985-86-87-88
McCurty, Damon — 1979
McDaniel, Ed — 1988-89
McDowell, Garry — 1974-75
McElmurray, Mac — 1964-65-66
McElveen, Norwood — 1939-40-41
McFadden, Banks — 1937-38-39
*McFadden, R.D. — 1908
*McFadden, R.H. (Doc) — 1906-07
McFadden, Wesley — 1985-87-88-89 (Capt.)
McGee, Edgar — 1965-66-67
*McGill, C.A. — 1925
McGlockton, Chester — 1989
McGlone, T.F. — 1925
McGuirt, Bill — 1960-61
*McIver, Rick — 1904-05
McKenny, Pat — 1985-86
McKenzie, W.W. — 1918
*McKeown, J.A. — 1903
McLane, Riley — 1966-67
McLaurin, Jewell — 1969-70
*McLaurin, J.N. — 1904-05-06-07 (Capt.)
McLellan, Bill — 1953-54
McLellan, Cliff — 1981
McLendon, Ed — 1939
McLendon, Lem — 1955
McMahan, Dave — 1969-70
McMakin, John — 1969-70-71 (Capt.)
McMillan, Goat — 1928-29
McMillan, Raiford — 1926-27-28
*McMillan, W.L. (Red) — 1913-14-15
McSwain, Chuck — 1979-80-81-82
McSwain, Rodney — 1980-81-82-83
M
Mack, Terence — 1983-84-85-86 (Capt.)
Mack, Kevin — 1980-81-82-83
Mader, Eric — 1989
Magee, Watson — 1936-37-38
*Magill, Dick — 1927-28-29
*Magill, W.K. (Rummy) — 1913-14-15 (Capt.)
Magwood, Frank — 1980-81-82
*Major, C.W. (Dopey) — 1913-14-15-16 (Capt.)
Mann, Wes — 1983-84-85
Mannella, Dave — 1979
Manos, Pete — 1949-50-51
Marazza, Dick — 1954-55-56
Mariable, Dorian — 1986-87-88-89

Marion, Phil — 1964-65-66
Marler, Macolm — 1973-74-75-76 (Co-Capt.)
*Marshall, L.E. — 1926
Martin, Bob — 1946-47-48 (Co-Capt.)
Martin, Carl — 1981-82
*Martin, J.M. — 1909-10-11
Martin, Peanut — 1972-73-75
*Martin, W.N. — 1925-27
Masneri, Ray — 1956-57-58
Mass, Wayne — 1965-66-67
Massaro, Cary — 1980-81-82
Massengill, Wells — 1972
Mathews, Mike — 1971
Mathews, Ray — 1947-48-49-50
Mathews, Tony — 1973-74
*Mathis, A.J. — 1898
Mathis, Bill — 1957-58-59
*Matthews, Bill — 1915-16
Matthews, Mack — 1960-62-63
Mattos, Tommy — 1952-53-54
Mauldin, Hugh — 1963-64-65
Mauney, Tony — 1988-89
*Maxwell, Jeff — 1896-97
*Maxwell, John — 1902-03
Mayberry, Bob — 1979-80-81-82
Mayer, Charlie — 1969-70-71
Meadowcroft, Charlie — 1963-64-65
Meadows, Dwayne — 1984-85-86
Medlin, Rick — 1967-68-69
Meeks, Chuck — 1982
*Mellette, F.M. — 1911
*Melton, L.H. (Doc) — 1923-24
Michael, Benny — 1966-67-68
*Midkiff, Bob — 1926
Miller, Bill — 1962
Miller, Billy — 1943
*Miller, Bob — 1931-32 (Capt.)
Miller, H.E. — 1937-38
*Miller, Jack — 1944-47-48
Miller, Jim — 1948
Miller, Ron — 1958
Mills, Jeff — 1974-75
Milton, Eldridge — 1981-83-84-85
Milton, Fred — 1968-69-70
*Mimms, Charlie — 1946
Monledous, Zag — 1927-28
Monneyham, Jack — 1949-50-51
Montone, Neil — 1947
Moore, Gene — 1947-48-49 (Capt.)
Moore, Ken — 1952-53-54
Moore, Otis — 1986-87-88-89 (Capt.)
Moore, Ted — 1964
*Moorer, John — 1945-46-47 (Alt. Capt.)
Moorer, Tom — 1938-39
Morgan, Bobby — 1958-59
Morgan, Lewis — 1946
Morocco, Chris — 1986-87-88-89
Morris, David — 1973
Morrison, Pete — 1961
Moss, Charlie — 1930-31-32
Mouzon, Tyron — 1988-89
*Mulherin, Eddie — 1928
Mullen, Ray — 1965-66
Mulligan, Wayne — 1966-67-68
*Mullins, H.D. (Horse) — 1923-24
Murray, Al — 1972-73-74
Murray, John — 1978
Myrick, Rocky — 1979

N
Ness, Jim — 1972-73-74 (Co-Capt.)
Neville, J.L. — 1943
Newell, Andy — 1985
Newell, Mike — 1969-70
Nimitz, H.J. (Foots) — 1916
Nix, Eric — 1984-85-86

Noelte, Dave — 1982
Nunamacher, Jeff — 1985-86-87-88
Nunn, Arlington — 1987-88-89

O
O'Brien, Chuck — 1987-88
O'Cain, Mike — 1974-75-76 (Co-Capt.)
O'Dell, Billy — 1953-54-55
*O'Dell, John H. — 1918-19
O'Dell, Wayne — 1941
*Odom, W.F. — 1908
Ogle, Chris — 1989
Ohan, Chinedu — 1987-88
*O'Kurowski, Whitey — 1937-38-39
Olson, Dave — 1958-59-60
Olson, Harold — 1957-58-59
Olszewski, Harry — 1965-66-67
O'Neal, Belton (Speck) — 1920
O'Neal, Brad — 1969-70
O'Neal, Robert — 1989
Orban, Turk — 1936
Osborne, Ronnie — 1959-60-61
Otorubio, Adubarie — 1985
*Owens, J.C. (Susie) — 1919-20

P
Padgett, F.M. — 1918
*Padgett, G.D. — 1931
Padgett, Jim — 1957-58
*Padgett, O.D. — 1928-29 (Capt.)
Padgett, Wade — 1939-40-41 (Capt.)
Page, Wayne — 1965-66
Pagliei, Joe — 1953-54-55
Palmer, Cary — 1989
*Palmer, E.D. (Frog) — 1925
Palmer, Johnny — 1963-64-65
Paredes, Bob — 1951-54
Parete, Anthony — 1981-82-83-84
Parker, Ace — 1940-41
*Parker, Harry L. — 1912-13
Parker, Jim — 1961-62-63 (Alt. Capt.)
Pasley, Jim — 1939-40
Pate, Milton — 1951-52
Patrick, Chris — 1932
*Patterson, Gene — 1931-32
Patton, Bob — 1949-50-51 (Capt.)
Paulling, Bob — 1979-81-82-83
Pavilack, Harry — 1959-60-61
Payne, Booty — 1940-41
Payne, Jim — 1956-57-58
Payne, Joe — 1937-38-39 (Capt.)
Payne, Oliver — 1936-37
Pearce, Frank — 1963-64-65
Pearce, Roy — 1939-40
Pearman, Dan — 1985-86
*Pearman, Fred — 1899-1900-01
Pearson, Ben — 1937-38-39
Peeples, Ken — 1972-73-74 (Co-Capt.)
*Pegues, E.S. — 1899
Pengitore, Ken — 1971-72-73 (Capt.)
*Pennington, Clyde — 1935
Pennington, Curtis — 1936-37-38 (Alt. Capt.)
*Perry, Bill — 1911
*Perry, L. (Tom) — 1911
Perry, Michael Dean — 1984-85-86-87 (Capt.)
*Perry, Tracy — 1976-77-78-79
Perry, William — 1981-82-83-84 (Capt.)
Petoskey, Ted — 1963-64
Phillips, Hank — 1986-87-88-89
Phillips, Harley — 1943-44
Phillips, Jim — 1945
Phillips, John — 1984-85-86-87 (Capt.)
Pickett, Edgar — 1980-81-82-83

Pierce, Hal — 1940-41-42
Pilot, Joe — 1958
*Pinckney, E.H. — 1909
*Pitts, Lewis — 1927-28
Pleasant, Reggie — 1982-83-84
Poe, Billy — 1944-45-46
*Pollitzer, H.R. (Polly) — 1902
Poole, Bob — 1961-62-63
*Poole, R.F. (Sarg) — 1915-16
Pope, Jamie — 1979
Portas, Lou — 1964-65
Potts, R.C. (Daddy) — 1917-18-19
*Pressley, E.H. (Buck) — 1912-13
Pressley, O.K. — 1926-27-28 (Capt.)
Pressly, Harlan — 1927
Price, John — 1970-71-72
Price, L.C. — 1925
Priester, Buck — 1930-31
Priester, Buck — 1953-54-55
Prince, Phil — 1944-46-47-48 (Co-Capt.)
*Pritchett, Jess — 1937
Proctor, Landrum — 1930-31
*Pruett, Chip — 1978-79
Pruitt, June — 1945-46
Puckett, David — 1988-89
Pusey, Mike — 1975

Q
Quarles, Jimmy — 1951-52
Quick, Rodney — 1983-84-85
Quinn, Dewey — 1945-46
Quisenbury, Sonny — 1957-58

R
Raber, Brian — 1983-84-85-86
*Radcliff, Charles — 1950-51-52
Radford, Kevin — 1980
*Randle, E.L. (Cat) — 1913-14-15
*Randle, M.B. (Little Cat) — 1918-19-20
Rankin, Gary — 1963-64
Ratchford, Warren — 1974-76-77-78
Ray, Thomas — 1963-64-65
Rayburn, Lee — 1966-67-68
*Reams, T. Jack — 1918-22
Reed, David — 1978-79
Reese, Archie — 1974-75-76-77
Reese, Steve — 1982-83-84-85 (Capt.)
Reeves, Marion — 1971-72-73
Rembert, Johnny — 1981-82
*Reynolds, Clifford M. (Pete) — 1926
Reynolds, Jim — 1945-47-48-49
Rhinehart, Jim — 1955
Rhodes, John — 1971-72
Richard, Al — 1989
Richardson, Chuckle — 1980-82-83-84
Richardson, Cotton — 1943-44
*Richardson, Joe — 1940
Richardson, Mark — 1980-81-82
Riddle, Leonard — 1943
*Riggs, A.F. — 1897-98-99
Riggs, Jim — 1983-84-85-86
Riggs, Matt — 1985-86-87
*Rion, Aubrey — 1939-40
Rivers, Dalton — 1955-56
Robbins, Butch — 1963-64
*Robbs, C.M. — 1907-08-09 (Capt.)
*Robinson, Charlie — 1922-23-24 (Capt.)
*Robinson, E.D. — 1934
Robinson, James — 1979-80-82-83 (Capt.)
*Robinson, Joe — 1927

Rodgers, George — 1950-51-52 (Co-Capt.)
Rogers, Bill — 1943-46
Rogers, Billy G. — 1944-46
Rogers, Floyd — 1965-66 (Capt.)
*Rogers, Johnny — 1929
*Rogers, Phil — 1965-66-67
Rogers, Rodney — 1961-62
Rogers, Shot — 1955-56
Rollins, Bubba — 1978
Rome, Stan — 1975
*Roper, T.H. (Pug) — 1918-19
Rose, Anthony — 1979-80-81
Rose, Chuck — 1978-79-80
Ross, Don — 1952-53-54
Ross, Jack — 1942-46-47
*Rothell, Claude — 1941-42
Roulhac, Terrance — 1983-84-85-86
Rowell, Spivey — 1944
Roy, Wallace — 1923-24-25
Ruffner, Bo — 1965-66-67
Ruffner, Jim — 1964
Rushton, Gil — 1945-48-49-50
Russell, J.A. — 1943
Russell, Jimmy — 1976
Rutledge, Bill — 1943
Ryans, Larry — 1989
Ryan, Steve — 1977-78

S
*Sadler, Hope — 1902 (Capt.) -03 (Capt.)
Salisbury, Tom — 1943-44-47-48
Salley, Grady — 1928-29-30
*Sams, Hal — 1916
*Sanders, Al — 1935-36-37
Sanders, Smiley — 1971-72-73
Sanford, Chuck — 1983-84-85
Sandifer, Red — 1940-41
Sasser, David — 1971-72-73
Saunders, Bo — 1945-46
*Schilletter, W.A. (Shorty) — 1911-12-13-14 (Capt.)
*Schneck, J.R. — 1918-19
Schonhar, Todd — 1985-86
Schroder, F.E. — 1912
Scott, James — 1981-82-83
Scott, Randy — 1975 (Co-Capt.) 1977 (Capt.)-1978 (Capt.)
Scott, Shane — 1989
Scott, William — 1974-75
Scrudato, Ron — 1959-60-61
Sealy, Sonny — 1982
Sease, Jody — 1984-85
Sease, Tommy — 1955-56
Seay, Pitts — 1943
Seigler, Eddie — 1970-71-72
*Segars, Al — 1937
*Segars, Kent — 1936
Sellers, Joe — 1963-65
Setzekorn, Ken — 1984-85
Seyle, Rusty — 1986-87-88
Sharpe, Bill — 1964
Sharpe, Bob — 1938-39-40 (Capt.)
Sharpe, Bob Jr. — 1975-76
*Sharpe, F.J. — 1931
*Shealy, A.S. (Shack) — 1896-97-98 (Capt.)-99
Shealy, Pat — 1971-72
Shell, Bob — 1970-72-73
Sheppard, Ashley — 1989
Shields, John — 1968-69
*Shingler, Lowndes — 1958-59-60 (Co-Capt.)
Shirley, Jim — 1950-51-52
Shish, Paul — 1969
*Shockley, J.A. — 1922
Shore, Henry — 1933-34-35 (Capt.)

Shown, Jack — 1952-53
Shuford, Don — 1934-35-36
Siegel, Reuben — 1929-30-31
Siepe, Jeff — 1970-71-72
Silver, Dennis — 1974
Simmons, T.D. (Shag) — 1919
Simmons, Ralph — 1937
Simmons, Wayne — 1989
Simpson, Don — 1943
Simpson, Tyrone — 1989
Sims, David — 1977-78-79-80
Sims, Marvin — 1977-78-79
*Sitton, Vet — 1902-03
Sizer, Danny — 1988-89
Skiffey, Jim — 1962
Smalls, Andy — 1950-52-53
Smartt, Bill — 1944
Smith, Bill — 1977-78-79-81
Smith, Dennis — 1973-74-75
   (Co-Capt.)
Smith, Glenn — 1949-50-51
Smith, Gregg — 1976
Smith, Harold — 1959
Smith, Jack — 1958-59
Smith, Joey — 1979-80
Smith, Lynn — 1979
Smith, Matt — 1977-78-79
Smith, Randy — 1965
Smith, Richard — 1985-86-87-88
Smith, Ronnie — 1974-75-76-77
Smith, Sterling — 1949-50
Smith, Thorny — 1968
Smith, Willie — 1954-55-57
*Snead, W.F. (Bill) — 1901
*Snowden, Moon — 1927
Snyder, Paul — 1957-58-59
   (Co-Capt.)
Soloman, Homer — 1930
Soowal, Jeff — 1976-77-78
Southerland, Ivan — 1967-68-69
   (Capt.)
*Sowell, Frank — 1930
Sox, Greg — 1986
*Spearman, Jack — 1920-21 (Capt.)
Spector, Robbie — 1988-89
Speros, Jim — 1980
Spiers, Bill — 1986
Spooner, Bob — 1955-56-57
Spry, David — 1983-85-86-87
Squires, Tappey — 1969
Stacey, Jack — 1942
Stanford, M.C. — 1940
Stephens, Tony — 1986-87
Stevens, Alex — 1932-33-34
*Stevens, R.G. — 1909
*Stewart, J.D. — 1924
Stewart, Watt — 1944
Stocks, Jeff — 1971-72-73
Stockstill, Jeff — 1980-81-82
Stone, Don — 1973
Stough, Tim — 1973-74-75-76
Strayer, Phyil — 1969
Stribling, J.W. — 1913-14-15
*Strother, Frank — 1923
Stuckey, Jim — 1976-77-78-79
Sublette, Dick — 1948
*Suggs, H.L. — 1914-15
*Sullivan, Frank — 1897-98-99
Sultis, Jim — 1945-46-47
*Summers, J.C. (Chuck) — 1905-06
Sursavage, Butch — 1965-66-67
Sursavage, Jim — 1968-69-70 (Capt.)
Suttle, Jeff — 1980-81-82-83
Sutton, George — 1962
Sweatte, Johnny — 1941
*Swetenburg, J.R. — 1920-21
Swift, Bob — 1963
Swing, Dale — 1982-83-84

Swofford, Bob — 1927-28-29
*Swygert, George — 1896-97

T
Talley, J.H. — 1926
Taylor, Jeff — 1989
*Taylor, Jerry — 1961-62
Taylor, J.W. — 1943
Taylor, Vince — 1986-87-88-89
*Tennant, A.B. (Dutch) — 1921-22-23-24
Testerman, Don — 1974-75
*Thackston, L.P. — 1917-18-19
Thomas, Bill — 1956-57-58 (Capt.)
Thomas, David — 1972
Thomas, Doug — 1987-88-89
Thomason, Johnny — 1955
Thompson, Dave — 1968-69-70
*Thompson, Doug — 1955
*Thompson, J.W. — 1916
Thompson, Marion — 1950-51-52
Thompson, Oscar — 1946-47-48
Thornton, Mark — 1978-79
Thornton, R.E. — 1918
Thorsland, Oscar — 1960-61-62
Tice, Johnny — 1954
*Tillman, Henry — 1902
Timmerman, W.P. (Pap) — 1926-27
Timmons, Charlie — 1939-40-41
Tinsley, Sid — 1940-41-44 (Alt. Capt.)
Tisdale, Charlie — 1938-39-40
Todd, Moe — 1969
Tolley, Charlie — 1967-69 (Capt.)
*Tompkins, F.G. — 1896
Tompkins, James — 1966-67-68
Trapp, James — 1989
Trayham, Arden — 1943
Treadwell, David — 1985-86-87
Trembley, Jimmy — 1959
Trexler, Bru — 1937-39
Triplett, Danny — 1979-80-81-82
*Trobaugh, Allen — 1938
*Trobaugh, Earl — 1938
Troy, Mike — 1963-64
Trumpore, Arthur — 1943
*Troutman, John — 1933-34-35
Tucker, Richard — 1988
*Turbeville, A.C. — 1912
Turbeville, Horace — 1956
Turner, Bo — 1945-46
*Turner, H.M. (Tuck) — 1907
*Turnipseed, Rhett — 1922
Turpin, Bucky — 1966-67
Tuten, Rich — 1976-77-78
Tuttle, Perry — 1978-79-80-81 (Capt.)
Tyler, O.J. — 1974-76
Tyner, Mitch — 1973-74

U
Underwood, Willie — 1977-78-79-80
   (Capt.)
Usry, George — 1957-58-59

V
*Valentine, Jack — 1926
Varn, Guy — 1983
Varn, Rex — 1976-77-78
Vaughan, Mark — 1985
Veronee, Jack — 1959-60-61
*Vogel, R.T. — 1896-97

W
Wade, Connie — 1966-67
Wade, D.A. — 1952
Wade, Don — 1950-51
*Wade, Grady — 1920
Wade, Mike — 1981
Wagner, Larry — 1958

Waldrep, Joe — 1964-65
Waldrep, Perry — 1967
Walker, Duane — 1984-85-86-87
Walker, Henry — 1946-47
*Walker, John E. — 1923-24-25
*Walker, Norman — 1897-98-99
   (Capt.); 1900 (Capt.)
*Walker, R.H. — 1909-10
*Wall, J.E. — 1926
Wall, Pete — 1953-55
Wallace, Nelson — 1973-74-75-76
Walls, Henry — 1983-84-85
Walters, Joey — 1974-75-76
   (Co-Capt.)
Walters, Henry — 1970-71
Ward, Billy — 1962-63-64
Ward, Jimmy — 1950-51-52
Ware, Billy — 1966-67-68
*Warr, Elza — 1926-27
*Warren, George — 1906-07
Washington, Jay — 1972-73
Waters, Charlie — 1967-68-69
Watson, Ben — 1969-70
Watson, C.W. — 1933-34
Watson, John — 1985
Watson, Ronald — 1981-82-83-84
Watts, Waldo — 1969-70
Weaver, Billy — 1962-63
*Webb, Clare (Tanny) —
   1911-12-13-14
Webb, Gary — 1976-77-78
*Webb, H.B. — 1922
Webb, Hugh — 1940
Webb, Jack — 1957-58
*Webb, Mike — 1904
Webb, Travers — 1973-75-76-77
Weddington, Rick — 1976-77
Weeks, Jimmy — 1975-76-77
Weeks, Scott — 1981
Welchel, Ken — 1976-77
*Welch, Maxcey — 1930
Wells, Jeff — 1980-82-83-84
Wells, Jim — 1976-77
Wells, Jimmy — 1951-52-53
Wells, Joel — 1954-55-56 (Alt. Capt.)
Werner, Chuck — 1966-68-69
Werntz, Eddie — 1960-61-62
*Werts, Rufus — 1931-32
Wertz, J.B. — 1922-23
Wessinger, Ron — 1989
West, Calvin — 1959-60-61 (Capt.)
West, Fernandez — 1988-89
West, Ron — 1978
White, Clyde — 1952-53-54 (Capt.)
White, Harvey — 1957-58-59
   (Co-Capt.)
*White, J.D. — 1896
*White, W.P. — 1908-09
Whitley, Curtis — 1988
Whitmire, Jim — 1943-46-47-48
Whitten, Red — 1952-53-54
*Wiehl, E.M. — 1916
Wiggins, Don — 1969-70
Wiggs, Milton — 1945
*Wild, Ormond — 1953
*Wiles, Bill — 1935-36-37
*Wilhite, F.T. (Rusty) — 1921
Williams, Bobby — 1947-48-49
*Williams, Bratton — 1923-24
Williams, Braxton — 1982-83
Williams, Jack — 1920-21-22
Williams, Jerome — 1986-89
Williams, Keith — 1983-84-85
Williams, M.H. — 1917-19
Williams, Pat — 1985-86-87-88
Williams, Paul — 1978
Williams, Perry — 1983-84-85-86
Williams, Ray — 1983-84-85-86

Williams, Rodney — 1985-86-87-88
   (Capt.)
Williams, Scott — 1981-82-83-84
*Williams, Tommie — 1904
Williams, Tommy — 1953-54
Williams, Toney — 1976-77-78
Williamson, Jimmy - 1972-74-75
   (Co-Capt.)
Willimon, Gene — 1932-33
Wills, Albert — 1950
*Willis, Don — 1936-37-38
Wilson, C.C. (Red) — 1921-22-23-24
Wilson, Jim — 1959
Wilson, Mac — 1969-70-71
Wilson, Ralph — 1944
Windham, E.E. — 1907
Windham, Kermit — 1936
Wingo, Bill — 1973-74-75-76
Wirth, Frank — 1979-71-72 (Capt.)
Wise, Frank — 1972-73-74-75
*Withers, George — 1950-51-52
*Witsell, F.L. (Fish) — 1915-16-17
   (Capt.)
Woodruff, Foggy — 1928-29-30
*Woods, Charlie — 1936-37-38 (Capt.)
Woods, Footsie — 1941-45
*Woods, Smith — 1903
*Woodward, Henry — 1932-33-34
   (Capt.)
*Woodward, H.M. (Jake) — 1909-10
*Woodward, Jake — 1900
Woolford, Donnell — 1985-86-87-88
   (Capt.)
Wray, A.F. (Bull) — 1921-22
Wray, Jack — 1924-25
Wright, Charlie — 1940-41-42 (Capt.)
Wright, Tom — 1940-41
Wrightenberry, Earl — 1950-51-52
Wurst, Jim — 1980-81-82
Wyatt, Charlie — 1952-53
Wyatt, Rick — 1977-78-79
*Wyndham, Dumb-Dumb —
   1948-49-50
Wyse, Fred — 1935-36-37

Y
*Yarborough, Mule — 1929-30
Yarbrough, Al — 1933-34-35
Yauger, Ray — 1968-69-70 (Capt.)
Yeomans, Ken — 1980
Young, Eric — 1977-78-79
Yow, Ken — 1983

Z
Zager, Emil — 1958
*Zeigler, F.M. — 1920-21-22

NEW 1990 LETTERMEN

Blunt, Rodney	Harris, Rudy
Bryant, Dwayne	Joye, David
Buckner, Brentson	McLees, Jimmy
Bussie, Arthur	Moncrief, Richard
Calhoun, Darren	Samnik, Mike
Caputo, Paul	Seegars, Stacy
Davis, Jason	Smith, Terry
Derriso, Steve	Taylor, Bruce
Eaves, Robin	Williams, Ronald
Fewster, Butch	Wilson, Pierre
Goudelock, David	Witherspoon, Derrick
Harris, John	

*Deceased